A John Catt Publication

"As cool as a Smeg fridge/freezer and a..."
Phil Beadle - Author

THE
SLIGHTLY
AWESOME
TEACHER

Edu-Research meets common sense

Dominic Salles

First Published 2016

by John Catt Educational Ltd,
12 Deben Mill Business Centre, Old Maltings Approach,
Melton, Woodbridge IP12 1BL

Tel: +44 (0) 1394 389850 Fax: +44 (0) 1394 386893
Email: enquiries@johncatt.com
Website: www.johncatt.com

ISBN: 978 1 911382 027
Set and designed by John Catt Educational Limited

Praise for *The Slightly Awesome Teacher*

"Dominic Salles seems to be under the misapprehension that he is neither cool nor awesome. I beg to differ, and this is why: many of us rejoiced at the idea of Professor Hattie's 'Visible Learning', paid our dosh on Amazon and cracked open the spine ... to find ... that it was not only really bloody boring but completely impenetrable too. From what I read there are some teachers who have read and understood it, even some who have gone as far as challenging some of the maths. Me? I didn't understand hide nor hair of it.

"Dominic's book is a sane and playful attempt at translating what 'evidence led' means for those of us who need such a translation. It is the work of a very experienced, very popular teacher with a stupendous record of results, and it is also an insight into the mind of someone at the chalk face who is attempting to make 'evidence-led' a reality. I finally understood some things that had always foxed me from reading this book and, because of this, have no hesitation in describing it, and its author, as being both as cool as a Smeg fridge/freezer and as awesome as a Jimi Hendrix solo."

Phil Beadle, author of How to Teach

Acknowledgements

Mike Salt, who gave me my first teaching job even though I was entirely unqualified.

Deirdre Fitzpatrick, who married me and inspired me to become an English teacher.

Phil (Chaz) Leslie, my first mentor.

Cara Galeozzie and Shelley Morgan (Shecara) who helped me lead a slightly awesome team and curriculum.

John Saunders who asked me to lead CPD and then suggested I go lead it somewhere else.

John Sanderson who asked me to write a teaching and learning handbook that turned into The Slightly Awesome Teacher.

Professor John Hattie who showed teachers how to look at research in 2009.

David Didau who provoked me to think deeply about the claims of research.

My family, who have read not a single word of it, and gave me not a single word of encouragement – the slightly awesome teacher needs no external ratification!

Alex Sharratt, of John Catt Educational, who took a moment's look at it, and told me to halve the number of words (because teachers only have time to read in the summer holidays).

Julie Higgins and Lee Simpson, my critical readers – thank you both.

Phil Beadle, an inspirational teacher and writer who gave me one great piece of advice which I ignored, and encouragement that I cherished.

All my students who taught me to see teaching through the learner's eyes, especially Jess and Harry, my own children.

Contents

Foreword

Certainty and over confidence can prevent us from thinking; the more certain we are that we're right, the less we'll consider other possibilities. This tendency not to think too much about the possibility that we might be mistaken stems in part from a whole suite of well-documented cognitive biases, but also arises from institutional pressures. Schools put pressure on teachers to explain away their mistakes rather than to explore them and this leads to teachers repeating the same old mistakes often unaware that anything could be better.

We tend to believe that experiences leads inexorably to expertise and so, the longer we've been teaching, the better our judgements become. Whilst I don't want to claim that this is flat-out wrong, I do think there are very clear limits to our ability to make reliable intuitive judgements. Of course, I could be mistaken about this but I think the benefits to exploring the ways we think we develop professionally far outweigh the costs. Dominic Salles' sharp, insightful and self-deprecating book is a useful antidote to the sort of unthinking practice of the same old same old which, contrary to our intuition, may be making teachers less rather than more effective.

That sounds like rather a strong claim to make. Surely teachers, like fine wines and good cheese, just get better and better with age and experience? Surprisingly, there have been a number of studies which seem to indicate that although teachers seem to improve rapidly – in terms of student outcomes – over the first three years of practice, they subsequently plateau and perhaps even begin to decline.[1] This is not uncontroversial and there are also many other studies that show the opposite and actually experience increases effectiveness

---

1   See for instance Hanuskek, Rivkin & Kain (2005) Teachers, Schools, And Academic Achievement Econometrica, Vol. 73, No. 2 (March, 2005), 417–458

throughout a teacher's career.[2] Both sides claim their opponents' results are based poor statistical models. The problem with anyone without a statistical background is that these claims and counter claims revolve around arguing who has the better maths. As the mathematician John Ewing says, "Whether naïfs or experts, mathematicians need to confront people who misuse their subject to intimidate others into accepting conclusions simply because they are based on some mathematics."[3]

In short, I have no real idea who's right, but the claims that teachers just get better and better are based on the assumption that everyone – surgeons, software developers, business executives – tends to get better with practice. If this axiom holds true for everyone else, why would it be different for teachers?

Sadly, surgery, software development and business are all examples of domains where experience does **not** automatically confer expertise. Take the example of radiologists. A 2004 analysis of 500,000 mammograms and 124 radiologists was unable to find any evidence that years of experience leads to increased skill in diagnosis resulting many thousands of unnecessary biopsies and hundreds of cases were malignant tumours were missed.[4] What typically happens is that a radiologist will be sent a mammogram of a patient she will never meet, make a diagnosis and return it, never to find out whether it was correct. Although her ability to correctly diagnose tumours may be by increasing, her confidence in her own expertise certainly is.

What about clinical psychologists? In his 1994 book *House of Cards*, Robin Dawes details how clinical psychologists with over 10 years experience are no better at diagnosing and treating mental illnesses than those fresh out of medical school. This pattern has been repeated in many many different domains. So much so that Robin Hogarth has identified what he calls 'wicked domains' in which experience routinely fails to lead to expertise. But all experienced clinical psychologists believe they are genuine experts.

A 'wicked domain' is one where feedback on performance is absent or biased. This is equivalent to playing golf in the dark – you never find out where the ball

---

2   The recent study from Kini & Podolsky (2016) makes exactly this claim: Does Teaching Experience Increase Teacher Effectiveness? A Review of the Research https://learningpolicyinstitute.org/wp-content/uploads/2016/06/Teaching_Experience_Report_June_2016.pdf
3   Strauss, V. Leading mathematician debunks 'value-added', The Washington Post, 9th May 2011
4   Ericsson, K.A. Deliberate practice and the acquisition and maintenance of expert performance in medicine and related domains. Acad Med. 2004 Oct;79(10 Suppl):S70-81.

went so you never get better at hitting the ball. But it's worse than that. Because feedback in wicked domains is biased, it leads us to believe we're becoming experts even when we're not. We become ever more confident and certain that we're right: a dangerous combination. This is connected to the Dunning-Kruger effect: the finding that those without expertise lack the knowledge to realise their own deficits.

He also identified so-called 'kind domains' which provide accurate and reliable feedback. Gary Klein has led research into these 'kind domains' and shown that where we get solid feedback, we become genuinely intuitive. He studies into fire-fighters, neonatal nurses, military commanders and other professions have shown that in these fields, experienced practitioners 'just know' the right course of action to take in seconds.

Hogarth shows that even where a domain may have some 'kind' aspects, it can also have a 'wicked' effect on the genuine development of expert intuition:

> *The physician in the emergency room …must make speedy decisions and will not always receive adequate feedback. Indeed, **the typical feedback he receives is short term: how the patient responds to his immediate actions**. It is rare that the physician ever really finds out what happened to the patients he treated within a longer, and perhaps more relevant time frame. Some patients simply go home after treatment and never return to the hospital; others are cared for in different departments of the hospital, and so on.*[5]

Although surgeons' short-term survival rates dramatically improve with years on the job, long-term survival rates and other complications don't.

Teaching may be similar to surgery. Although we get better at certain aspects of the job, we may not improve in others. For instance, teachers improve rapidly at managing classrooms. We get excellent feedback from students on the effectiveness of our decisions; they either behave or they don't. We get daily opportunities to learn from our mistakes and we can see our practice improve as we hone in on the best way to interact with different classes. But we don't necessarily get any better at actually *teaching*. Hamre et al (2009) have shown that 'quality of instruction' is the aspect of teaching least likely to improve over time. This may be because the feedback we get is biased. We see that students can answer our questions and respond productively to our suggestions and we think we see learning when in reality all we're seeing is their current performance from which we are *inferring* learning. Current performance may

---

5   Hogarth, R. (2003) Educating Intuition: A Challenge for the 21st Century http://crei.cat/files/filesOpuscle/12/090429180657_ENG_op13ang.pdf p. 14.

be 'mere mimicry'. If we assume our instruction is effective and move on, we'll often be mistaken.

The frustrating thing is that we know quite a lot about how to develop expertise. Anders Ericsson – the expert expert – has been researching expertise across many different fields for decades and for teachers I think there are 4 key principles we can take from his findings.

Firstly, teachers need frequent, low stakes lesson observations that are focussed on developing and honing key teaching skills. Too often teachers are afraid to make mistakes for fear of judgement. The truth is, we all make mistakes but we only learn from them if we acknowledge them, hold up to the light of critical enquiry and make sure we never make them again. If teachers are worried about consequences of mistakes they'll be tempted to explain them away, make excuses and repeat them. Let's find ways to break this stupid cycle.

Second, teachers need much better feedback on how effectively they teach. Most of the feedback teachers get is on students' performance during lessons; we see that they appear to have learned something as a result of our instruction and conclude that whatever we're doing must be effective. But unless we collect data on whether our teaching is effective over the longer term, we could be improving students' current performance at the cost of their future learning.

Third, teachers can benefit from guided, purposeful practice – once we have automated a skill we stop getting better at it. When you start learning to drive (or teach) there's a hell of a lot to focus on and this effort keeps us conscious of what we're doing. The more we think about our practice the more we're likely to improve. We've all experience the phenomenon of driving on auto-pilot with no memory of the last 50 miles, and the same can be true for experienced teachers – you can get to the end of the day without having had to think all that much about what you were doing. Purposeful practice would require us to remain in the conscious stage of skill acquisition in order that we continue to improve.

Finally, teachers would benefit hugely from having a codified body of knowledge to refer to. In most fields were practice results in genuine expertise – sports, chess, ballet, classical music – there is a well-defined body of content to master. This isn't the case in education because we don't agree on what effective teaching looks like. If we did, we could start to break down and work on individual components in the knowledge that improving *these things* would definitely make us better. But because we rely on faulty intuitive judgement about what *these things* are, our practice is often purposeless and maybe even degrades our ability to teach effectively.

This is where this book comes in. Dominic Salles has synthesised much of the best of what we have learned from science and research with his own hard won, practical experience of what leads to students making progress and getting excellent results. No gimmicks, no frills, just sold, sensible advice on actually teaching children to do better than they ever believed possible. Oh, and a smattering of wisdom from that well-known educational thinker Arnold Schwarzenegger.

David Didau, Backwell, June 2016

"You know, nothing is more important than education,
because nowhere are our stakes higher; our future depends
on the quality of education of our children today.

Help others and give something back. I guarantee you will discover that
while public service improves the lives and the world around you, its greatest
reward is the enrichment and new meaning it will bring your own life."

Arnold Schwarzenegger

Introduction

Page 1. The sales pitch. Talk about pressure – this is the page that will decide whether you buy this book. This book isn't *1001 Cool Ways to be Cool and Awesome* – Jim Smith has already written that book. It isn't *How to be Truly Cool and Awesome* – Phil Beadle has already written that book. It isn't *Teach Like A Truly Cool and Awesome American* – Doug Lemov has already written that. Nor is it *Visibly Cool and Awesome Research* – Professor John Hattie has already written that book.

I am not cool and awesome. I have been nominated for teacher of the year twice – got nowhere. I entered Jamie Oliver's Teacher competition. I came second. I have an English Language and Literature YouTube channel with under a million views. It comes second. I used to enter strong man competitions, but I am not Swindon's strongest man – I came second. I entered indoor rowing competitions when I gave up weight lifting – in the 2000m I came 50th in the UK (it get's worse, this was in my age group). In 2007 I was the 106th fastest marathon rower in the world. I am not a Head Teacher, but assistant head in charge of teaching and learning. Not even second.

So, will this book make you slightly awesome?

Yes, of course it will – as you've seen, how to be slightly awesome is my middle name. You could buy the four books above – this book is in part their lovechild, in a test tube sort of a way – I love those books. But plenty of teachers read great books, without necessarily becoming better teachers. This book wants to make you a better teacher. The first message is, you don't have to be awesome to get great results from your students.

How do I have anything to offer? Well, in 23 years, my classes have always made excellent progress. This is just as true for my bottom sets as my top sets. (In the jargon, they have beaten their FFTD predictions or, before The Fischer Family Trust was invented, their Yellis predictions, and their Relative Performance Indicators, or residuals. This year 57% of them made 5 levels of progress, and it has been the same story in every school I've taught in).

Bear with me here. Schools are full of people who can talk the talk – but if it doesn't result in students making great progress, what's the point? I recently attended a whole school literacy course led by an expert, recommended by Ofsted as a case study in awesome practice, who had been a head in two schools. Yet a brief analysis of his schools' results showed great impact on English, but nothing visible to any other subject, even the ones that are full of reading and writing.

I'm the kind of teacher who would point that out, which is not cool, but I hope a tiny bit awesome. I can't stand flim flam. That is the second reason to buy this book, or to edge nervously back to your Kindle library.

There was, however, one year when both my GCSE classes failed to get excellent value added. It was the first year in which I introduced 'intervention'. Intervention is a panic measure, and is always robbing Peter to pay Paul. Peter, in this metaphor, is your available time – what economists and now teachers are starting to call 'opportunity cost'. This book should give you a way out of interventions, and help you become a really effective teacher. "Back off SLT, my kids are doing just fine – read my value added". I hope that feeling will be a little bit awesome. In fact, what I tend to do is the opposite of 'intervention'.

As head of English I allowed 55% of my mixed ability year 9 students to study no English at all, all year. Instead, they sat GCSE media studies in one year, sitting the exam at the end of year 9. Didn't reduce our excellent progress in English, but 90% got C and above in GCSE media studies. We didn't work any harder, but the students did. So again, no flim flam.

The fourth reason to buy this book is that it will get you to forget about *teaching* and think about *learning*. This is another way of saying, for you to stop stressing about what you do, and get the students to work harder and smarter at what they do. This book couldn't be called 'How to Teach' but 'How to Get Students to Learn'. In a climate where most teachers feel they are never good enough, this is a big deal. You can really enjoy the job when you feel a little bit awesome.

OK, enough now. You've probably decided whether to buy this book.

Read this book because:

Your students will make great progress and you will be a little bit cool and awesome.

I won't give you any flim flam, just stuff which is *proven* to work.

It isn't a guide to all the extra stuff you should do to become cool and awesome. Instead it will show you how to get your students to learn what you teach, *without you working any harder.*

By focusing on learning, instead of teaching, you can ditch the guilt and enjoy: being just a little bit cool and awesome is enough.

So, buy this book, and skip to a chapter that interests you. If you are pressed for time, the quickest way to improve your teaching will be to jump to "Worked Examples". Think of this book as a library, with short books between its covers, and browse.

Introduction Part Two

Taking the Fifth

Still here? The fifth reason to buy this book I'm a little bit embarrassed about, and in many ways I'd prefer if you skipped it and just went to chapter one, that would be best. Very little in this book is about me, but this bit is, because you are still making up your mind whether to trust me. I'd hoped our first impression was enough.

The fifth reason is that I really believe you could be awesome. Most teachers feel they already work very hard. Most like their students, even when some classes appear more than we can bear. Most teachers feel their SLT are fairly nice people, but ask, shouldn't they be more effective – what difference do they make? So, most teachers feel that being awesome is impossible. "Don't ask me to do more, instead give me harder working kids, and get the SLT off our backs." I've been that teacher, anyway. But ultimately, I don't think that matters, – I think most teachers could be awesome. Better than that, I think this is what the research tells us.

Awesomeness is all around you. Let me begin with sport.

In *Bounce*, Matthew Syed reflects on his journey towards being awesome. He doesn't call it that, but he is British champion for a long time, three times Commonwealth champion, and went to the Olympics twice. However, for a long time, he is not even the best table tennis player in his own house – the best junior in the country is his brother, Andrew, until Andrew is injured. But as he looks back, Matthew is also struck that a majority of the best table tennis players in the country live in his street, Silverdale road. "For a period in the 1980s one street, and the surrounding vicinity, produced more outstanding tennis players than the rest of the nation combined." And this is in a country where over one million people play table tennis.

The premise of Syed's book is that the ability to be awesome is everywhere. Two things are required – practice and opportunity. He uses the figure of ten years, or 10,000 hours of practice. But it has to be *deliberate practice.*

Although this is a hell of a lot of hours to rack up as a sports person, it isn't for a teacher. After teaching for 4 hours a day, 39 weeks a year, a teacher will hit 10,000 hours in under 13 years. But your free lesson is also taken up with marking and feedback, lesson preparation, etc, all part of becoming an expert teacher. So, if you only worked 5 hours a day, your 10,000 hours would be reached in just over 10 years – you are practising for 975 hours a year.

The opportunity to be awesome is built into the job. In fact, on hours alone, it should be inevitable. But, the key is deliberate practice. The other reason I've written this book is that too many of those hours are spent practising the wrong things. I'd like to help you make that practice deliberate. As David Didau says, practice doesn't make perfect. Practice makes permanent. So, this book wants you to practise the right things.

You might also feel that Syed's experience is atypical – the world is not really like that, it is only with hindsight that so many brilliant table tennis players comes to look like proof that being brilliant is the result of practice. Weren't there plenty of other clubs where people practised relentlessly, but where people didn't reach such high standards? Yes, but his was the only one open 24 hours a day – so 10,000 hours could be reached earlier. Arguably, his club also had the best national coach.

But my argument here is that there probably were. If you found the clubs where coaches pursued excellence, you would probably find exactly that – a number of excellent players, clustered round a small area. They would not all have to be internationally ranked in order to be awesome, or at least slightly awesome.

If you know your school well enough, start there, or in your street, or village. In my first school I was the netball coach (not awesome – I was the teacher presence, while an outside club coach taught, before I eventually knew what I was doing). My first team went to the national finals, losing by one goal in the semi-finals. Two players from that team played for England at U16 level, one at U19. One, Anna Mayes, went on to captain Wales and eventually become England netball coach – the only coach to take England to a series win over Australia, winning 3-0.

This should be impossible, unless Syed is right. Now take my street. Next door to me lives Gerry, who is an ex international marathon runner. In the familiar way, he is not even the best marathon runner in his own home – growing up with a brother who was also an international, but faster.

A few doors up is one of the top ten child athletes in the country for her age. Two doors from me is a county rugby player. My daughter is selected for the South West as a rugby player. My son, and his friend the rugby player, fool about with athletics, and could represent the county at several throwing events. My son is county wrestling champion. All these children go to the same school – in fact they went to the same primary school. A little older, three county netballers are also within a dozen houses from my door. There are other streets like this at the same school, I just don't live in them.

In my current school, in my current year 11 class I teach the world under 16 dressage champion. Two years ago, it was the top UK under 16 canoeist. Both schools are normal comprehensives. There are at least two other international athletes in the school, I just don't teach them.

My point – the opportunities to be awesome are everywhere. What stops people being awesome is a choice. And this choice is often dictated by their view of the world. Do they choose to take the opportunity, or not? This is the embarrassing bit – I want to change your view of the world. Because the only thing that will stop you being awesome is your view of the world.

To change that view you need to be objective about your experience. Are you listening to your feelings, or questioning them through the lens of your students' progress? Let's return to sport for a moment.

Now this is early 2000, and my five year old daughter is at her best friend's birthday party. Her father is an Olympic swimming coach at Bath University's high performance centre.

In 2000, I am an ex strength athlete, pulling lorries etc. I've been around heavy lifting for a long time. My lifts are stronger than any player at the Rugby World Cup, which has just turned professional. Even now, in 2015, there are only a handful of players in the world, full time athletes, who could out-lift me.

But, in a twist that should be getting familiar, I wasn't even the strongest drug free lifter in my own gym, never mind the hundreds of lifting gyms around the country. My friend Perry was stronger than any professional rugby player there has ever been. My other training partner, Martin, had been an England schoolboy sprinter. In 2000, at 5' 8" and 15.5 stones, he could run the 100m under 11 seconds. He was both faster and stronger than Jonah Lomu, at 19 stones, the most famous rugby player in the world. My other training partner, Brian, is a national champion as a natural body builder. His sister Lesley – Ann is a Commonwealth Games Bronze medallist in the 100m hurdles, who also competes at two Olympics. This predisposes me to a world view – being awesome at something is only a small part natural ability, in the sense that many, many people have natural ability. Mainly it is about opportunity and deliberate practice. This isn't just an analogy for teaching – it is the same thing – deliberate practice will transform your natural ability. And very few teachers become teachers because they're rubbish at it – if you get through your first year, the Darwinian attrition suggests you are already blessed with natural ability.

So, the dad and I discuss his job as Olympic swimming coach, and I enquire about weight training, which I'm surprised to learn is minimal. Muscles slow you down, making your body too bulky, is his expert view.

This is the prevailing orthodoxy. This is interesting, because the Chinese are starting to dominate swimming. Rumours are they've inherited East German coaches. Rumours of drug use are widespread, because it is now known this is how the East Germans dominated swimming. In 1992, China's women swimmers dominate the Olympics. They are muscular.

The father agrees that drug use is a probable cause, I think. But he seems to ignore the effect of muscle. So I point out that drugs do not make you swim faster. Steroids allow you to build stronger muscles more quickly. It is the increase in muscle power that helps you swim faster. This is an important distinction, because if you could find a different way to gain the muscle power, you'd become a faster swimmer. Steroids are therefore not the direct cause of improvement. But to an Olympic swimming coach, I was talking nonsense. I was an English teacher, with no background in swimming, so I did not expect him to see my point. What expert would? His view of the world, at least in so far as it affected swimming, had to trump mine.

This is much like you – if you have taught for 10 years, you could quite rightly see yourself as an expert. But, has your practice been deliberate enough? What if I could change your teaching-world view?

One of the coach's athletes at the time was Mark Foster, a 50m sprint swimmer. The 50m is a power event, the shortest in the sport, taking 22 seconds and requiring only one breath. The first three seconds are not really explosive at all, but a glide under water, so the explosive element lasts 19 seconds. If you watch Usain Bolt run 200m you are looking at the same idea, an athlete generating immense power for 19 seconds.

So, I was very interested later in 2000 when Mark Foster left his coach, and indeed left the whole traditional, Olympic swimming set up. Instead he took to coaching himself. (No, I hadn't emailed him with my brilliant insights into weight training).

His inspiration, however, was the athletics set up at Bath. Colin Jackson, the 110m hurdle world record holder was his lodger. Malcom Arnold, Jackson's coach, also trained at Bath, and taught him about weight training and nutrition for power. Suddenly, powerful muscles made sense. He began proper weight lifting, dramatically increasing his longevity in the sport. In a world in which Rebecca Adlington can retire, spent at 23, Mark Foster competed at the highest level till the age of 38. As a definition of awesome, this takes some beating. He had been England's fastest swimmer since the age of 15, and he still set a 50m course personal best aged 38. I would ascribe much of this to much smarter training – what I referred to earlier, as deliberate practice.

This is how Mark Foster described it to Sam Murphy in The Observer, in 2008:

"Has Foster made changes to the way he trains over the years? 'Definitely,' he says. 'The old ethic was: "You're a swimmer, so swim." Now I do about 50 per cent of my training in the gym and 50 per cent in the water.'

In the gym, Foster's workout centres around heavy weights with low repetitions... 'I might get on a machine, like the lat pulldown, and go mad for 20 seconds, and then rest. I also use the arm crank – just doing lots of really fast spins. And I've started doing a lot of calf raises, because that's the last muscle you use to dive off the block.'

Another important – and fairly new – part of his training is core work. 'I've really got into the core stuff over the last couple of years,' he says. 'It's made a real difference to my back, which I've had problems with in the past.'"

You can see what I mean about deliberate practice. Here is someone with a different world view to the coaching community, to the experts. He is looking for what surprises him in other sports, and asking if it would make sense in swimming. Notice that he starts emphasising core work at 36, 21 years into his swimming career. Educational research allows us, similarly, to look beyond our own expert experience, and find better ideas, no matter how long we have been teaching.

I don't raise this example in order to say I was right all along, "Hey, I'm so awesome, read my book, I'm always right!" I raise it because it is *still* the orthodox view that weight training should be minimised. In 2008 Foster was still being described as a maverick and an outsider. His success, which by any comparison is awesome, was not causing coaches to re-evaluate everything they do with their sprinters. I don't know what the set up now is at Bath, but the top internet swimming coach in 2015, who has coached internationals in Australia, writes at theswimmingexpert.com. His advice to a 50m sprinter is this:

"You also need to work on your upper body strength by doing some pull work. I have found using a band around my feet and sprinting for 15 to 25 metres as a useful way to improve this."

Really? This just turns the water into a greater form of resistance – in other words, it becomes the weight. But not much weight, not much resistance. Why do that when you can generate much more power with real weights? Why do that when you have seen Mark Foster? In a world where Mark Foster exists, weight training has to be compulsory for any sprinter, until a better technique comes along. This will be my argument when I personalise the research for you – exploiting it is compulsory, until a better technique comes along.

Our view of research is very similar to this. We assume that our experience is far more valid than the conclusions of studies which are all different from our context. Twitter is awash with teachers bemoaning the fact that research studies are too unlike the context we teach in. To them, we're mixing apples and oranges. But, by that measure, Mark Foster would never have picked up a weight – weights came from a different context: they were apples in a world of orange growers. He would never have started swimming less, because that went against everything in the world of swimming. He wouldn't have bothered with core work – how balanced do you need to be in a pool, right? You can't exactly fall out of the water. But for me apples and oranges are the same thing – they're both fruit. And hey, they both float. So it is with research – learning is learning, and it is going to help us float in a slightly cool and awesome way.

Chapter 1

"I suppose nothing hurts you."
"Only pain."
Conan, 'Conan the Destroyer'

"Political courage is not political suicide."
Arnold Schwarzenneger

Most Teachers Have 10 Years' Experience. So What's the Problem?

The problem with our classrooms is that they act like mirrors – they only reflect back to us ourselves. Our experiences, assumptions and painfully learned insights are constantly reinforced. This leads to us practising the wrong things, becoming experts at the wrong skills.

Your Academic Qualifications

Your degree is worth very little to your students. Hattie tells us that the average impact of an "intervention" is d 0.4 while your qualifications have an impact of d 0.11. So, having a degree is better than not having a degree. But a teacher who has no degree in your subject can pick numerous strategies that far outweigh the effect of your degree on the progress of students. The Sutton Trust, in *What Makes Great Teaching?*:

"The search for a relationship between characteristics such as academic qualifications or general ability and student performance has been rather disappointing: correlations are typically very small or non-existent (Rockoff et al, 2011)."

What will make a difference is your knowledge of the exam syllabus, "in particular the kinds of content knowledge that are relevant to teaching, to student gains". This means putting yourself in your students' shoes, predicting and reacting to the difficulties they are likely to have. You need to sit the exam your students sit to fully appreciate this, at each change of syllabus.

Sadler et al (2013) tested a group of science teachers: "Overall, teachers answered 83% correctly, compared with 38% by their students." So their subject knowledge did not actually benefit their students that much. A reason why: "The teachers' ability to identify common misconceptions was hardly above chance". This strongly suggests most teachers do not truly understand the exam.

If your degree matters very little, but your ability to think through the subject from the point of view of the student matters so much, what should we do in schools? A rational education system would pick the best teachers, and allocate them to subjects later. It would thoroughly train them in the syllabus they need to teach, and then watch them go. Their degree would be largely irrelevant.

Now you'll have a problem with this. It does not describe your secondary school, nor my school, nor any secondary school I know. It seems a ridiculous idea. Please rank it on a scale of 1 – 10, where 10 is totally unrealistic, and 1 is "let's do it now".

You went for a high number? Ok, now take a look at a primary school. Here, it is the norm. In a special school, it is the norm. But if you are an expert in a secondary setting, it looks entirely alien to you, because your classroom is a mirror, your school is a mirror, reflecting back to you only yourself.

Yes, teaching A level is hard without an advanced subject knowledge (but many of us have still done it). But GCSE? Unless you are having to learn a subject completely from scratch, say music or German in my case, it wouldn't take long to reach A*. You could do it within one year, easily, (because a 15 year old does it in two) and a teaching career lasts a lot longer than that.

So, in order to get the best progress for students in your 11-16 school, we don't have to hire subject specialists. That's what the evidence shows. It's not even a discussion point, it's not even really a subject of debate.

Still troubled? Let me show you this way: that's what your 10,000 hours will have shown you. If I suggested those 10,000 hours of building up skills as a teacher were less important than the degree you spent less than 1500 hours on, you'd be outraged.

But this illustrates a fundamental problem of this book. It's rational approach will rub up against your experience in a number of ways. This really isn't my fault. I'd just like to show you the way things are, not the way they seem to be.

Chapter 2

Some Uncomfortable Truths

Setting by Ability   d 0.12

The Sutton Trust tells us that setting does not really work:

"Evidence on the effects of grouping by ability, either by allocating students to different classes, or to within-class groups, suggests that it makes very little difference to learning outcomes (Higgins et al, 2014). This can result in teachers... going too fast with the high-ability groups and too slow with the low."

So, you see the problem again. We think ability grouping is the best way to differentiate. It turns out it is not *even* a way to differentiate. Hattie tells us that the more-able do tend to gain from being set together, but these gains are outweighed by the negative effects on everyone else. Robert Coe suggests that even this view is optimistic.

Behaviour Management

Now, let's talk about behaviour. Clearly you still need behaviour that enables you to teach. But a brilliant disciplinarian who does not pay enough attention to learning will never do as well as the teacher with average discipline, and a clear focus on learning. Again, from *What Makes Great Teaching?*

"Classroom management (moderate evidence of impact on student outcomes) are a teacher's abilities to make efficient use of lesson time, to coordinate classroom resources and space, and to manage students' behaviour with clear rules that are consistently enforced. They are all relevant to maximising the learning that can take place. These environmental factors are necessary for good learning rather than its direct components."

But there are three aspects of learning that have higher impact than how well you manage your classroom and behaviour:

1: Seeing the subject's learning through the eyes of the student,

2: Quality of feedback, assessment, modeling, scaffolding,

3: High expectations.

That teacher down the corridor with the noisy classroom and messy desk may get more from her students than the highly organised, uber efficient, promotion candidate next door.

Yet, who is likely to get the higher grade in a lesson observation? Who earns more respect in school? Who is more likely to be promoted? The disciplinarian, every day of the week. Because, in school, we value proxies for learning far more than the evidence of learning itself.

Be the Guide on the Side, Not the Sage on the Stage

Here's Hattie again, on the interventions of teacher as "activator", and the effect of the teacher as "facilitator".

"Effect sizes for teacher as activator and teacher as facilitator

Teacher as Activator d		Teacher as Facilitator d	
Reciprocal teaching	0.74	Simulations and gaming	0.32
Feedback	0.72	Inquiry based teaching	0.31
Teaching students self-verbalisation	0.67	Smaller class sizes	0.21
Meta-cognition strategies	0.67	Individualised instruction	0.20
Direct instruction	0.59	Problem based learning	0.15
Mastery learning	0.57	Different teaching for boys and girls	0.12
Goals – challenging	0.56	Web-based learning	0.09
Frequent effects of testing	0.46	Whole language – reading	0.06
Behavioural organisers	0.41	Inductive teaching	0.06
Average activator	**0.60**	**Average facilitator**	**0.17"**

How many times have you heard the idea, "be the guide on the side, not the sage on the stage"? Perhaps you have even believed it. The research appears to be quite clear though. This book is very much about activating you, so that you deliberately practise the right things.

Reciprocal teaching doesn't involve being a 'facilitator'. It does indeed call for you to stop teaching and watch the students teach each other – but it presupposes you have taught them directly first; you are in this sense an "activator", not a "facilitator". In this way, students are teaching what they already know, not having to find everything out for themselves.

This is dramatically different from most classrooms in most schools. In most classes I visit, whichever school I work in, teachers facilitate and elicit.

If we really try to impress, pulling out all the stops in search of excellent learning, we do two stupid things: we throw in group work, and we make students discover things for themselves. We have been programmed to believe that organizing our classroom so that students learn independently is the gold standard of teaching. It isn't.

We may throw in Bloom's Taxonomy, SOLO Taxonomy, DeBono's hats, Personal Learning and Thinking Skills etc to shape the tasks that students do. We obsess about their skills as learners. Again, we assume this is the gold standard of teaching. But it is of only secondary importance. I know this sounds wrong – how can the students' skills at learning not be the most important aspect of our teaching? Let me show you through an example:

Think Through the Eyes of a Learner (Why I Love Mixed Metaphors)

To help you see beyond the mirror of your classroom, let's look at a subject you probably don't teach. Imagine you are learning to swim butterfly, in a 50m pool (which represents our classroom). The other 27 students are divided into two groups of 14, one at each end of the pool. The teacher gets one student to demonstrate the stroke (to represent the modeling you do in lessons). Or, the teacher explains what butterfly looks like, and while standing on the side, moves both her arms simultaneously, so that they look like the butterfly arms (to represent the sort of explanation I see in many classrooms – partial, wordy, without a clear view of the whole model).

The swimming teacher excels at classroom management, so you all know to set off at once toward the middle. To avoid colliding, you all know to stop, tread water, change direction and swim back to. 28 of you all make some progress. The teacher watches, and after a few more goes, offers advice that is pertinent to many students. She has a word with a couple who are struggling. Again, many students make progress. Clearly, this is outstanding teaching – excellent classroom management and feedback has led to progress.

Ok. But if you had spent your 10,000 hours with more deliberate practice, you wouldn't be thinking about the SLT or Ofsted observer, and you'd look beyond the 'outstanding' label. Instead, you'd look at learning. This would be far from an outstanding lesson. Your complete focus would be on learning. You would always ask yourself this question: ***How can my class learn this best?***

Let's rerun the lesson, from this point of view. Your teacher knows that, because of the mix of abilities, at best her advice will be relevant to half of the class. That's 14 students. Of those, perhaps only 11 will listen closely enough to learn from her advice.

But now compare that to a fellow student teaching you. Your teacher selects pairs, having worked out from previous lessons who is likely to know what they are doing, or to learn it quickest – they become the student teachers in the pair.

Your student teacher swims next to you, watching your technique, and then telling you what to change. You still don't quite get it, so he shows you in his own stroke. Meanwhile, this happens with everyone else, in teaching pairs. Obviously, your adult teacher is still watching, giving general advice, and having quiet words with those who are struggling. She is working no harder and no differently, but her class are now making much more progress.

Some of the advice the student teachers give will be wrong, but research says an astonishing 50% will be right. On average. But if your pairing is based on how well you had learned backstroke, the chances are your student teacher would be correct more often than 50%. And where they were wrong, you could self correct. When your teacher stops the class to draw everyone's attention to an aspect of the stroke, you check yourself again, even correcting your student teacher, if you spot something that contradicts with the class teacher. Now, learning happens all the time.

Now your swimming teacher reverses the roles, so that you watch your student teacher. Teaching them further clarifies what to look for in your own stroke. Even better, it is easy for you to see, because it is happening right in front of you – you don't have to imagine what really good butterfly looks like. This is much more effective than being told how to improve, when you can't see what that eventual improvement will look like.

That's reciprocal teaching, d 0.74. This is clearly a much better way for you to teach, but you are likely to resist it. This is odd, because intellectually, it makes sense. Incredibly, it takes no more effort – you will still give the same number of instructions, and intervene with the same number of students. Your interactions, in terms of effort, will be exactly the same. But it demands a complete change in your behaviour. Are you willing to address this? Are you willing to change your view of teaching, so that you can instead focus on learning?

Why Learning to Learn Can be Secondary

Now, let's look at the learning to learn agenda I said was secondary. Did the swimming teacher teach her class *how* to learn? No, she got her class to see the model, then copy it, however imperfectly. Then she kept getting her students to compare their stroke to the model, by having a student correct it. She didn't teach her students how to use a model – she simply got them doing it.

Did she have to teach that student to *analyse* the other student's stroke? No. They learned to anlayse by looking at the model, then comparing what their student was doing. Students got better at analysing by analysing, not by being told how to analyse.

Did she teach them how to *synthesise*? No, she just asked all her students to put the whole stroke together each time, so that synthesis at some level was always present.

This is why teaching your students how to learn is secondary. The trick is always to give students a model, so that they have to learn. Simply putting your students in pairs where one student teaches the other will keep them learning, comparing themselves to the model.

Would this approach get you an outstanding lesson observation? Yes. But that is not why it's here. It's to show you how to get outstanding learning. I hope to reconnect you with why you started teaching in the first place. It was to make a difference, wasn't it?

The Impact of CPD Reveals Teachers are not Very Reflective

The impact of CPD is low. How can this be?

I am the senior leader in charge of teaching and learning at my school. When I began teaching, there was no such thing as an Assistant Head. No such thing as a leader in charge of teacher training. There were no training days. What a revolution there has been! And now I'm going to ask you to buy this book, as your own personal form of CPD. What could be more powerful than that? This is how *What Makes Great Teaching?* rates the impact of CPD:

"Behaviours exhibited by teachers such as reflecting on and developing professional practice, participation in professional development, supporting colleagues, and liaising and communicating with parents" have only "some evidence of impact on student outcome." Oops.

Why is the impact of CPD is so low? Most schools offer whole school training days, twilight sessions, department meetings and several trips to external providers for each faculty. A typical school CPD budget might be in the range of £30,000. Add to that the cost of 60 teachers at £180 per day for 5 training days a year, and the cost of lost teaching time is another £54,000. Why is this £80,000+ so unproductive?

Let's start with the idea of "reflecting on ... professional practice". We hit our 10,000 hours relatively quickly. But is it deliberate practice? Only if we are reflective. Many teachers are weak at this. I have lost count of the number of candidates at interview who have been unable to reflect meaningfully on what learning happened in the lesson they had just taught. This is just as likely to be so for interviews of Assistant Heads and Deputy Heads. I'm not dismissing them because they had a different interpretation to mine, rather that they had a real difficulty talking about the learning in the lesson. Instead they talk about the students' engagement, or the teacher's use of time.

They simply don't look for evidence of learning. This is not a criticism of the teacher's intent; I'm not suggesting they deliberately failed to reflect, but that this is a difficult skill to master. Because it requires painful honesty.

Unless you are honest with yourself, you won't be able to change the way you view teaching.

Few of us are that honest. If we were, would we fear observation? I have overcome this barrier to honesty many times by simply filming lessons. However, that has not overcome the barrier of fear. Because, as a profession, we are reluctant to accept too much honesty. It reminds me of the headteacher who received a "requires improvement" grade on an Ofsted inspection and wrote to parents to point out that this meant they were "on a journey to outstanding".

We are all on this journey. But it really helps to have a map. If you are reflective, you are much more likely to see the map. The problem with CPD is that we latch on to two kinds of information – that which confirms what we already believe, and that which looks shiny, new and likely to impress an observer. Rarely do we focus on what will transform learning in our classrooms.

There is no fair measure of my impact on students

It is very difficult to change our own beliefs. Consider that the single most important piece of information in your school about your teaching is the progress your students made.

Most SLTs I know don't look at this year on year – they are very unlikely to know your value added over the last 5 years. They usually get very excited when things go wrong in a single year – why did this subject, or this class bomb? – which is often short sighted. Sample size plays a large part then. Listen to them drawing meaningful conclusions from the last A level class, which had only 8 students in it. Or the last three years' A level results which still only totals 24 students. They often won't look at how those same students did in other classes. It is very rare indeed that they will aggregate your last 3 years, or 5 years' progress data, to give you a very meaningful sample size.

But what's stopping you from doing this? Why are you waiting passively for your SLT to comment? Indeed, why are you happy to accept the excellent results of this year's students, without looking at the last 3 or 5 or 8 yourself? You're the teacher who wants to be a little bit awesome. When will you start to measure your impact properly to see how you're doing?

Even teachers with low impact get glowing emails from past students, by the way: teachers are lovely and have students' best interests at heart. The fact that you get Christmas cards and friends requests on Facebook, and some students who think you are the best thing since I'm a Celebrity is not proof of your impact. We all have stories about individual students like that. Let's not get warm and fuzzy here – this is about honesty.

It is your beliefs that need changing. I'm sorry, there isn't an easier way to put this. Let's develop the example with your classes:

- their progress against FFTD targets
- against where they were when you inherited them
- against their progress in all their other subjects

That's three separate measures of value added.

Put these together, and you have a good measure of how effective you are. Do this every year, and your picture gets more and more real, less and less influenced by sample size.

You will also be able to find every teacher in your school who had a similar ability class, or a class with many of the same students as your class. You can clearly see your value added compared to theirs. This will tell you who to advise, and from whom to seek advice. This is the most relevant CPD you could possibly do – and I bet you've never done it.

So here's the thing. All the data you need to work out how effective you have been is sitting there. Have you found it? How do you know whether you are making a difference unless you measure it? And if you are not making a difference, then what are you making?

Let's pause to consider the reasons we come up with to suggest that it is not a viable question to ask about a teacher's value added, the progress of their students.

1. We can't be sure what the effect of their previous teacher was.

2. The class is dominated by boys.

3. It is a middle set.

4. FFTD is not always right.

5. We can't believe a level 5 in primary school is the same as a level 5 in secondary school.

6. Too many students had high absence rates.

7. School trips, exams, careers, training days (insert whatever) took too much of my teaching time.

8. Too many of their lessons were in the afternoon.

9. James was in the lesson and had a pervasive influence on too many others.

10. And Jamil, Jason, and Jessica.

11. They have poor parenting.

12. They're disadvantaged.

13. Thirty is much too small a sample to draw meaningful conclusions from.

14. I shared the class with so and so.

Yadayadayada. Yes, each of these might be true, but they are very likely to be true in many of the other classes, and indeed in the whole cohort FFTD predictions come from.

Year upon year, your sample size will get bigger, and the reliability of your results will consequently grow. And there will be plenty of teachers in your school who consistently do well, every year, regardless of the class – this is not a random occurrence. If results just depend on the quality of your class, we would expect teachers with reputations as poor teachers to often get very good progress. I have found this to be very unusual (and I always look). But I find plenty of examples the other way, teachers with excellent reputations who have average or poor value added.

If you will accept that the progress of your students is the key to your improvement, then this book will have done its job. Put the book down and find out what your effect has been. Then find the teachers who have had similar classes to you, but performed better. Seek them out for a discussion of what they did. Share this. Go to your SLT and ask them to do the same with all teachers. If you do that, this book will already have paid for itself. Everything you hear will be directly relevant to you – real teachers, whom you know, teaching real kids in the real world, in a context exactly like yours. All you have to do is change your beliefs.

Many of you might find this focus on progress and your students' results difficult. It's bad form to ask what effect we have had on our students' results. Instead we have checklists of behaviours that make for good and outstanding teaching. But it is usually a common sense list, not one grounded in research. And it is often wrong. (Remember how progress had to be visible in twenty minutes, then over the course of the lesson, then 'over time'?) What was 'right' can only become 'wrong' so very quickly because we value the wrong things.

The research says my experience is typical. We do something else instead to measure our effectiveness. Robert Coe again:

"Interestingly, a number of teacher characteristics (such as teachers' self-reported self-efficacy, extraversion and conscientiousness) were found by Rockoff et al (2011) to be related to supervisor ratings of effectiveness but not to actual student achievement gains."

Leadership teams are rewarding the wrong behaviours, because they are merely common sense, visible behaviours, which are not based on student progress. Perhaps you are familiar with this already – being instructed to develop auditory, visual and kinaesthetic learning styles:

"A recent survey found that over 90% of teachers in several countries (including the UK) agreed with the claim that "Individuals learn better when they receive information in their preferred learning style (for example, visual, auditory or kinaesthetic)" (Howard-Jones, 2014)…but the psychological evidence is clear that there are no benefits for learning from trying to present information to learners in their preferred learning style (Pashler et al, 2008; Geake, 2008; Riener and Willingham, 2010; Howard-Jones, 2014)."

This can only happen because of the prevalence of the checklist in schools. An Amazon search of "The perfect Ofsted" delivers 17 books with these words in their title. Try a search with "outstanding" to see the effect of Ofsted on our thoughts. We are constantly in search of what will be *perceived* to be brilliant. The attention to surface detail is a plague in schools, because it directs our attention to what looks good, rather than what has an impact on our students' learning.

This is not that kind of book. This is about what works. Everything else is subjective, negotiable and potential flim flam.

Chapter 3

"I welcome and seek your ideas, but do not bring me small ideas; bring me big ideas to match our future."

Arnold Schwarzenegger

A Word About Research

I've noticed an increase in criticism about educational research. Coe himself argues that much of the research is poor quality (studies which are therefore not included as having high impact in *What Makes Great Teaching?*).

Some argue that effect sizes are too imprecise because the conditions of each piece of research will be different. Younger students will perform with a higher effect size because they know less, and therefore add more knowledge; the study might focus on one ability group and distort the results; the time taken for the intervention may vary; the researcher is likely to be biased towards confirming a conclusion they set out to find; the class being observed will receive better teaching because they are being observed, etc. etc.

Well yes. This, and no doubt dozens of other problems do exist with interpreting the research. But the more studies included in the meta analysis, the greater the chance of these variables cancelling each other out. Merely because our measurements are not exact, does not mean that they are not broadly accurate.

Probably like the majority of teachers, David Didau, author of *The Secret of Literacy*, and *What if Everything You Knew About School is Wrong*, disagrees, stating on his blog, *The Learning Spy* that:

"In Hattie's meta analysis there's little attempt to control for these problems. This doesn't mean we shouldn't trust that those things he puts at the top of his list don't have greater impact than those at the bottom, but it does mean we should think twice before bandying about effect sizes as evidence of potential impact."

Moreover, it is in our teaching DNA to distrust research, because it is remote, it is ivory tower, and most of all, it often does not correspond to our experience. But our experience is not a window on the world, it is merely a mirror, reflecting back to us what we have learned, however imperfectly, through trial, error, and a good deal of pain. So, we have passionate views about uniform on either side of the debate. It then infuriates all of us when research claims uniform has no impact – uniform or non uniform, it's all the same. Our subject knowledge, our degrees, three or four years of hard work and student debt. Makes nearly no difference to the progress of our students. Are you kidding, Hattie? I mean that just defies all logic, doesn't it Robert Coe? Your effect sizes must be completely, utterly, blindly wrong. The Emperor has no clothes.

But if we look at our experience through the lens of research, we might see things differently.

From Professor Robert Coe again, in *Improving Education: A Triumph of Hope Over Experience*

"The teachers who believe strongly and unshakably that reducing class size from 30 to 15, or adding a teaching assistant into a mainstream classroom, or setting learners into ability groups will make a big difference to learning are often justifying this belief by drawing on an understanding of 'learning' that is at odds with the one being measured in research studies.

For example, in discussing why they believe smaller classes are much better, a teacher will often say, 'You can give students more individual attention.' My question is then, 'Does more individual teacher attention mean more learning? What makes you think that?' In fact, much of the learning that happens in classrooms can be unexpectedly unrelated to what teachers intend, assume or do (Nuthall, 2005, 2007). But somehow the idea that 'I have taught it' becomes a proxy for 'they have learned it', without a need for any independent check on what (if anything) has actually been learned."

This is the heart of the problem. We look for evidence that confirms what we believe or feel. Instead we should look at evidence of progress.

Mixed Ability Teaching

Here's a story of how my experience had to give way to research. Years of teaching mixed ability year 7 had convinced me that a teacher needed to be too skilled to differentiate. In my first years of teaching, I sat all my year 7s in groups to work on mixed ability teaching. I took in an extra shirt to work each day, as I would need to change it at lunch, having sweated too much. It was unsustainable. How much better to set by ability, and allow the more-able to fly. Because lower ability students with similar needs would be grouped together, lesson planning would need little differentiation. Being in smaller classes, they'd get better feedback and individual instruction. In fact, this is what nearly all teachers believe.

When head of English, my head teacher had the bare-faced cheek to suggest that we accelerate our students through Key Stage 3 by the end of year 8. All students, while still teaching in mixed ability year 7, with setting only in year 8. Worse than that, they had to make two levels of progress, ridiculously getting to the same point they would have reached at the end of year 9. Madness. Stupidity.

Yes, I'd read enough research by then to believe this was an opportunity. Acceleration, a deeper curriculum, higher expectations, the lack of ambition of our GCSE exams all led me to believe it was achievable. But with mixed ability classes? Give me a break.

Revaluate Your Curriculum

The only solution to this was not to tinker with the curriculum, but to start from scratch.

I drew a life-size outline of a body on wallpaper roll.

Inside the body, we wrote all the subject knowledge and skills we wanted our perfect English student in year 7 to have. Outside the body we noted all the experiences we wanted them to have in English.

We found that very few were open to debate – we pretty much agreed. Teachers put some bold things down, because this was our ideal student, and our ideal experiences.

What was a little bit awesome came next. We looked at our KS3 curriculum, and we matched all the units of work that fitted the knowledge, skills and experiences that we valued. This meant we had a purpose for keeping parts of the curriculum. And a clear purpose of chucking some away. We instantly saw where the gaps were, and planned new units. This gave us faith in the moral purpose, the English purpose of our curriculum.

At the end of year 7, we gave all our students an old KS3 Sats paper, took a Sats examiner and got them all marked. We wanted to find out the worst, to see what we were up against with this idiotic forced marriage of mixed ability teaching and high aspirations.

Astonishingly, they averaged 92% of a level of progress in one year, in mixed ability classes. There were many things at play. High teacher expectations, an accelerated curriculum, peer teaching where the more-able taught the less able, an element of mastery teaching, worked examples, etc. All techniques that the research said would work. And they did. With mixed ability teaching that none of us believed could work. By and large without differentiation (which the research also suggests does not work).

By the end of year 8 they averaged nearly two levels of progress. All our experience (getting on for 100 years of teaching) told us this would not be possible with mixed ability teaching in year 7. But we were wrong.

Do You Have Split Classes?

In the following year our expectations were floored again. The timetable became more complicated, so that our classes were often split in year 7, between two teachers, and sometimes three. How could we possibly do our jobs properly with our hands tied so ridiculously by the SLT? How could we meet their impossible demands on progress? Idiots. A year of teaching this way only confirmed our worst fears. We were convinced that we had been sabotaged.

But now it gets very interesting. I analysed the results of each class, and compared it to the number of teachers it had had – one, two or three. The progress of the class was greater in that order – the more teachers a class had, the more progress the students made. Surely an anomaly? But no. The pattern continued for the next two years, when I stopped looking.

It is worth pausing here to consider some implications of this. I did not learn from this that the best way to design a timetable is therefore to split all your classes (although we assume it is the best way to teach A level because, well, just because.)

Hopefully, we begin to see that some of our beliefs have no foundation in logic, and are not objective, they are emotional responses. Often, our emotional responses will be right, but we must look for evidence of impact first, to see if this is true.

How We Made Split Classes Work

Clearly split classes shouldn't work. Our feelings were unanimous: they didn't work. We did not believe the evidence of our own eyes – our emotions or preconceptions would not allow us to believe students progressed better this way *even when the evidence proved that they did*. Here are some tentative reasons why I think split classes worked.

1. No one had to plan a lesson. All the lessons were already planned, and the resources for the lesson were also included in a single software, Flipchart for Promethean boards, equivalent to PowerPoint.

2. All our classes were mixed ability, so you would expect us to differentiate the objectives and the resources for each class. But actually, I refused to do this. I figured that if you taught the whole class how to achieve level 6+, those at 4- would pick up some stuff that took them to level 4+, or level 5. If you look at how bottom sets cope with Shakespeare, you'll get a hint of why this works. To them, everything is difficult, so Shakespeare is no harder than *The Hobbit* or Enid Blyton. To them, level 5 is just as hard as level 6, it's just something they can't fully grasp yet.

3. We organised the curriculum so that each teacher was responsible for a unit. So they had their own exercise book for their class.

4. An unexpected benefit is feedback. If you have a split class, it is likely that you have a gap between lessons. In this gap, you have a much better opportunity to mark, and for that marking to lead to something. Even better, on some days, you would get the class twice. This meant they learned something, had a break, and relearned it, and then went in to more depth. This meant they learned more and more quickly.

5. Again, unexpectedly, but entirely in line with the research on memory, the increased gap between lessons also allowed students to forget. This is important, as when they think about this learning, revisiting it, memory is improved – next time they forget more slowly. This is called the 'forgetting curve' which we'll meet later with Robert Bjork to learn more about this amazing feature of memory.

6. This brings us to interleaving. Memory works better if learners move from one topic to another. This is because it helps with the forgetting curve – they forget, revisit, develop better neural pathways, forget less, and so on. This is very difficult to do as a single class teacher. It feels wrong and (as the research says) the kids don't like it. It is hard. But it works. And having more than one teacher made it inevitable that our students would have time for the forgetting curve, and for interleaving learning, changing topics every week.

7. We all did assessments where each student had to aim for at least level 6 by the end of year 7, even though those entering at level 3 would not get there. There were relatively few of these. And we wanted lots to get to level 7, so we taught them how. To do this, every assessed skill had to be modelled. We started with a level 7 example, and then gradually built

up a bank written by students at different levels. We did this for every unit of work, and every assessment. So differentiated resources were built in where necessary. This was always done through modelling, never dumbing down by giving easier texts.

8. To keep us on track, we standardised testing with the SAT paper. This was also efficient because we had always used it as a year 9 mock. We made it the end of year paper in year 8 and year 7, giving us reliable marks. To make it more reliable, we took off timetable for a day one teacher, an SAT marker. This gave us consistency. Finally, we didn't want the year to be dictated by the SAT test, so we prepared a two-week unit – this was the *only* time we were able to teach to the test. And we kept this when SATs disappeared, because it worked.

Why Your Beliefs Will Get in the Way of the Facts

Because we did not like having our classes split, because it was alien to us, because it was simply logical for it to disrupt learning, our experience was that it was a disaster. This forced us to find ways to overcome the disaster.

Yet our experience was completely at odds with the facts, with what was unfolding in front of our eyes. We were literally blind to it. Our beliefs will do that. Your beliefs will do that.

Here is Dylan Wiliam, co-author of *Inside the Black Box*, and assessment for learning guru, in reply to David Didau's objections to the research above. I believe he was agreeing that research results, and the idea of ranking through d effects, are valid for teachers:

"Here is the full Kelvin quote:

"I often say that when you can measure what you are speaking about, and express it in numbers, you know something about it; but when you cannot express it in numbers, your knowledge is of a meagre and unsatisfactory kind; it may be the beginning of knowledge, but you have scarcely, in your thoughts, advanced to the stage of science, whatever the matter may be."

www.learningspy.co.uk/education/unit-education/#comments

So ranking educational research is valid. But in the same discussion, he claims, "Actually, the effect sizes proposed by Hattie are, at least in the context of schooling, just plain wrong. Anyone who thinks they can generate an effect size on student learning in secondary schools above 0.5 is talking nonsense."

And there it is again. "This doesn't match my experience, therefore it must be wrong". "This just isn't logical, it must be wrong". "I don't know of a school that is doing this, it must be wrong." This is what we all say. It's what I used to say, until I started looking at learning, looking at impact.

So I described a real curriculum to him. Here it is. Having accelerated KS2 to end in year 8, we revolutionised year 9. We set up an English option curriculum. We advised, but did not dictate, that students who had not reached level 4a by the end of year 8 could opt to do English language GCSE over year 9 and 10, taking it a year early, but having two years to learn it instead of one. Or students could opt for a creative writing course with an anthology book vanity published at the end of the year. Alternatively, any student at level 6a or better could opt to do English language and literature GCSEs by the end of year 10, and AS literature in year 11. We aimed this at students who suspected they would take science and maths in sixth form.

Finally, anyone of any ability or prior attainment could opt to take GCSE media studies (instead of English) in year 9 – done and dusted, in two and half terms, with the GCSE taken in year 9.

What was the result of this madness? 100 out of 186 students took GCSE media studies and gained 90% C to A*, with the full range of grades. Their results exceeded the national grades for GCSE media studies of students in year 11. They exceeded their FFTD predictions for taking GCSE media studies in year 11. And of course many of the most able in the cohort, 20 or so, had opted for AS Literature, so were not able to inflate the grades of the media cohort. This continued to happen every year, with results always over 85%.

If d 0.4 represents a year's extra progress, that would be the effect of giving our year 11 students only one year to study media studies. What is the effect size of making two years' progress two years early? Do the math.

I should also add that I simply created the curriculum here – I did not lead the teaching of GCSE media studies, nor even teach any of the classes. My delight is because the research was right. In this case, acceleration at d 0.62. It felt like a leap of faith, but actually was simply a logical step.

My opinions are therefore improved when I view them through the lens of research. I can justify virtually anything from my own experience, because, hey, I lived through it, no one can deny me that. But to write about my opinions as gospel is a blog. I'm not interested in my own experience here except in so far as it throws a light on the research, and vice versa.

Each chapter consequently begins with an aspect of teaching with Hattie's effect size, and then offers suggestions on what that might look like in the real world of the classroom, and I hope, in your subject. Each chapter will deal with a higher effect size than the one preceding it – so that there is always a reason to read on, or so I hope. I have been very fortunate to have had so many of my beliefs challenged by the research. It's been painful at times, and often annoying. But if only one chapter helps you improve the way you teach, or how you lead your team, your time will have been well spent. There are a lot of chapters. Hopefully we can start panning for gold.

Chapter 4

"Milk is for babies. When you grow up you have to drink beer."

"'I'll be back' always sounded a little girly to me."

Arnold Schwarzenegger

Getting the Best out of Boys

Surprisingly the difference in boys' and girls' achievement is overstated in schools and the press. Research shows a d = 0.12. This is based on 2926 studies, covering 5,594,832 students. Hattie tells us boys and girls "are more alike than they are different. The evidence for this claim is overwhelming."

The research is quite clear on gender differences, and it shows that the difference in progress is cultural. In most countries, it seems, your gender does matter; gender does affect your progress. However, there are just as many countries where it helps to be a boy, which is why the actual effect of gender is tiny. However, in England as we all know, girls outperform boys:

"The gap between the proportion of girls getting A*-C and boys is at its highest rate since 2003 despite boys getting a slightly higher share of A* grades.

The *GCSE results today showed the female A*-C rate* was 73.1% compared to 64.3% for males, a gap of 8.8 percentage points and a small increase on last year.

Looking back at the results since GCSEs were introduced in 1989, *using data from the Centre for Education and Employment Research (CEER)*, it's quite striking just how wide the gap has remained over that time."

www.theguardian.com/news/datablog/2014/aug/21/gcse-results-2014-biggest-gap-11-boys-and-girls-a-c-pass-rate

How to Solve the Gender Gap in England

In my time as head of English we got this gap down to below 2% while 85% of students made the expected 3 levels of progress for several years running. How did we buck the trend? Not the best in the country, but not bad. We didn't double enter everyone for exams either – over 80% of students took their exam only once. We didn't care if some took their GCSE a year or two early. We didn't care that 100 out of 186 didn't study any English at all in year 9. We didn't collapse the timetable for a day's intensive English before the exam. We didn't force students to come in at the weekend, or in their holidays. We didn't stage interventions. We didn't redraft lots of coursework. We didn't have endless mocks. We didn't increase the amount of curriculum time because we were a 'core' subject. I point this out because, morally, I believe we should aim to be excellent teachers. But too often, leaders take the moral view that we should simply do much more in response to raised stakes. This book is in part a desire to mediate that conflict, and to alleviate teachers and leaders from that unsustainable pressure.

We could have done even better if we had pursued results more energetically, but we still wanted job satisfaction and a work life balance. I hope this book helps you to do the same.

Whenever I looked at results, I could find no pattern that explained the high performance of boys – whether they were taught by NQTs, experienced teachers, whether the teacher was male or female made no difference. This suggested it is what we had in common as a department that mattered, not our differences.

How did we manage to do so well with boys, in a subject where the gap nationally is massive, over 16% and growing? There are boy friendly techniques you'll meet in this chapter, but their impact is small. Your expectations will make the most difference, and these expectations begin with setting.

A Word About Setting

As we have seen, The Sutton Trust and Hattie both point out that setting is not a reliable way to improve students' results.

If you want to see just how ridiculous the impulse to set students is, look at a grammar school where all students have passed the eleven plus and at least 90% of them arrive with three level 5s. In a comprehensive school they would all be expected to get an A or an A* in every subject. But in a grammar school, they are just as likely to be set. Really, this is true.

You can easily see what this does to those not in the top set – not only are they labelled by their teachers, but they begin to label themselves as not good enough, not clever enough and (no doubt confirming their teachers' wise judgements) probably proceed to do less well than those in the higher sets. In this way, two nearby grammar schools to my own comprehensive achieved an average B+ for the GCSE grades of their students. In the same year our students entering at level 5 averaged an A-. Last year, this dropped to a B+ – and we are disappointed, believing we are not challenging the more-able enough. In this way, the grammar school setting of able students has actually lead to poorer results.

So powerful is this effect, whereby we compare ourselves to those around us, rather than against a more objective measure, that it causes 75% of students at Harvard, the world's top university, to underachieve. How can this be? Malcolm Gladwell in *David and Goliath* shows us. The graduates from the top 25% of scientists at a mid ranking university will produce more research papers, published in better journals than scientists graduating from the bottom 75% of Harvard. Even more remarkably, all of those Harvard graduates will have had entry scores on their SATs far in excess of the top 25% of the mid ranking university. But they stop believing in themselves, because they are not in the top 25% of their own cohort.

We convince ourselves that setting is necessary in order to get the best out of the top 25% and sacrifice the chances of the rest. But parents also expect this, and consequently we set. We need middle class parents with high expectations, because they provide students with high expectations and good work ethics, and fewer problems in family background, and more support at home with homework and wider culture. They make our schools calmer, harder working and more polite. And of course they attract other parents with similar students. They protect our jobs, because it is easier for the school to escape a poor Ofsted judgement, there are arguably fewer disruptions, and rolls are less likely to fall.

The Education Endowment Foundation sees setting as producing a negative effect, "Low attaining learners fall behind by one or two months a year, on average, when compared with the progress of similar students in classes without ability grouping. It appears likely that routine setting or streaming arrangements undermine low attainers' confidence and discourage the belief that attainment can be improved through effort.."

educationendowmentfoundation.org.uk/toolkit/

This becomes even more heated when we consider that those of us who are parents also expect our own children to be stretched in top sets. Most of our friends are also tooled up with degrees, MAs and PHDs, who also expect their children to get in to top sets. Our world view is pretty much centred on this principle of setting. Ok, the research might suggest setting is a false god, but Gove, Nicky Morgan-Gove and future-Gove, government, our friends and, above all, prospective parents of hard working kids, beg to differ.

And in a world where we have to compete for students, why wouldn't we seek those who work hardest and whose parents already get what school is about? Who wants to teach in a constantly challenging school, or one with falling rolls, improbable floor targets and consequent jobs at risk?

So this is not an attack on setting in your school. Indeed, there are schools in which setting does work, as the EEF observes, "it should be noted that there are some exceptions to this average, where ability grouping has benefitted all learners. Further study could be undertaken to understand what happened differently in these examples." However, the myth cited in defence of setting is attacked here. Differentiation – the myth is that setting does it better. How can you teach a mixed ability class and differentiate for everyone? How can you personalise for that variety of abilities? Impossible right? Setting is the answer...

The EEF Toolkit ranks the gold standard of differentiation, individual instruction, as conferring only 2 months extra progress. "Individualised instruction provides different tasks for each learner and provides support at the individual level. It is based on the idea that all learners are different and therefore have different needs, so an individualised or personally tailored approach to instruction ought to be more effective, particularly in terms of the tasks and activities that students undertake and the pace at which they make progress through the curriculum." This is twice as effective as it ranks the use of a TA, at one month. But given the amount of effort involved in this 'perfect' form of differentiation, is it worth the effort compared to doing something else? Because it is very unlikely that your attempts at differentiation are anywhere near as comprehensive as the individualised instruction described above. Moreover, the Toolkit lists 18 interventions with higher impact than this gold standard, and only 9 with worse.

But we should also bear in mind the damaging effect of setting on learning. Then, we should try to repair as much of that damage as we can.

How to Make Setting Work

Ok, so you're stuck with setting by ability. But look closer. Are your bottom sets dominated by boys? Are your middle sets' populations two thirds boys? Are your top sets filled with more girls, even in maths and science? Hang on, don't boys do worse than girls in English schools? Could this be more than correlation?

Consequently, as head of English I ranked my teachers' assessment of students' work as less important than other data. I trusted their assessments. I just decided they were less important in determining setting. Most important was their predicted grade, in our case FFTD. Why? Because this is based on past performance. If a student has got a level 5 in year 6, at worst it will mean that they have been coached to within an inch of their lives. You'll have heard this is not a real level 5, it is performance enhanced. But even if this were true, it means that before you sits a highly motivated, and incredibly teachable child. This may be much more valuable than a student who is simply able, but may not know how to cope when work becomes challenging.

Next I go to the IQ test your school probably uses, CATs or Midyis, and put all the students with a verbal score of over 114 in a top set. (For other subjects you might choose the overall score, or the numeracy score). Then do the same with those who have a non verbal reasoning score of over 114. Suddenly this promotes a significant number of boys into top sets. In other words, if I simply relied on how the boys had performed in year 7, many of them would not make it into a top set. I trusted my department's assessments, but these will ignore underachievement. My job is to tell those underachieving that this is not good enough – the only reason they have potential is because they have not reached it yet.

It is not your head of department's job to do the setting themselves. You can offer to do this for your department, or shadow whoever does it, and compare the difference in sets when you produce new ones, as above.

Now you have to look at your setting structure. It might mean that instead of two top sets, you have to have three, or indeed four. I often had to have four, or 60% of the year group. Although it was never perfect, we still got an enormous number of A and A* results from it. It also allowed me to move disruptive students into a top set, where they would find few allies and generally knuckle down. It is very common for a school to have 35% of its students arrive with a level 5. In a year group of 200, this is 70 students. Add to this another 5 – 10% who came in at a level 4, but are now beginning to excel at the end of year 7, and you have another 15 top set students. Then, another 5% of students who have very high IQ scores, but who have underachieved in primary schools and in year 7. Another 10 students. Suddenly there are 95 top set students, minimum in your year group.

But if you ignore this, persisting with two top sets, you have only 64 out of these 95 students in a top set. Suddenly, by the end of year 7, you have rendered it almost inevitable that 31% of your best students will underachieve. This is bonkers. You are creating a setting system that forces large numbers of students to underachieve. Even at the level of whole school results, these 95, minus the 64 you put in two top sets, leaves 31 students who should be top set, but are told they are not. 15% of your students will automatically underachieve simply because you have mis-set them. Before they enter the room, before you have taught them. Now, because these are more-able students, only a few of them will show up in your 5A* to C figures, and our failure has been hidden. But in your progress 8 all of them will matter, which is a good thing.

At the other extreme, very occasionally we had a cohort of students who would not work well for many of their teachers. Here we have been quite open, writing to parents and pointing out that if their behaviour for learning over year 9 continued to disrupt their class, then they would be put in one class, together, in year 10. These 12 to 15 students would then be given to one of our strongest teachers. They would all, of course, be boys. They would still do ok, but the classes they left could now excel.

This might seem shocking. But actually it is much less shocking than what probably happens in your own school. We never told these boys they were stupid. We told them their behaviour was preventing their peers from learning. In your school it is likely that, through the message of your setting, you have told them that because they are male, they are stupid, and because they are stupid, they behave inappropriately, and because of their combined poor behaviour and stupidity they deserve to be in a bottom set.

Which message would you rather give? Which message is more likely to get the best out of the class? Which message convince boys in the rest of the year group that they are expected to succeed?

What is the problem with boys?

'Boys' is a four letter word. Boys top the league tables for truancy, for detentions, for exclusions temporary and permanent, for calling out in lessons, for lack of homework, for poor effort, for untidy handwriting, for arriving late, for disturbances at break and lunchtime, for vandalism, for forgetting equipment, for not taking letters home to parents, for provoking each other, for tapping desks and clicking pens, for prodding friends, and drawing on them, for verbal put downs of others in and out of class ... Girls simply cannot compete, except academically, where the gap between them and boys continues to grow, much remarked upon, but still unchecked.

So, what are we to do? The research is vague in many ways: we can teach boys and girls in separate schools, but find that both boys and girls do better academically this way, yet the gap between them increases. We can set by gender in our school, but this tends to benefit the girls alone (and we can't have that, can we?). But, what if we want girls to take risks, and speculate like boys, and what if we want boys to be considerate, supportive and reflect like girls? Can we do this if we divide them, and so teach them not to value the skills the others have?

Are You Part of the Problem?

Try this test. Below is a list of the typical ways that boys and girls learn. Which ones do you reward, or value in the classroom?

Students who are good at:

1. Collaborating
2. Articulating thoughts
3. Answering questions
4. Planning and organising
5. Apply learning from other subjects
6. Interrupting
7. Asking for help
8. Get work done quickly
9. Engage in practical work
10. Good at literacy
11. Review their learning
12. Respond to feedback
13. Calling out answers
14. Students who help other students
15. Making jokes, laughing
16. Taking creative risks
17. Openly trying to beat their peers

Here is the list again, with a guide as to whether it is a male or female way of learning in the classroom.

Students who are good at:

1. Collaborating   g
2. Articulating thoughts   g
3. Answering questions   b
4. Planning and organising   g
5. Apply learning from other subjects   g
6. Interrupting   b
7. Asking for help   g
8. Get work done quickly   b
9. Engage in practical work   b
10. Good at literacy   g
11. Review their learning   g
12. Respond to feedback   g
13. Calling out answers   b
14. Students who help other students   g
15. Making jokes, laughing   b
16. Taking creative risks   b
17. Openly trying to beat their peers   b

Now, like our staff, you know that some of these are typically male, some typically female. We looked at teachers' reports on students. The results were fascinating: they showed a huge bias towards praising girls and criticizing boys, even where attainment was similar.

However, when we asked teachers to look at this list, many teachers found it very hard to admit this in their own teaching, and identified male characteristics as ones that they rewarded. In other words, so alert were they to being judged as sexist, that they simply retold their story differently.

Perhaps you think I am too hard on them? Not at all, theirs is a natural reaction: no one enjoys implied criticism. You decide for yourself. Total up whatever reward system operates in your school. Find the top 30 students in each year. Take the head of year and the Head teacher, praise the children to the hilt, then photograph them by year group. Group the boys at the front, and the girls everywhere else. You know what you will see, but seeing it is all the more powerful. In every year group, the smiling faces will be almost entirely girls'.

Try it with year seven, after their first half term. The result will be the same. Compare these to their KS2 results, and you will see the problem straight away: the boys have just arrived, and we have already stereotyped them, we have already told them that they are not good enough. If you still need convincing, photograph the top ten boys in year seven and eight who do not make the top 30 students overall for effort grades, or for attitude to learning grades. Talk to their teachers and tutors. These boys, it will be universally claimed, are wonderful, a pleasure to teach; if only all boys were like this. Then tell the teachers what you have found, how little reward for effort they have had. Perhaps most boys could be like this. Perhaps they already are.

Yes, you might see my point, but still say that the problem with boys is not the school's, but social: it is single parent families, and absent fathers, and the addiction to Play Stations and X boxes, the fact that many of them have computers, phones or tablets for best friends, that boys don't read, that they are quicker to try drugs and crime, that they eat too much sugar, that parents don't discipline them properly anymore. But stop. Let's say this is all true. Yet, if a school can't make a difference to its students, what is the point of having a school, of being a teacher? Again, your expectations will have far greater impact than boy friendly teaching techniques.

Praising Boys

Thanks to the work of Carol Dweck on growth mindset, many teachers assume that praise is wrong. It isn't. Dweck's work asks us to be careful to praise directed effort and perseverance, not intelligence or ability.

Consider your reaction to your leadership team. How often do you get told what a great job you are doing? It doesn't happen often, does it? You might well remember times when you have put yourself out, and no one has mentioned it. In fact this probably happens all the time.

I've just deleted a list of 27 changes I've had to cope with this year. And I have hardly even scratched the surface of changes affecting you, and I haven't even mentioned the photocopier, which attacks you once a week, exactly when you don't have a plan B. It is constant change, and yet you rarely get any praise for coping with it, and often feel you might not be coping at all.

And the effect is predictable. You defend your corner. You start to compare yourself to teachers in other subjects and notice that they seem to have it easier than you. You start to realise that many of you feel management have an easy ride, or are not working hard enough, or are ignoring what staff really want. And before you know it, you've become one of them. You have started to moan.

You complain. You are feeling low, but you are starting to drag others down with you. Or perhaps it is not you, but you have seen it in others.

They are the drowning teachers. Do you join in and drown with them, or stay away from the corners of the staff room they complain in, let them drown?

Neither. Instead, throw them a lifeline, offer them praise.

If I haven't convinced you how important this is, and how easy, lets look at the implications it might have for your teaching. Take the bottom ten students in your class. Let your criteria be either effort, performance, or behaviour. How often do they get praise at home? Do their parents take an interest in their school day, do they ever sit down to homework together? How likely is it that they live with both parents? How much of their time at home is left entirely supervised by TV, video, PlayStation, computer, phone, tablet? How many of them go to sleep before midnight?

Now, picture them at school. It isn't just in your lessons that they are a problem, it is most of them, isn't it? How often do they get told off, told to sort out uniform, told to be quiet, told to stop calling out or stop doodling, or told to stay after class, or spoken to by tutors or heads of year. Add up the times that they are criticised, and compare them to the number of times they are praised. The ratio is huge; it feels entirely negative. And it takes little imagination to see how they start to see themselves in this entirely negative light; it takes little time for them to get locked in to the cycle of negative behaviours rewarded by negative responses. They come to expect it of themselves and they expect it of you.

So, how can you find a way to praise these students so that it is meaningful, and not just a comment on improved behaviour? How can we praise for worthwhile achievement, without dumbing down standards so that they'll reach them? How can you praise them if they continue to lack anything praiseworthy?

How to Motivate Students and Improve Behaviour (Without Working Harder)

All these techniques work with boys. All these techniques work with girls. Because they are aimed at improving behaviour in the classroom, they are all designed to be motivational.

Many of them depend on consistency: if you are like me, this is the hardest part of the job to learn; in other words they are designed to help you to be consistent even if this is your most difficult challenge.

Finally, I am not a super teacher who has devised all these; usually I have stolen them and adapted them from someone else. I have, however, used them all. I should stress that there are some awesome teachers who don't have to do this – they are the legends in your school, the teachers students dare not cross, for whom they dare not miss a homework. This chapter isn't for them. Their personality demands consistency from everyone, beginning with themselves. I simply don't have that level of self control.

Managing Behaviour, Particularly of Boys, Through Competition and Reward.

Most of us find it difficult to meaningfully reward class work each lesson: it will rarely be worth a whole merit, credit or house-point (insert whatever reward system you use here) so we don't give one. Here is a solution.

Rewarding Boys

Organise competitions for absolutely anything that the class do. I award thirds of merits to my winners, and these very quickly build up. And because my organisation is not impeccable, a student enters them in my mark book for me. There are dozens of things you might reward for in your subject. However, below are ways that reward the process of student work.

Managing Writing

- The first two people to copy down the information with perfect spelling and punctuation. Very good for speed and getting students to underline, date, spell, punctuate etc. Sometimes you will find individuals in your class who keep winning. When this happens, nominate them as an expert, and then handicap them. Get them to stand for five or ten seconds after everyone else has been allowed to start.

- Quick spelling tests of key words you are going to use in the lesson. Do these on white boards or scrap paper; you can get a student, a top speller, to mark them instantly. It works just as well as a test of prior learning on subject specific words. It will also play well with whatever literacy initiative is in the school – but this is not why you do it; it is because improving their spelling in your subject makes them more of an expert in your subject. Nominate a boy to check the answer. Boys love the recognition of being chosen as the expert.

- Often, especially with students in year 7 and 8, you will find that your school ethos has deskilled the once highly independent year 6 student, so that they constantly feed you pointless questions that simply delay the task. My solutions with younger students is: "if the question is about the work, the answer is yes. If it is not about the work, don't ask it. If you still have a question, write it down on a line next to your work." Boys also enjoy an extra level of punishment here – if the question could have had the answer "yes" the student has to stand while they work, until I tell them they can sit (usually around 2 or 3 minutes).

- Ask them always to write their question in their book, for you to write a reply. If they are engaged in an extended piece of writing that will take twenty minutes or more, ask them to type a question on the computer. Answer it there. Your typed answer is available to everyone, so this minimises the amount of repeated questions. You also have a record of all the feedback you have needed to give the class, which informs your planning for the next lesson. It also provides you with a perfect starter in another lesson – test them on your replies, to see what they have learned from it. Finally, you are able to reinforce their learning by uploading this dialogue to your school platform.

- During shorter silent writing, do not answer any questions out loud; make students write their questions in their books, so that you can provide a written answer. If you answer even one question aloud, they will start to talk. This seems to be an unwritten law of classrooms. This also provides useful feedback to you, so that you can return to it several lessons later, and see if has been mastered.

- If any student claims 'I don't understand' (which they will!) be very specific; ask them to write down the word or phrase they don't understand. This forces them to think and not waste time.

- Where students are reluctant to check work in draft form, get them to underline say five words that they think might be spelled incorrectly, and reward them when they have been corrected.

- Where students are writing, put a mark in the margin that will stretch the reluctant writers, give them a third of your school reward if they reach this target in your time limit.

- When setting homework or class writing, set specific minimum word limits. You can also set exact word counts, such as 50 or 87 or 22. This can also be done for short writing tasks in class. Boys delight in reaching the exact word number.

Managing Talk

- Many of us spend a lot of time expecting students to work well in pairs and groups. However, we spend very little time showing them how to do it well. Here's how.

- Steal 'Just a Minute', getting students to speak for 1 minute on the topic you are looking at: thirds if they get through it with no pauses or ums or repetition. This can be done in pairs; the winners go forward to the class, or simply open up to volunteers. This works very well as a starter or a plenary.

- Having a method for getting quiet. This is doubly important in group work. When you want silence, have a signal you are comfortable with. This is a very quick way of getting silence, and you are always able to reward the class with praise when they succeed. If they are slow, you can try to beat a time limit. This way, you never have to raise your voice.

- The very best method I've seen used is by a drama teacher at my school – she claps once, her students reply with one clap – she claps three times, her students reply with three claps. They are all silent by this stage, and the whole thing has taken less than 5 seconds.

- Another huge advantage of this is that it reminds you never to talk while your students are still talking. This is a fundamental skill which teachers frequently forget, because they want to move on. It is the easiest way to lose a class, though. If they keep talking while you are talking, not only do they find it difficult to follow what you are saying, you are giving them permission to ignore you. Phil Beadle (in *How to Teach*) advocates a longer than normal pause here, before you speak, so that there is a sense of drama, and so that you can signal your authority.

As a shorthand, any learning that takes place in public will motivate most boys to seek the reward of being recognised, or work harder to avoid producing something poor in case they are summoned. The chapters on feedback, direct instruction, modelling and reciprocal teaching will be particularly useful for you here.

Managing Note Taking

Student Scribes

Ask students to be scribes, so that they take others' ideas while you monitor the responses and behaviour of the class. This is very easy to do now that most classrooms have a computer connected to a projector. Now you can model what good note-taking looks like, either by having it live as the student records notes from the class discussion, or by keeping it off screen until you are ready to reveal, and compare it to notes that students have taken in their books. This allows you to be very explicit about what note-taking looks like.

Students who have good ideas that need to be shared with the class, (e.g. what do we learn about a character in a chapter?), come up to the computer and write up their idea, so that they are rewarded by attention this way.

Get students to be explicit about why they organised notes in a particular way.

Test Students From Their Notes

Validate any form of note taking by testing students on it. For example, if they have devised a mind map to remember everything to comment on when analysing media texts, or the causes of WW1, or the way Buddhist belief affects behaviour, or even British values, take their notes away and ask them to reconstruct the map. Reward straight away.

Ask students to take notes in colour, or to colour code it. This will organise ideas, but also give you a quick way to test and reward: e.g. ask what notes an individual wrote or underlined in green, what diagram they drew in red, what word linked the blue idea to the yellow one. This also models for students how revision works and why mind maps work. This makes it much easier to follow the notes, to categorise them, and therefore to remember them. It also helps that is much easier to look at: they will be a pleasure to mark.

Teach students how to remember. Behaviour is improved if students are aware of their own growing success. For example, give students several facts/ideas/spellings to learn. Get them to visualise it, tell them you will not be testing them by asking them questions, but by getting them to reproduce the whole lot. I have even done this very successfully with bottom sets: here are twelve spellings, or twelve facts, learn them in this order. The test is a blank page; they have to reproduce as many as they can. Thirds to anyone who gets all, or at least ten out of twelve. Merit to anyone who gets all of them in the right order.

Teach Note Taking From Google

Teach students to take notes from the Internet. Begin by copying and pasting in to Word. Present 10 pieces of evidence, all numbered. Group them under at least two headings. Rank the headings in order of importance, and similarly rank the points under each heading. Copy and paste the website address that is the source for each point. Consequently, they must read, understand, précis, prioritise and consider presentation. A very worthwhile task, which takes little marking. It is very easy to reward straight away too: e.g. most sources, or most succinct bullet points, or anyone with a relevant fact that no one else found etc.

If you are researching, tell students in advance that the research will be your teaching resource for the next lesson. This means that it has an audience and a purpose, you are far more likely to get all the work in, and ensure that they try their best at it.

Finance a Note Selling Business

A real audience always motivates students. If you are preparing revision notes, or notes that will form the basis of coursework, offer them the chance to pay for notes. So, the students present their notes, word-processed, or mind-mapped, or in diagrams with symbols, or as real maps, or flow charts etc, to suit their own revison. They then set themselves up as a shop: other students browse, and sign up for a copy of anything they will find most useful. The student who designed the notes collects in the money, say 3 pence per sheet. Students then hand you the orders for photocopying. The author keeps their profits.

If you have been paying attention, you will notice that all these techniques and many in the other sections minimise your marking considerably. At the same time, it increases the number of times that students are assessing themselves, and the number of times that they are being assessed.

Word Process Homework

Set some written work to be done on Word or Publisher or Excel. If it is a homework, you can reward anyone who uses IT. This will be most students in the class, which is fair: if they have used IT they are automatically trying hard. (Clearly you will also have to reward work that also meets your success criteria, so if it doesn't use IT it will still be rewarded). Boys in particular are motivated by this. Moreover, many of the weaker writers will prefer the presentation of their work, and you'll find that they therefore write in greater detail and with more focus. Curiously, they are just as likely not to use a spelling and grammar check, so you can make the reward contingent on them doing so before handing it in.

Publically Displaying Marks

It may feel controversial to display students' marks. However, before dismissing it, look for impact. Boys in my classes significantly improve their efforts when I publish the results of the whole class in the quizzes I set. Because these are tests of memory, and students get three goes at each quiz, everyone can reasonably expect to aim for 100%. Any low mark is therefore richly deserved, and most boys will work harder to avoid this.

A word of warning from Daniel Pink, author of 'Drive'.

Students are likely to perform better if they are intrinsically motivated, rather than extrinsically. To encourage this, you might wish to reward effort, rather than outcome. There is a danger that this will automatically favour girls, however, because of our biased perception of their effort. To compensate for this, it is useful to think in terms of personal bests. This has the advantage of measuring a student's starting point, and thereby rewarding all abilities. I find it particularly useful when setting a maximum number of mistakes, say in ten lines of writing. If students set their own such measureable targets for improvement, then there is a higher chance that they will be intrinsically motivated to meet them.

Chapter 5

*"Strength does not come from winning. Your struggles develop your strengths.
When you go through hardships and decide not to surrender, that is strength."*

Arnold Schwarzenegger

School wide teaching reform   d = 0.22

Hattie wonders why the effect of school wide reform is so low when many of the reforms are clearly based on very good teaching, and when they are clearly aimed at reducing the achievement gap.

If we know the initiative will simply be overtaken by a new one in a year's time, why bother investing emotionally in it? Perhaps it also tells us about the school environment – we are not actually encouraged to think critically about student progress and learning week by week, we just look at final key stage assessments. Even then we tend to look at the level of individual departments, not individual teachers – and it's only an annual event. We don't analyse learning. Instead, during the year, we focus on what can be ticked off our Ofsted/government/SLT inspired checklist – intervention, differentiation, consistency, intervention, feedback, more curriculum time, intervention. During the year, we are more accountable for keeping to the checklist, than for the progress of our individual classes.

To illustrate, let's look at a topical school system reform, the demise of levels.

Life Without Levels

Whose life? My impression, when we frame the problem this way, is that we mean our lives. Teachers. Assessing differently, perhaps in less time, perhaps less frequently.

Imagine that you have your progress data to hand. You've looked back over the last few years, and you've found that your students have progressed really well. This gives you 'back off' money, as in you can suggest to the SLT that they should 'back off' a change you don't need. For example, you can legitimately ask whether removing levels and putting in some other form of assessment is going to affect how your students learn, because your students are making excellent progress anyway.

Now converesely, imagine instead that your results do not show very good progress. Was it because you were using levels to assess your students at KS3? No. That would be ridiculous. You taught them for an exam in KS4 or KS5. There must be other reasons why your students are not progressing, and you and the SLT need to address these, not your KS3 levels.

Ask yourself this. Are any of the skills in levels not real skills in your subject? Is any of the subject knowledge not real subject knowledge? For most of the levels, no, and again no. The words we use, 'life without levels' reveal why the school reform is likely to fail. We are focusing, once again, on the superficial. "Yes, we have moved on getting rid of levels inspector, look at how we assess and report to parents now..." My thought experiment above was designed to reveal that your students' progress, or lack of it, had little to do with the terms of your assessment. Moreover, the decision not to expect schools to assess in levels I think is motivated a lot more by a desire to improve the curriculum, rather than the things teachers assess. Schools take the message, and then distort it. Let me explain.

There seem to me to be three real objections to a reliance on level descriptors.

1. The skills and knowledge attached to levels can seem arbitrary. Why is x in level 6 while y is in level 4? Y looks harder than x.

2. Some of the skills are vague, and therefore open to huge interpretation.

3. Instead of teaching a curriculum that was valuable, and then assessing students' knowledge using levels, teachers teach to the levels. Gradually, the enriching curriculum becomes fragmented, compartmentalised, lacking in depth.

The first two points are inconsequential when weighed against the progress students make. However, the choice of curriculum will dramatically affect your students' progress. When you get caught up in the 'life without levels' changes remember this – how you assess matters a lot less than *what* you assess, and what you teach.

If you are a head of department, it is your job to make sure that the curriculum is inspired. Don't get sidetracked with the mechanics and labels of assessment. Later you will see what a high impact feedback has, which has nothing to do with how students are graded. If schools use the opportunity to rethink their curriculum, it might have a powerful effect.

For example, cohorts taking a language GCSE early in order to take AS in year 10 and 11. Cohorts taking a design technology GCSE in year 9 or 10, to make room for the academic subjects league tables and progress 8 measures force on students now. For example a KS3 curriculum in all practical subjects that involves no writing, only designing and making things. These changes would be profound and serve all our students much better. If you think with an open mind about your curriculum you would no doubt think of many other ways to make it vibrant, relevant, creative, empowering for students and teachers alike. Altering the curriculum can have profound effects. Instead, we are likely to ignore this opportunity. Instead, we will focus on pieces of paper – "look at this lovely piece of paper – it explains how we assess now".

The Focus on Student Premium

What has student premium funding achieved? Much of it is wasted on TAs, because we haven't measured the impact of interventions.

We are all up against this. I am an ex student premium student myself – I'm not in the business of claiming this shouldn't be a focus. But I am going to claim that the way we measure that focus is all wrong.

I recently worked with a head teacher who had a tiny cohort of 15 student premium students in year 11. Two of them had catastrophic histories and absence, which meant that they failed to take exams, or performed terribly in those they took. The gap between her student premium students and the rest was inevitably too large. She received a section 8 inspection which condemned their progress.

This is intolerable. A maths teacher in your school could easily show the inaccuracy of using such a small sample size to draw conclusions. It is your duty as a school to look at bigger sample sizes – take several year's data until you have sufficient numbers of students to draw meaningful conclusions. I would suggest at least 100 students, but the more the better. You should also be aware of the predictive power of a student's background.

The student's background has a profound effect:

- Parental education d = 0.60
- Parental occupation d = 0.58
- Parental income d = 0.58

Hattie notes that the effect on the school, rather than the individual, is even greater, so that the socio-economic status of its students has an effect of d = 0.73. The greater your number of well off students, or the greater the education of their parents, the better all your students progress. This is true regardless of prior attainment.

Presumably, therefore, having a higher range of deprived students results in lower achievement for all. Deprived students in a school with many disadvantaged students are likely to have poorer progress. We can infer from this that middle class students do as well wherever they go to school, but for the disadvantaged, there is a clear advantage in choosing the right school.

The problem is also very clear when you consider sample size. The effect of a small sample size in any one year group, of say 50 students or less, makes it highly likely that in any given year your disadvantaged students will achieve badly because poor performance by only 5 of them is 10% of your cohort and will dramatically affect your value added.

A fair system will therefore add the results of disadvantaged students year on year, looking at trends with much larger sample sizes. Schools need to do this, so that they are not the victims of a blinkered value added analysis, which is the lead inspector's analysis of Raiseonline.

Schools have to own their own data, to have a more detailed picture than Ofsted has. This is a protection against Ofsted, and allows you to measure the effect of your school. And of course, over time, it may reveal that your disadvantaged students are not making good progress – in which case you will want to do something to improve it.

Are You Serious About Student Premium?

Every school in the country updates its computers every 3 to 5 years. Most would be suitable to give away to families who are most in need. I've yet to see it happen though. How many schools hold parents' evenings specifically for parents who don't have at least an A level education, or who have a measure of disadvantage? How many organise cultural events – trips to museums, theatre, literature festivals where disadvantaged students attend with their parents, with the school paying for their tickets? We simply ignore parents, as though they weren't the most significant factor in their child's progress. And yet the research keeps reminding us that parents are key.

Students do gain a slight advantage from having two parents, where $d = 0.17$. More significantly, the effects of divorce are negative, -0.12. This does suggest we should be ready to intervene more explicitly when we know a student's circumstances change, and their parents divorce. At the moment we do this only for levels of disadvantage that have the right label: pupil premium, SEN etc. And even here, we rarely consult the parents.

Parental control over when homework is done, hours of television watched, time spent going out with friends etc actually has a negative effect on achievement. Parental aspiration has the highest effect, $d = 0.58 - 0.88$, depending on the study. Parental participation has an effect of $d = 0.56$, getting a tutor $d = 0.49$. This research clearly suggests that we should take, not just the disadvantaged student, but also their parents to visit universities, to hear outside speakers etc. But again, do you know of schools where this is happening?

This is because we focus on managing change, not embedding reform.

Chapter 6

"We all lived in fear that the Russian tanks would roll in and we'd be swallowed up into the Soviet empire."

Arnold Schwarzenegger

Individual Instruction   d = 0.23

Individual instruction designs the learning at the level of the individual, responding to their specific needs. This is differentiation in its purest form – it is the gold standard. This seems a stunningly low effect, going against what we would naturally expect.

We should beware of following our natural instincts to pounce upon counterintuitive data – yes, extreme joggers die early, I knew it, thank God for my couch – and see this objectively. Differentiation clearly works. But is it worth the effort? We shall explore that question in this chapter.

Closely allied to this is mentoring, another gold standard of differentiation. This fares even less impressively, but is probably even more costly in terms of effort.

Mentoring   d = 0.15

This is astonishing – it has no greater effect than simple maturation. There is no discussion of assertive mentoring in Hattie's books. Here, mentoring is seen as merely a supportive relationship.

Why is getting to know the student as an individual not much more powerful? A clue perhaps is that getting to know the student as an individual misleads us. For example, giving a student control over learning, treating them entirely as an individual: d = 0.04

One of the problems with differentiation might be that it encourages us to make allowances for the individual, to be sympathetic towards them in ways that prevent us having truly high expectations for them.

How should we interpret these findings? It seems that personalised learning is actually a social activity, and students will learn better with and from other students, rather than from one to one attention.

So much of what we will see in the research is that learning is much more successful when it is shared with others, and tested by others. In a school, learning is necessarily a social activity. Students personalise their learning best through their feedback to and from others – this seems to be the key. If 50% of what students teach each other is wrong, one key to successful differentiation ought to be training students to support each other more accurately. Students also teach each other constantly, not simply on the occasions that teachers ask for peer feedback. Because it is happening all the time, in every class, it is well worth spending some time developing it as a skill. First, let's look at some problems with differentiation.

The Myth of Differentiation

Teaching is full of myths, because our experience can confirm most views. As Hattie points out in *Visible Learning*, "everything works". Teaching is prey to our experience, which entrenches opinion. If you want to see quite how far entrenched we are, suggest we might abandon setting or uniform, and watch battle lines be drawn around contradictory experience.

On the other hand, if you just want to get on with differentiation that works, skip to: **A Teaching Sequence That Always Differentiates**

So why might differentiation be the wrong answer?

Here I stray into the realms of opinion. Remember, I don't need to prove that differentiation does not work, the evidence has already proved it. You've just read it. I am trying to work out what is wrong with it, so we might find a cure: differentiation that works.

Here's an experiment. Next time you teach a dyslexic student, ask them, "What are you doing about your dyslexia? YOU have a problem, what are YOU doing to overcome it?" I ask this because the student and the parent both assume you will do something about it. That's the wrong way round, isn't it?

No matter how hard you try, you can't devote more than 10 % of your teaching time to that student. But they can devote 100 % of their lesson time to trying to overcome it, and a good percentage of their evenings and weekends. This is not to say that dyslexia is not real. It is to say that the way to overcome a problem is to overcome it, not to make allowances for it and let it become the responsibility of ten disparate teachers.

I will be very surprised if the dyslexic student will lay out to you a series of steps they are taking to overcome their dyslexia. How often are they reading? Are they timing their reading, so that they improve in speed or quantity over time? Do they have their own spelling book for words that cause them problems? Do they check their work for accuracy before they hand it in? Do they practise look, cover, write, SAY, check with their spellings? Do they volunteer to read aloud in class? Do they reread pages in order to attain familiarity or mastery? Have they worked out which spelling patterns cause them most problems, and devised a plan of attack for these? Etc.

Most of our support in school runs that very danger. You tell the child they have a difficulty, you put in support which becomes a label the student at best struggles to overcome, and often the student regularly opts out, expecting someone else to do the work for them.

We are also to blame. Our differentiation does the opposite of what we want. We dumb down. The last thing we do is ask them to rise to the challenge.

Let's look at what differentiation looks like in a learning objective. "All will, most will, some will." This looks personalised, but instead gives the class two levels at which to opt out. This is the opposite of differentiation, the opposite of mastery learning, which we will meet later. Here, the "all will" is also likely to be a small degree of subject knowledge or skill – after all, the teacher has set it *knowing* that everyone in the class will be able to do it, no matter what their starting points. Despite the teacher's best intentions, and the SLT's best intentions (for they are likely to have asked for it to be standardized across the school, to engender differentiation), it is likely to have the opposite effect. How else to explain the poor return?

Ok, to answer that, let's look at the impact of another panacea of intervention, the use of TAs. This is how the EEF reports on it:

"Research that examines the impact of TAs providing general classroom support suggests that students in a class with a teaching assistant present do not, on average, outperform those in one where only a teacher is present. This average finding covers a range of impacts. In some cases teachers and TAs work together effectively, leading to increases in attainment. In other cases students, *particularly those who are low attaining or identified as having special educational needs, can perform worse in classes with teaching assistants.*"

These are my italics. Every school is conditioned to believe that their TAs are doing a good job – working with the right students, working hard. Fine, but are they making a difference? Imagine a conference of 500 senior leaders listening to a professor present on educational research. Before she gives them the low down, she gets them to raise a hand if TAs are used effectively in their school. 490 hands are raised. The professor scans the room. She pauses. She says, "I've got some good news and bad news. Either you all come from the only 500 schools in the country where TAs are used effectively, or most of you are idiots."

The truth is, we are more likely to be idiots. We probably have not quantified the value added of having TAs in our school. We definitely won't have costed this. Your school's TA budget is likely to be way over £250,000, for what Coe shows is about one month's extra progress. If you really wanted to make a difference, how else might you spend that money?

How could you spend the money your school now spends on TAs?

Let's start with maths teachers in Shanghai. This is from Nick Gibb in The Guardian, 26th November 2015: "Why are we so keen to learn about Shanghai mathematics teaching? ... At the age of 15, Shanghai students are studying work equivalent to the second year of A-level, while our students are still studying for their GCSE. What's more, the children of the poorest 30% of Shanghai's population are outstripping at mathematics the children of our wealthiest 10% in England. Clearly, Shanghai teachers are doing something right."

If we look beyond the politics, at what those maths teachers actually do, we might find an alternative to our use of TAs. This is from Salop Teaching School, which looks at implementing the Shanghai maths system:

"Work collaboratively – provide two way link

1. Practice and consolidation – Keith, Steve...

2. Specialist Maths teaching – Kieran, Amy, Helen...

3. Efficient teaching – Colin, Rachael, Sarah...

4. Immediacy of feedback and interventions – Colin...

5. Preventing the gap – Graham, Emma (Y1), Louise"

Items 3, 4 and 5 are where an alternative model to the use of TAs comes in. This is from The Center for International Benchmarking:

www.ncee.org/programs-affiliates/center-on-international-education-benchmarking/ top-performing-countries/shanghai-china/shanghai-china-teacher-and-principal- quality/

"Teachers also often meet in regularly scheduled (often weekly) groups based on subject and level in order to discuss best practices, share advice, and create common lesson plans for the upcoming week. Occasionally, teachers will give demonstration lessons; these serve either as a means of sharing best practice with other teachers or as a means of feedback and critique to the teacher giving the lesson.. Teachers in Shanghai spend less than 50 percent of their working hours teaching."

Because they teach fewer than three days a week, these teachers have time for immediacy of feedback. No student is allowed to fall behind – the teacher intervenes with them straight away, probably on the same day, but certainly that week, to go over what the student has not understood.

What if your school employed just 6 specialist teachers, who taught half a time table, and for the other half intervened directly with students, in small groups, straight away? What might they achieve? What if your school had 10 such teachers? How many students would still fail to make progress in reading, maths, or writing? Those numbers would be small. Test it. Think of the 8 students with the worst progress in your lessons. What would happen if every other day you could take them in groups of 4 and find different ways to get them to learn what they haven't grasped? If you put names and faces to this experiment, the results will feel more real.

Now, what would have greater impact on your students, 10 TAs, or 10 teachers working in this way, on 50% timetables? Feels like a rhetorical question, doesn't it? A better question would be, what would be the magnitude of improvement? If a good TA adds about 1 month to a student's learning per year, how many months could you add if you were that teacher with the 50% timetable, and 50% of your time to intervene, every single day, with every single student?

And let me point out, this is far from blue sky thinking, because in Shanghai it happens for every teacher in the school. It is far from blue sky thinking because, in your very own school, 10 TAs really are being paid a sum which really could be spent on 10 teachers like you, doing their job much, much, much more effectively. You are highly trained, years ahead of a TA's training and thousands of hours ahead of their experience. And, where the TA might be competent with one or two students, you'll be highly skilled with at least four students at a time.

The comparison isn't even a fair one. Except it is, because your school really is paying that money to your TAs, who have to be working less efficiently than the same number of teachers could in half the time, but with more than double the students.

So I do want to change your thinking. This is real. If you are a head teacher, you could plan for this to begin in September, simply by not replacing TAs who leave, you wouldn't even need to make TAs reduntant initially, possibly ever. You could start with two in maths and two in English and, and, and...please fill in the blanks, and let the logic of it carry you through.

Given that you probably aren't a head teacher, let me give you differentiation for your classroom. This will always work, and involves no extra work for you.

A Teaching Sequence That Always Differentiates

Compare the differentiated learning objectives to setting the lesson at a level or grade *above* the ability of the group, where there is no opt out, and *everyone is in difficulty*. How can you make this lesson a success? Here is the solution in brief:

See
Firstly, show students what success looks like. That means you have to model it, and then explain the model.

Try
Now, perhaps some students will get it clearly from the model, but possibly most won't. So now put the students in a pair to try to produce their version of the model. Let's imagine it is a longer exam answer. You simply can't get round those who are having difficulties – there will be too many. So students have to support each other in pairs. One pair can type these at your computer.

Apply
Then you ask your students in pairs to grade each other's answers using your version of the criteria. Effectively, you are modeling a second time. A third time if you display the paired computer work.

Secure
Now students try a new question that tests the same skills, this time on their own. Again, an individual types at your computer.

When you mark this you have two opportunities to shape their learning. Firstly, one or two specific things that the student individually MUST improve, based on the model.

Secondly, the next opportunity it provides is that of the exit slip. You now know what your class most lacks, because you can see what they produced in the 'secure' phase. This will be what you next teach or set for homework.

This teaching sequence can be summarised as **See, Try, Apply, Secure**. I stole this from the national strategies. If you would like to know more:

www.teachfind.com/national-strategies/writing-challenge-handbook-school-organisers

webarchive.nationalarchives.gov.uk/20110809101133/nsonline.org.uk/node/97441

How have you differentiated? Through modelling. You showed what successful performance looks like in your model, looked at the criteria to pick on the key skills that made the difference, supported the individual by giving them a partner to talk these through with and to test understanding, revisited the model to apply what they've learned, revisited the model again to assess their success, before finally securing what they know.

All this has been achieved without a single change of resource and without a single one to one intervention. Not only will this work, it is entirely sustainable for all those lessons where you are not being observed. This means it won't just be wheeled out twice a year for lesson observation: it can easily become a sustainable habit that helps all your students to shine.

Your feedback is immediately differentiated, because you give each student exactly what they need to improve on. But for now let us consider the main reason teachers don't force their students to redraft part of their work based on feedback: we don't want to give up our curriculum time; we have so much to get through. "Spend another fifteen minutes at the beginning of the lesson to get them to improve...I'll lose an hour every four weeks, or about one week per term...you might as well let the kids go on holiday during term time".

Ok, I hear you. Here's another thought experiment. What would happen if a student learned their year 10 science curriculum in year 10, and then we did not teach them any new science in the first term of year 11, but retaught year 10 again, and made sure they knew it? Which students would get higher marks in their GCSEs? Probably the ones who currently get E, D and C. Arguably those who are also getting a B. We would actually raise standards with these students by teaching less, and making the students more accountable, testing them more on everything they learned in year 10.

This is a thought experiment by the way, not a curriculum model. I am posing it this way to try to get an insight into the relative importance of spending time mastering subject knowledge, compared to learning new knowledge. Mastery is much more effective than new knowledge. When we look at interleaving and spaced learning later, we will see that it is possible to gain mastery of elements taught earlier, even while we move on to new learning. These also will suggest that you simply have to make time for students to revisit what you have taught them and get it right. So, differentiation means making sure that students master knowledge, redrafting after your feedback.

Use of Pictures in Differentiation

Although I am proposing using pictures as a way to differentiate successfully, they have an impact all on their own.

Adjunct aids   d = 0.37

Animation is more effective than a still picture. If it is used for representational purposes, it has an effect of d = 0.89, but even if it is only decorative, its effect is 0.29. "Learning is better with pictures in most cases". To me this seems an extraordinary idea, because it is so simple. It suggests that pictures should always be used on the IWB, and students should be asked to draw as often as possible. The gains to be made from virtually no effort are what make this so exciting.

This is why diagrams are such an excellent way to organise learning. Scientists, PE teachers, DT teachers and geographers will have no problem accepting this. But what about mathematicians? Yes, a 3D drawing of a pyramid might well help students learn many aspects of trigonometry, and more importantly, retain them.

MFL teachers? Yes, a video of students talking with a bit of gesture and a few props will be much more memorable than much or all of their practice in class. This might not be the way a languages teacher would teach, but it is the way they themselves learned, being immersed in another country. No, you don't need a department camera – most of your students have phones that will do the job. Some of them will even have green screen apps that allow them to impose backgrounds from anywhere Google images can take them.

Evidence for how useful pictures are was confirmed for me when we introduced GCSEpod. This is a revision guide. But students don't read it, they stream it from the internet, or download it as podcasts. Because the file size has to be small, this does not download as a large video file, but as a small one, with images, and limited movement within and between images. These are matched to text and voiceover.

When I analysed the top performing students for progress, I found a clear pattern. The more GCSEpod students used, the better their progress. Ok, but that could simply mean, the more revision students did, the better their progress? So I compared their progress in subjects where the same students didn't used GCSEpod, but used some other sort of revision. Yes, progress with GCSEpod was better. Animated pictures do appear to make a difference.

Still pictures are a great way to differentiate, as they allow the student to access what they know, and apply it to a new context. These can be done logically. For example, a before and after tsunami shot. Or what will this picture of Chernobyl look like in twelve months? In five years? Two competing photographs: a hurricane and eruption. Which one is worse for the economy? Which is more important to a geographer? Which will create better literature (and how could you find out?)

Alternatively, pick pictures of people famous in your subject. Which one is most important to the topic you are studying? For example, Stalin, Hitler, Roosevelt. Which one was most of an influence on Churchill?

Who would win in a fight? A picture of Ghandi and another of Martin Luther King. A picture of Electricity and Combustion. A picture of coastal erosion and another of a rubbish dump in India. A picture of two actresses – the debate to be had in a MFL. A picture of Pythagoras and Newton. These differentiate, because all students are able to bring their existing subject knowledge to the debate. In addition, they revisit that subject knowledge, making connections, revisiting the neural pathways to retrieve it (which you'll be familiar with if you looked up Robert Bjork and why this works).

Some of these ideas are stolen from *The Secret of Literacy*, by David Didau, and *The Lazy Teacher*, by Jim Smith, I think. Both of which are great if you like collecting ideas to energise your teaching.

Or pictures can be abstract. Which one best represents your topic? E.g. a tree and an elephant. Which one best represents the passage in the French book you are reading? Or to your studying of Christianity? Or to your understanding of osmosis?

This is a very good way of extending thinking. For example, in English, you might pick several images that are easily matched to a character, but then increase the level of difficulty. A great example I've used is a picture of Ronnie Coleman, a huge bodybuilder, who is also black. In a text like *The Tempest*, which explores notions of power, and to a modern audience, colonialism or empire, it is a great stimulus to deeper understanding of the play.

Students can easily match Caliban's status as a slave to the fact that the body builder is black, and they might make something of the nomenclature,

African-American. Caliban too wants to assert his cultural heritage and battle the effects of a colonial ruler. Coleman's size and power are more difficult to reconcile with Caliban's powerlessness. It also raises interesting questions about his relationship with Miranda – the black man as rapist stereotype of newspapers counterpoints the possibility of stereotyping by Prospero. Perhaps Caliban is less malevolent, but is simply perceived in this way because of his otherness, an appearance they choose to see as subhuman. Here Prospero is not even aware of his own racism.

It also leads to a discussion of sexual desire, how something that one person views as monstrous, another finds compelling. What if Miranda desired Caliban?

Ok, now let's push the students further. What if the picture of the bodybuilder was Ariel? How might Ariel be more powerful than Prospero? Is Ariel's magic black, or its opposite? What about Ariel's gender or sexuality? How does that match the photograph? You can extend this further through androgyny. Steroids cause the testes to atrophy because they are no longer required to produce the male hormone, testosterone. How does this match Ariel?

Ok. Now, what if the image is Prospero? I hope you can see what a rich way this is of using the image, as it always forces the student to *make connections with different areas of their learning.*

The same image could be used to justify a representation of electro magnetism, friction, a circuit, convection. A major reason for its success is the sheer difficulty of doing it. A major complaint of teachers is that students don't make connections in their learning, not just across a subject, but within it.

And this is the final problem with differentiation: even when you raise the level of challenge, your students often remain dependent on you to challenge them. Without you, they can quickly revert to a less thoughtful state. If we return to the teaching sequence, we can therefore see why the secure stage, with students working on their own, is so important.

Time on Task   d = 0.38

Hattie tells us "At best half of student time in class involves engagement with class activity". This low to average d effect would suggest it is difficult to increase the amount of time students are engaged. Surprisingly, the effects are higher when students are working in groups, which suggests that group work can indeed be engaging, and many students request group work as a method of learning. But engagement and time on task do not necessarily cause good learning.

The low figure of time engaged on task does offer us an opportunity. If we can construct activities that engage students for even 40 minutes out of the hour, we have increased their time on task by 33%!

Let's look at some ways to make it happen during group work.

You are testing a hypothesis – what if Napoleon had won in Russia? What if Pluto were half way closer to the sun? What if a mathematical problem was made as complex as possible, but still solvable by the group? What if William Golding was an atheist? What if sea levels rose two metres next year? Here the group can decide on lots of different approaches to the task, allocate lines of enquiry, come back and test each other's findings, then propose a final outcome.

Hopefully, when I frame questions in this way, you can see that this sort of investigation forces students to use the top levels of Blooms – analyse, evaluate and synthesise. Another point that may seem obvious, but is often missed, is that group work is a terrible way to teach content. Instead, this line of enquiry is only possible *once* sufficient knowledge has been acquired. Such acquisition has to be the major part of your teaching, which is why group work should not be your dominant teaching style, unless you are charismatic and brilliant, like your man Beadle. But our job is to be only slightly awesome. Once knowledge is mastered, it is therefore an excellent differentiation tool, especially for the more-able.

The flipside of this however, is that if you are not teaching these skills, then you should not be using group work – it will just be a much slower way of teaching something you could have done in pairs or individually.

Chapter 7

*"Money doesn't make you happy. I now have $50 million
but I was just as happy when I had $48 million."*

Arnold Schwarzenegger

Some Notes on Praise and Reward   d = 0.12

There is much evidence cited about the difference between intrinsic and extrinsic motivation. The question then is, how can your use of rewards lead to better relationships? And will a use of reward damage intrinsic motivation?

You are rewarding effortful performance. You need to be explicit about this. "You were able to disprove that idea using two pieces, rather than one piece of evidence." "You used an alternative interpretation in your conclusion, well done." "You were able to use Pythagoras in a three dimensional shape, without giving in to panic – well done". In other words, it is their skills as learners in your subject for which students are rewarded.

The research in growth mindsets also clearly shows that a student's effort is most closely linked to success. Therefore, the effort a student puts in should be rewarded. This means that the quality of work is not the only determiner. A more-able student will often produce something very good with little effort.

Reward students for academic improvement, in terms of grades or levels. This again means rewarding students of all abilities, but who exhibit the right learning behaviours – resilience, effort, reflectiveness.

The test of your reward system is not whether students value it, by the way. They may not value the whole school system when it is not applied consistently. And dare I suggest, it is hardly ever applied consistently. The test is whether they think you value their hard work. That is the main goal of your rewards, to get your students working hard to improve.

Why won't you reward?

1. Well, other teachers don't.

2. The students are too old for it.

3. You often don't remember.

4. The effort was good, but not worth a full house point/merit/credit/Vivo etc.

5. You just reward homework.

6. It takes too much time.

The solution is simple. Allocate the recording of rewards to a student in your class. I use my mark book. As soon as I have heard or seen some excellent example of learning or thinking like an expert in my subject, I reward. We use Vivos, so the student in charge enters a V in the register for the student I want to reward. I am much more likely to be consistent, as it involves no effort from me. And I have a built in monitoring system – the student recorder, who won't let me forget.

Moreover, this also means the students immediately know they are being rewarded. If you simply award your rewards later, without the student knowing, it will have next to no effect.

We are reluctant to reward the little things, and often resort simply to rewarding homework. But it is the learning in your classroom that will lead to most progress. Most teachers forget to do this. Consequently I award Vivos in thirds. This means I never worry that I am rewarding too cheaply – students obviously need three occasions where I reward them before they get the actual symbol of reward.

You will give many thirds to more students, whereas you would often struggle to give a whole school reward. 6 thirds to 6 students in one lesson will give no one a Vivo, but over time is the equivalent of two Vivos in each lesson.

The students finishing work first, with no mistakes, should always be rewarded, especially if you narrate who is close during the task itself. This is especially true of copying from the board which, in learning terms, is dead time.

This is also a great way to model the standards that you expect. Hands go up as soon as they are finished. "Ah, that date isn't underlined." The next hand goes up: "Yes, all your spellings are correct. But your last paragraph doesn't end with a full stop." It only takes a few of these before students attempt to get everything right. It works best if they cannot be rewarded for a second attempt – only the perfect first attempt counts, because it is simply copying – there is no excuse for a mistake. In this way you can reward easy tasks, because you have pointed out their difficulty. This also improves performance, because intrinsic reward is not damaged – it is very difficult to be intrinsically motivated with mundane tasks. Daniel Pink describes how extrinsic reward boosts performance in a mundane task, "Since participants simply had to race down an obvious path, the carrot waiting for them at the finish line simply encouraged them to gallop faster."

Ok, having said that...

Reward and Praise

What Makes Great Teaching? describes praise as being ineffective.

"Praise for students may be seen as affirming and positive, but a number of studies suggest that *the wrong kinds of praise can be very harmful to learning.* For example, Dweck (1999), Hattie & Timperley (2007). (My italics)

Stipek (2010) argues that praise that is meant to be encouraging and protective of low attaining students actually conveys a message of the teacher's low expectations. Children whose failure was responded to with sympathy were more likely to attribute their failure to lack of ability than those who were presented with anger.

"Praise for successful performance on an easy task can be interpreted by a student as evidence that the teacher has a low perception of his or her ability. As a consequence, it can actually lower rather than enhance self-confidence. Criticism following poor performance can, under some circumstances, be interpreted as an indication of the teacher's high perception of the student's ability." (ibid)"

The key, then, is to praise a response to challenge. I can square this with my moral purpose, because I instinctively feel that getting students to accept challenge is my job. If I've taught my students to accept challenge, and this lesson lasts into adulthood. Arguably accepting challenge will be more important than their ability to remember Macbeth's reaction to Lady Macbeth's death, the point of the cosine, why Sarajevo was important, what Kant believed, or whether frogs could be heliotropic.

How do you model good learning behaviour?

What is the discipline of the task you have set?

Is it to redraft, using the feedback from the teacher or peers? Is it to offer feedback that is specific and gives precise examples of what the student could do? Is it reaching a personal best in effort, or standard of work, or even in presentation? Is it making sure that everyone is involved in the group and that the least confident learner knows everything that the group knows?

Is it being a student who accepts failure, volunteering to show work that they know is not good enough, but which they would like improved?

Or is it the student teaching an explanation in a new way so that a fellow, struggling student understands it?

Or is it for reaching a certain percentage in a test (because you have first set an appropriate level of challenge for that individual student)?

Reward these. None of these behaviours are performed *in order to receive the reward*. They are done because they improve learning. Your giving of a reward is not therefore expected, it is a simple thank you. Indeed, a hearth felt "thank you" can be the reward itself. This is important. As Daniel Pink has already pointed out in *Drive*, extrinsic rewards are counterproductive unless they are aimed at getting students to complete boring, routine tasks. For example, being among the first to copy something down, accurately, without mistake. (But then, of course, what should actually be copied down..?)

None of these rewards a student for simply not disrupting the lesson or not ruining the learning of others, or for completing an easy task.

You Won't Change Behaviour Through Bribery

Every school I have ever taught in has many of the poorest behaved students achieving among the highest rewards in a year group. Lazy teaching, not lazy teachers, rewards students for simply choosing not to disrupt lessons. But this sends completely the wrong message to the misbehaving student. It tells them that you do not think they can behave, and that indeed you expect them to relapse soon. This is a self-fulfilling prophecy. And of course it undermines the whole reward system in your school.

Rewarding challenge and learning will stop your natural focus on the content of what you teach. Instead, you will ask yourself, 'how will my students master this content?' And this is the same question as 'what learning behaviours will my students need to master this content?' Having to reward will make you a better teacher.

Example: in order to get to grips with area you will have to learn the formula for two dimensional and three dimensional shapes. Try two questions on each. If you make mistakes, you must try two more, until you have two correct in a row. Once you have made a mistake you can't understand, ask another student to explain why it is wrong and how to correct it. Do it again until you have two which are correct.

Now increase the level of difficulty by trying a similar question with less information.

Now create a question that combines more than one shape, so that it is more difficult than the examples you have been working on.

Or look at this example from Salop teaching school (which incidentally I think is primary school maths from Shanghai). How might you reward the acceptance of challenge in this problem?

If the length of the square is 10cm, what are the dimensions and areas of the other shapes?

You might choose to reward at any point where the learning behaviour is what you want: mastery of the initial problems, or teaching another student to help them achieve mastery, accepting the greater challenge of setting a new question that is more difficult and also solving it, etc. Of course, this will also lead to better behaviour in your class. If students try to achieve mastery, and accept challenge, they will be predisposed to use the right behaviours to achieve this. Just as certainly, some will struggle with this, fear failure, misbehave, and distract others. But if you persevere rewarding what you want, they will begin to change their behaviours and manage their fears.

Challenge as a way to think about rewarding learning behaviour

Have you ever spoken to a student and found that they really didn't want to succeed? I haven't. I have spoken to plenty of students who didn't think they could, were scared of trying, and who thought the teacher didn't like them, or that other students in the class were the problem, or who had put in an effort that wasn't enough, and so become demoralised. The only way to change this is to give the students challenges that you show them how to meet. This is why I have such a problem with the differentiated learning objective we met earlier: all will, most will, some will. All will? How challenging can that possibly be? Worse, what is the learning behaviour you are encouraging?

"I am setting you a minimum standard, and it is ok if you only reach that mimimum". That is an un-learning behaviour, it is anti-learning.

Instead set up a challenge: "This is difficult. But I am still going to ask you to try to master it."

Then ask the student to help someone else figure out why they are still finding it too difficult. Then help them overcome this. Peer teaching is hard, but if you ask your student how they feel about peer assessment, they usually reply that they don't like it. Why? Because they don't treat it as a challenge. They make a simplistic comment that helps no one – 'you could have written in more detail'. But what if you asked them to give a specific example of what could be improved, and the words 'so that' to explain why it will help. 'Your conclusion needs to explain why the increase in temperature led to an increase in volume in the gas so that Miss Jones can see you understand cause and effect. Say what units this was measured in.' Model the feedback you want students to give, then reward it.

Narrating what you want

Another way of rewarding behaviour is to narrate what you want, by describing it as it happens: "three seconds, excellent. Waiting for two more hands to go up. Thank you."

If a student extends an answer, moves their thinking, or the thinking of the class on, praise them. Articulate what it is they have done – "you've revealed a problem in our original thinking", "you've solved that in a new way, and helped us see a different way of doing it", "you've interpreted that in a way I hadn't thought of before." Again, these are the aspects of learning behaviour that you want to encourage and model, so call attention to them.

These are the right kinds of praise. They don't tell the student that they have succeeded because they are clever. (Dweck tells us this is counter productive, as the moment they encounter difficulty, or failure, their self image is attacked – it means that they are not clever).

Dopamine and Reward

Amazingly, your body has its own reward system that deepens memory. In other words, a reward system that creates learning. It's called dopamine.

Raised dopamine causes improved memory. The important fact about dopamine is that it is connected with novelty and reward. Does this mean learning has to be exciting – the same old unrealistic rubbish that forces teachers to think that they have to entertain students? Not quite. The role of chance is your friend. Chance will allow your lessons to be exciting:

For a full account of how this might be useful, visit Zondle: *www.zondle.com/ publicPages/theScienceBehindZondle.aspx*

"When a stimulus associated with 50% likely reward is seen, it generates a spike and then the dopamine ramps up until the outcome is revealed. Averaged over time, the uncertain reward thus generates a greater dopaminergic response than either certain or totally unexpected reward (for original research and image see Fiorillo et al. 2003*4*).

Measurements suggest the brain's reward response peaks when rewards are 50% likely – which is the probability of success offered by Team Play's wheel of chance."

This releases dopamine, which makes the learning more memorable, so that learning becomes sticky. Think of dopamine as glue for learning. Pairs or groups choose an answer. The correct answer is revealed. A spinning wheel spins to music, to decide whether or not the points are doubled. Scores are maintained for each group, and at the end a trophy is displayed for the winning team/teams.

This is well worth doing as a bit of fun, and it feels impossible that it leads to better learning. But it does. For our purposes, it also leads to much greater engagement with boys – they usually want to gamble. This is win win for you . There are of course problems with this approach – am I condoning gambling?

I deal with this by explaining the science to students – it is the dopamine that makes gambling addictive. But the same effect can be gained without any recourse to money, or stakes that you are not prepared to lose.

Competition

"Our brain's reward system doesn't just respond to our own fortunes, but also to those of our competitors. To help develop Team Play, researchers carried out a study of what happens in the brain when we observe our competitors. This revealed that our brains (including our reward system) respond chiefly to our own successes but also to the failures of our competitors."

Yes, there is also that wonderful, vicarious pleasure in seeing someone else not succeed. How wonderful it is when your children do better at school than those of your friends – yes, a dark, enticing place we've all been to. When your friend buys a top just like yours, but it looks nowhere near as good on her. When your neighbour gets a new car/tv/holiday which doesn't quite compare to yours. You know how it is. One of the secrets to a longer and happier life is not to earn lots of money, but just enough to be more than your friends and neighbours.

You can read more about this with the help of the deutche bank here: *www. dbresearch.com/PROD/DBR_INTERNET_EN-PROD/PROD0000000000202587.pdf*

Or from the US Library of medicine here: *www.ncbi.nlm.nih.gov/pmc/articles/PMC4041613/*

Excellent though Zondle is, it is now a service which charges. The fool proof way to do the same job is to open up a spreadsheet, put in your team names, put in one formula so that each of the columns add up cumulatively in one column (a maths teacher will show you this in thirty seconds – trust me). You need 50/50 odds, and a coin toss will do.

Once teams have answered, ask them to decide whether or not to gamble. The gamble is – if you win, your points for the question are doubled. If you lose, even if you had the answer right, you get no points. Another alternative is that you get no points, but some of the points you might have won go to another team, such as the one in last position.

I find this is more dramatic when the group know they have the answer right, and the points are already potentially in the bag. Then loss aversion kicks in. You might also observe that it is a ploy that really motivates boys.

Quizzing to Hone Your Curriculum

Another advantage is that it gets you to look at your curriculum in terms of essential knowledge and understanding. You can test facts, theories, processes, and vocabulary very easily. This forces you to pick out what your students most need to know, which is always a very revealing exercise. This alone will make you a better teacher – giving the students exactly what they need to know – even if you never actually get the students to gamble. Knowledge organisers will also do this (see later).

It is also very easy to adapt to problem solving, or to a demonstration of skills. It will work in every subject. You can award points for a group of students who evaluate two conflicting sources on the dissolution of the monasteries in a paragraph with two quotations; the group who can write about their weekend adventures with a chimpanzee using three tenses in a MFL; the group that can prove the value of 'n' in a sophisticated equation, or finish a set number of these problems in a given time; the group that can score a netball goal in the quickest time, or in exactly 5 passes...it is infinitely adaptable. The key is that there must be a 50% chance of losing their points or doubling them. If this release of dopamine will make your learning memorable, can you afford not to try it?

I'll toss you for it...

Chapter 8

"Even when acting in a movie, I would not shoot a stunt
if I hadn't rehearsed it a minimum of ten times."

Arnold Schwarzenegger

Teacher's Notes   d = 0.41

Having teacher's notes, written or in the form of video, adds d 0.41. Reviewing notes also means the student doesn't have to think about the note taking process itself, just about content. It lowers mental effort in favour of mental efficiency.

This is direct instruction, because your notes tell the students exactly what they need to learn. When you talk, they often have to sift through your words to pick out the key learning. It is often easier not to bother. Your notes are nearly always more powerful than your talk.

Making a video of your notes is even more effective. It prevents you forgetting what you've once taught well, and it makes you give very clear explanations to your students. Now, when I have fully researched a topic, including past papers and examiners' reports, I make an instructional video. I put it on YouTube, for any student or teacher to use if they wish. The result is that, a year or two later I will revisit it, and realise how much I have forgotten, but from which my students can still benefit.

Knowledge Organisers

A way round this is simply to write your own revision guides for students. Let's take a minute to imagine what this might look like. At its simplest level, it would be a knowledge organiser like the ones used at Michaela school. A history example is on the excellent blog, Pragmatic Education, at *pragmaticreform. wordpress.com/2015/03/28/knowledge-organisers/*

The idea is to distill key knowledge to just one A4 sheet. This includes a timeline of 15 dates; 10 key terms and definitions, like apartheid and segregation, connected to 'political vocabulary'; 5 Mandela quotations; 8 key anti – apartheid activists with one key fact about each, and 6 key words and definitions connected to 'legal vocabulary'.

Much complexity is involved in the selection of information, how it is presented and how it will be tested to aid memory. The simplicity is from the student's perspective – it is incredibly easy to navigate, all on a page of A4. We might make it more memorable if, in all history knowledge organisers, dates were in one colour, quotations in another, etc – the colours applied consistently across the year goups.

There are many subjects where this kind of revision organiser would be incredibly useful – science, geography, MFL, PE for example. Getting students to learn these simply involves different kinds of memory tests – removing words, letters, re-ordering text, removing vowels, removing consonants, every fifth word etc.

Apply Their Knowledge

Once memorised, it can now begin to have even greater impact. Because you have included key concepts and subject specific vocabulary, students are able to express themselves like experts in your subject. They can't do this simply by parroting – they use this vocabulary and key concepts in other contexts. This has transformed my teaching of literature, and the ability of my students predicted C grades, but instantly able to access B and A grades in essay writing. If this book makes you do a Google Image search on 'knowledge organisers' you've already had value for money.

At a more complex level for students, you could write your own guides. These lend themselves to subjects that involve ideas – English and English literature, history, RE. For example, when teaching Of Mice and Men, I give my students a revision guide containing the ideas beyond A and A*, that aren't available on other online sites, such as SparkNotes. In history you might do this by writing short, contrasting interpretations of the same events or historical figures. In Philopshy and Ethics you might write contrasting religious approaches to the war (in Syria?), from Budhist or Christian perspectives, or from the points of view of different philosophers.

Using Video as Teachers' Notes

And for those of you who wish to reach a far wider audience, tap in to a greater range of learning styles, and enhance your pension, you can also make video. Videos need to be between six and ten minutes long for most learners, as recommended by Khan Academy, probably the largest learning channel on YouTube. It is also near the the the average length of a view on my channel, six and a half minutes. However, the most popular videos are often the longest, so it is worth combining short ones in to one, long, definitive video on a topic also.

This would mean that soon every student you ever teach could learn the whole of the course on their own. Most won't, of course, but how many of your students would need to do this before it was worthwhile? 20%? Definitely. 10%? This would do for me. That is only three students per class, but if those three get A* instead of A or B, that will make a difference to you, and to them.

This is another way for students to learn more than you teach. I've been very amused when asking my students where they had encountered the idea that the Inspector, in *An Inspector Calls*, was like a vector (which in biology transmits disease), here transmitting ideas. "In your video sir," was the reply. It was a revision video made with my son, and his idea. Interestingly, I filmed all the revision my son did for his literature GCSE. Together, it is under four hours. He dropped only one UMS Mark. Yes, a small sample, but another indication of how teachers' notes will help your students. I hadn't given him any other help. And no, it wasn't the result of the teaching he had at school. His teacher did not approve of students offering any interpretation she had not taught them herself.

Ok, not many of you will leap to making videos. Here's a further nudge. You can appear only as a voiceover, and like the ones with my son, you can record them live, with no requirement to edit. Any time you work individually with a student, get out your phone or tablet and film the exercise book, textbook, or resource you are looking at. The conversation you have with your student forms the basis of your teaching. Only your voices appear, with fingers or pens pointing at the text or resource you are discussing. No effort, no extra time. And it is there forever, for you, your students, your department, trainee teachers, etc.

The night before an exam I will record my thoughts over a single image, for five to ten minutes. It is frequently about a question I think will come up, and often is the difference between grade boundaries. The quality has no production values. It is really just a podcast. But again, it is there forever.

Still not convinced? Fair enough. I promise this is my final push towards video. Ever left a cover lesson where the students learned what you wanted them to? But, if you had made a video...

Zero Effort Teachers' Notes

Finally, there is the zero effort approach to teachers notes which I have never seen done, but could be done in every school. Imagine there is a department in your school that has all its lessons for the term, or better still, for the year, on PowerPoint, with a folder of other resources.

What if they were made available to your students? You might object – they are written for teachers. Yes, but can your Initial Teacher Training students understand them? If so, why not make them available to all your students and their parents?

It is quite possible to be teaching in a department for some years, and still not know where to find everything you need. Making it available to your students and parents will help you also organise it for your team, improving everyone's teaching.

You might object, that you have personalised resources. In which case, put your personalised resources on your Virtual Learning platform for your students and parents, instead of making the whole world a better place.

There are no doubt other excuses teachers might find for not doing so – but they are likely to be equally as ropey. It can have a dramatic impact with minimal effort – can you afford not to?

Chapter 9

*"Learned helplessness is the giving-up reaction, the quitting response
that follows from the belief that whatever you do doesn't matter."*

Arnold Schwarzenegger

Teacher Expectations   d = 0.43

Hattie explains: "it is about how the way in which we think leads to the changes
that we want".

Your Expectations

We all think we have high expectations, just as we all think we are good drivers,
or have good taste in clothes, or are blessed with common sense. How do I write
a chapter about something we think we already have, and certainly don't need
any more of?

Here are some questions to help you look at your school, your subject, and your
class:

1. If it were just you, with a group of six of your and your friends' children,
   how would you teach them your subject? Imagine it is science – would
   you use video, textbook, revision guide, investigations? How different
   would this look to your school based curriculum?

2. Same scenario – would you give them an age related curriculum, or see
   what they could cope with?

3. At what age would they know enough to get an A at GCSE?

4. If you wanted them to make lots of progress, how and when would you test them?

5. If you wanted them to have a chance of loving your subject, what activities would you get them to do?

6. How much independent research would you want them to do?

7. How much would you want them to teach to the rest of your group?

8. What is the earliest you could teach your tutor group to answer the follwing question if the SLT told you they had to answer it within the next month, or you would not get paid?
   "'The positive impacts of population change on the character of rural and urban areas outweigh the negative impacts.'
   To what extent do you agree with this view? [15 marks]"

9. This is an A level AQA geography question, containing the most marks on the paper. Would you have the same answer if the SLT set you the same task, based on the question with the most marks on your A level paper?

10. If your answer suggests that your subject is more difficult, then I suggest you do not have high expectations – we all are prone to believe our own subject is more difficult because we see students struggle with it. This lowers our expectations, and limits the way we teach. That is why raised expectations has such a high impact – it changes the way we teach. Many experts at Ofqual, AQA and in schools decided that that was a really demanding question for A level students. But you could see that it was not impossible for many in your tutor group. The same *must* be true of your subject.

11. You set a memory recall test, as a multiple choice. What percentage do you demand students reach before they can stop retaking the test?

12. Why not 90%?

13. You give your class a longer exam question based on the content you taught yesterday. What will you set as the pass mark? See 12!

14. How often do you make students redo work that is scrappy? How often do you decide to write a comment, but not enforce it?

Hopefully these questions will help you to see the tension between the demands of getting through the curriculum, and the desire for your students to attain high standards. Usually, our curriculum is much too slow – we could all get through it much more quickly, and I have already described how this is possible using the example of more than half the year group not studying English, with no drop off in progress when they get to GCSE.

The difficulty is in seeing your world anew. The more it is unlike other schools, the harder it is to believe in your higher expectations. You'll also get bogged down in all the Black Hat thinking – how will we fit it in? How could it work with mixed ability? What would parents say? What if it doesn't work? How will we do it so quickly?

These are not really questions, they are just fears. Once you decide on the high expectations, so much else will fall into place and the questions will answer themselves.

Your Expectations as a School

For example, imagine the SLT said the top sets in year 7 science are going to be taught in French or Spanish. You are going to teach one of those sets, because you are a science teacher in this scenario.

They tell you this in May, intending to start in September.

1. You would try to timetable some languages teachers to at least team teach with you.

2. If no language teachers were available, you might decide to use July to get them to video themselves giving your top 20 classroom instructions, your pieces of equipment, and the scientific terms you would need – so you could use these with the students, and also for yourself to practise.

3. You'd pick the science teachers who were most confident in the foreign language, or failing that, have learned a foreign language.

4. Then you would do the same with all the explanations of scientific concepts you had to explain. This might lead to considerable clarity, as you probably give very little thought to how you define things in English.

5. Then you would organise some after school sessions where you could meet with your counterparts teaching the other top set/s, and with a languages teacher.

6. You'd work out what your assessments were going to be, so you knew the key vocabulary you and your students would have to master.

7. You'd decide on whether students would need phones with Google translate enabled in order to help out during lessons.

8. You'd look for online learning, like Duolingo or Memrise to help you, or insist that the SLT buy you the language course, e.g. from Rosetta stone.

The purpose of this thought experiment is to demonstrate a few principles:

- High expectations carry with them a leap of faith, an acceptance of risk.
- The risk is not catastrophic, and is always less than it feels – students will keep learning, even if it goes wrong. (This is a real example! To see how immersion of one subject in a foreign language works to raise both the language and the science results, visit Bohunt school's website.)
- You can't plan the whole curriculum – you simply have to embark on it and shape it as you go.
- High expectation happens when teachers often don't know the answer, and they and their students have to find out together – e.g. when the teacher is also a learner.
- Because you can't plan everything, put your energy into planning the assessments. Are you assessing the right things, in the right way?

If you are lucky enough to be in a school where Senior Leaders and Heads of Department have high expectations, you can look at ways to change the curriculum in this way.

In both the examples above – , and as a school – the key aspect that determines your high expectations is the curriculum. This is an issue of planning.

Planning as a Way of Transmitting High Expectations

Planning is arguably the most misunderstood skill in schools. Perhaps this is because it is paper based, and can consequently be monitored. In most schools it is a tyrannous checklist of everything you have to cram into the lesson to get an outstanding grade.

Differentiation? Check. Personalised resources? Check. Visual, Auditory and Kinaesthetic learning? Double check. Engaging starter? Check again. Plenary (which will probably be cut short anyway) check. Variety of activities? Check. How many cheques can you write before the bank account runs dry? No wonder planning seems so hard.

Worse, all of that is a distraction. It overwhelms us and makes us feel inadequate.

So let's start again.

Rationale

Planning is simply making sure that students are learning.

To do that, start with something they don't know. You'll find that in the success criteria of your scheme of work, or the exam board's requirements. Some teachers call this endpoint planning – working backwards from where you want the students to end up. Don't confuse this with an exam factory. The skills and knowledge required for a student to gain an A or A* grade have been fought over by senior examiners who are passionate about your subject. To start here is not to sell out to the system, but to make the system work for your students.

There is also a teaching sequence that never fails, which we met in the chapter on differentiation.

- **See**
- **Try**
- **Apply**
- **Secure**

This sequence covers all the things that may be in your school's impossible planning sheet. So:

Differentiation –

- You make the success criteria explicit in your modelling.
- Students support each other in pairs, correcting at least 50% of their misconceptions (according to Hattie, you will recall).
- They try the skill, and apply their knowledge a second time, having already worked out where the gaps are in their knowledge.
- Then they try it again, aiming to master it.
- Some, of course, will not do so, but you have maximized the chances that they will.

Personalised Resources –

- You modelled something that they did not know.
- They individually found out what they still needed to master and had another go at mastery.
- I include learning styles not to promote them (because we know there is little evidence for them) but to acknowledge that you may teach in a school that still values learning styles in its lesson planning.
  Visual? Yes, you've made the model explicit. **Auditory**? Students have taught each other. **Kinaesthetic**? You may be teaching a practical subject – easy. Working in books? Swap partners for the

'apply' stage. Get another pair to write theirs at the computer. Get another pair to come up to the board and assess it.

Engaging starter?

- Get students to memorise the model, and reconstruct it.
- Use the reveal tool of your Interactive White Board to get them to guess what is in the model.
- Present the model as a cloze, and students have to work out what is missing.
- Demonstrate the skill in the wrong sequence and get students to rework the sequence directly.
- Do the model physically and get the students to provide a commentary. Etc. You get the idea. What you mustn't do is go out and find something engaging to grip their attention – I've lost count of the starters I've seen that have nothing to do with the learning in the lesson.

Plenary.

1. Yes, once after the **'try'** phase.
2. Another after the **'apply'** phase.
3. And then another after they have tried individually. Count them – three plenaries. If that doesn't give you progress, nothing will.
4. (By the way, this isn't a whole class, let's hold up everyone's learning, while I, as your teacher, try to find out what you all know plenary. In pairs, or on their own, students will keep finding that out for themselves. Your sample of three or four students will be enough to give you an idea of what they don't know, and decide where to go next).

Variety of activities.

Well, there are at least 4 – **see, try, apply, secure.**

And of course, this is a teaching sequence. It does not have to begin and end in one lesson. This is why, in my plan below, the lesson begins by securing learning from previous lessons.

What This Means for Planning

The most popular planning tool on the internet is the 5 Minute Lesson Plan from Ross McGill, @TeacherTookit. It is very useful as a way of hitting all the buzzwords you might think of as being required in an 'outstanding' lesson: objectives, engagement, AfL, differentiation. Of these, only AfL will prove to have significant impact as we look at the research.

The buzzwords I have included above: differentiation, personalised, engaging starter, plenary, are also simply Ofsted words – they are not something that appear in my planning at all. I've included them to show you that simply planning the students' learning journey – See, Try, Apply, Secure, will automatically hit all the buzzwords you need. The buzzwords themselves are not the learning journey – they are a distraction from it.

The other buzzwords in the 5 Minute Lesson Plan are: the big picture, and stickability. These two are not what I would classify as Ofsted words – they are backed up by research. The big picture looks at goal setting and context. Both of these will be apparent in the 'see' stage. Stickability happens with the process of review, which is built in to 'apply' and 'secure'.

My point here is not that I have a form of lesson planning that will take you all of 5 minutes. My point is that if you focus on this very simple learning journey – **see, try, apply, secure** – your students will always make progress, and your lesson will always hit all of the buzzwords that Ofsted, SLT or a head of department might throw at you.

What Might Lesson Planning Look Like?

Let's imagine you are a maths teacher – (I'm doing this because maths teachers I train have a lot of difficulty in applying anything that involves writing to their own teaching, even though the 'writing' here is just a signifier for what you are teaching).

Most of the planning for a maths teacher has already been done by the textbook. This is not an attack, it is a celebration of a well designed resource. Here, students will see a worked example. There will typically be twenty easy, twenty moderate, twenty hard and ten very hard progression questions. Remember that, with high expectations, you are trying to get to learning the quickest way possible.

So, **See** would involve us going through the model on the board. Then in pairs students would **Try** two of the easy questions. One pair at random would show one of these on the board – if it is right, we can probably move on. If it is wrong, can they work out why?

Your job is to patrol the room while they work on each question – because there are only two, you can instantly assess whether it is safe to move on. Doug Lemov calls this standardizing the format. Then pairs will **Apply** learning to a more difficult question, or two.

Again, because you are patrolling, and have only two questions to focus on, you can constantly assess what the students do and don't know. If there are many mistakes, pick on a pair who are wrong in ways that are common to the class – get their work on the board and use it to teach from. If many are right, you can afford to pick at random.

You can **Apply** again, if they were struggling, or move to individual work for the **Secure** stage. In each case, choose two more difficult questions.

In the **Secure** phase you want students to think as mathematicians, rather than simply following a method. Anyone with a good memory can follow a method in a single lesson and achieve apparent mastery. But once a problem that looks slightly different arrives, such students panic – the method no longer suffices. It is a significant reason, I feel, why many otherwise academic students are convinced that they are no good at maths – it is because they have learned a method, but have not been made to secure knowledge.

The key to the **secure** stage is finding ways to test your students' understanding of the concept, rather than just what has happened in the lesson. To do this, you want to *alter the context.*

How Does Altering the Context Create High Expectations?

1. Your high expectations are communicated here in the **secure** stage, by asking for learning to be applied in a new context.

2. In order to make this possible, your expectations also had to be apparent in the model you chose at the beginning.

3. You also modeled each increased level of difficulty, by getting students to show their work at the board.

4. You communicated that everyone had to participate, with the pairing of students. You also achieved this because at each stage students know it could be them that are called to demonstrate.

5. Your questioning has not just been about knowledge, the method, but about understanding: why does the method work, what happens to it when problems become more difficult or less familiar?

Crucially, you did not have to think about this in your planning. You didn't have to ask yourself, "am I setting high enough expectations?" in the same way that you did not have to ask, "am I hitting the right buzzwords for this year's checklist of what should be in the lesson?"

This is important, because those questions introduce complexity into your thinking. Complexity takes time, and invites mistakes, and inconsistency.

Instead I am offering simplicity. Simplicity is always sustainable. It is also precise, and will consequently deliver high expectations, whatever you are teaching.

What Might An Individual Lesson Plan Look Like?

This is just a normal lesson I taught to my year 10 English class. There is nothing flashy in it, and nothing that would take more than 5 minutes to prepare – 10 if I dictated the students' work on my iPad, rather than just photographing it. I've never asked myself how will I differentiate or engage, because the **See, Try, Apply, Secure** structure does that for me.

AHFASTERCROCH is a mnemonic I use for remembering persuasive writing rhetorical devices, and students learn them in this order: alliteration, hyperbole, facts, anecdote, statistics, three (rule of), emotive language, rhetorical question, creating an enemy, repetition, opinion, contrasting pairs, humour. This itself communicates high expectations to the students.

Most schools teach AFOREST, alliteration, facts, opinons, rhetorical questions, emotive language, statistics, three (rule of), and some push the boat out with DAFOREST, where D = direct address to the reader.

Hopefully, you can see how much more interesting the piece of writing will be using A*H*FAS*TER*C*ROCH* – look at the techniques in bold italic, which are missing from DAFOREST.

The model you choose to set out from determines your high expectations. DAFOREST will help you analyse a persuasive speech by David Cameron. But it won't also help you write like Stephen Fry or Alison Pearson or even Jeremy Clarkeson, which AHFASTERCROCH will.

So, when selecting your model, pitch it the very highest you can for the class. Most teachers claim they do this, because they believe they do, but the prevalence of AFOREST and PEE should be a reality check.

The Lesson Plan

Year 10 – Target grades in the class B to A*

Objective:

Understand how paragraphs can be linked together using key words, topic sentences and a developing argument.

(There is much more than this that I will teach them, or that they might learn in the lesson – but I share only one objective, because that is the learning I really want to focus on in the lesson).

Student activity	Learning Points
Matt and Mark to rehearse – Charmain and Adnan in AHFASTERCROCH **Secure** (from previous lessons) As Matt and Mark were experts and Charmain and Adnan were weakest. Other students test each other in pairs.	Students rehearse the rhetorical techniques that Boris Johnson uses, and consolidate/learn to recognise them themselves for their own writing. Use of time limits secures memory, engages and therefore promotes learning.
Challenge to beat 15 seconds for reciting all of AHFASTERCROCH in the right order for a third of a stamp, merit, credit, housepoint, Vivo etc **Secure (from previous lessons)**	Reward promotes challenge and establishes the class culture that standards are hard, tasks are challenging, though achievable. 15 second time limit does this also.
Students look at the homework Annabel wrote to identify the writing skills, which come from AHFASTERCORCH. **See**	Randomly chosen students feed back so I can gauge what the class has retained. They will be practising these skills later in the lesson, so we rehearse them now. Crucially students see what the skills look like in writing.
Explore misconceptions **See**	If students miss particular points, we will return to them with the next text, so that they can immediately measure their learning. Call on volunteers in the class to explain to those who have misconceptions.
Philomena's homework, projected on the board – students identify what knits two paragraphs together **See**	Students see how key words in the final sentence of one paragraph are picked up in the first sentence of the next paragraph. This is a vital skill in constructing an essay, and is part of the B/A grade skill.
Students in pairs decide how to link a paragraph to the one that preceded it. They do this with their own writing. **Try**	Students immediately have the opportunity to test their learning from the previous activity. They are supported in pairs before having to try it themselves.
We watch a video of Boris Johnson on David Letterman's show. We analyse quotations in class discussion to see what message Johnson aims at different audiences **Apply**	Students consolidate their understanding that a single speech can have different aims for different audiences. This complexity is also at the A/A* grade, and this will be made explicit to them. Here I can allow volunteers, as we are developing new thinking and not looking for 'right' answers. Intersperse with random questioning so students can't afford to opt out.
A scribe types notes for us during this class discussion, otherwise learning is easily ignored, or lost. **Apply**	Students' note taking skills are developed – they decide what key words are necessary to help later reconstruction in paragraphs. This also allows them to decide what is vital, and what is less important. Additionally, limiting word choice highlights the importance of the right vocabulary – the more precise a word, the more it conveys.
Students write individually – two paragraphs using the quotations we have found, and the class notes just taken on the class discussion. They must LINK the paragraphs. **Apply/Secure**	This is an exit ticket, which will show me if they have learned this skill. The modeling of this will be achieved by having a student type theirs on the board. Hopefully, there will be a remote that allows me to hide this, until we are ready to reveal.
Pairs called at random to critique the paragraphs on the board: has the model met the learning objective? How far? **Apply/Secure**	Students will be more likely to apply what they see to their own paragraphs – does theirs look right in the same ways, or wrong in the same ways as the student model?

How Else Does The Lesson Convey High Expectations?

As usual, modelling will teach students more than I have planned. Here, the student models will introduce new analyses of Boris Johnson's language that each student can 'steal', or attack. I've chosen Annabel's and Philomena's work, as near A* and A* respectively. Annabel's work I've also chosen to motivate her – she has an SEN issue that demands 25% extra time, even though she is in a top set.

Students will meet new vocabulary in Annabel's and Philomena's work, and have it translated for them during class discussion, so they can 'steal' it.

They will notice that quotations are introduced with a comma before the opening speech marks. They will see how quotations are integrated into the sentence. They will realise integrated quotations are very short, even one word long.

They will notice how the point and example of PEE are conflated here, so that paragraphing is not mechanical and clunky. They will see how PEE has actually been dispensed with. They'll find how a student links more than one explanation or interpretation around a single quotation.

They will find that using key words to link paragraphs is a planning tool, which may save time in an exam.

They will hear new interpretations from a new speech, and apply what they already know.

They will find out whether they have the skill to write connecting paragraphs, and whether they can achieve this in a typical exam time limit.

My job is to be alert to these moments, and others that I have not anticipated.

And of course they will revise persuasive techniques from AHFASTERCROCH, and get better at both remembering them and spotting examples in others' speech and writing.

It is a totally sustainable way of teaching, because it takes so little effort and time. Yes, I will have had to mark the previous lesson's work – but that at least gives my marking a purpose. Similarly, I only have to read the work of five key students to identify two I want to use in the lesson – I can mark the books later if I choose.

In this way, the teaching sequence forces me to have high expectations, and forces me to motivate my students.

Motivation   d = 0.48

Often students have the wrong sort of motivation, what I call the completer finisher, which Daniel Pink calls "performance motivation...some just want to finish regardless of how they got there." The goal instead is to get students to value "the process of learning".

Daniel Pink shows us that motivation is highest when people achieve mastery, purpose and autonomy. This is a delightfully short section, as we've covered reward and praise, extrinsic and intrinsic reward already.

Jim Smith calls it WIIFM – what's in it for me. As long as you engage students in this process, you'll find out what motivates them. However, I like to simplify things, because then I know I'll probably do them. Students are motivated by doing better – so show them how, then test them so they can see their own improvement. Therefore, everything you do has to be public, so everyone can see who is learning, and who is not. To see how this is achieved, jump to my chapter on Worked Examples and Modelling.

Chapter 10

"Los Angeles stood out because it was the only big city that had after-school programs in every one of its 90 elementary schools."

Arnold Schwarzenegger

Writing Programs   d = 0.44

How do you teach students how to write in your own subject? This is disarmingly simple. It has to do with modeling the genres that your subject uses. Modeling itself has a higher impact, so I deal with it later. For now, let's think about how improving writing in your subject will also improve your students' subject knowledge.

We all imagine, perhaps, that this happens naturally in schools all the time. My experience, admittedly limited statistically, is that we focus on subject knowledge for 90% of the time, the structure of students' writing for 5%, and the remaining 5% concerns creativity.

Creative Writing Tasks Across the Curriculum

My way of testing this was to look at Google, with the search for "interesting homework". You will notice that all the hits on the first page are for primary schools – there is a clear message here. When I open the most popular one, it is from the TES. Below I list some creative ideas taken from this TES contributor, bluerose, in 'Creative Homework pack'. It is a wonderfully creative resource, downloaded 56,000 times. I pick it because it illustrates how useful writing is as a way of exploring the curriculum. I also pick it because it reveals what I think is our default position as teachers: we simply assume our students know how to write in the genres we demand:

So, here is the list of some of the written activities from bluerose.

1. Write a letter to a scientist with your questions.

2. Write your own creation myth/ How the birds got their colours etc

3. Write an encyclopaedia entry for ...

4. Write a book or film review – teacher can specify certain vocabulary that must be used (and perhaps some boring vocab that must not). Review could be presented on tape or as interview between two people. Present review as discursive text, poem, etc according to genre of writing being studied at time.

5. Write a short newspaper report announcing the discovery of Tutankhamen's tomb. (Include a Catchy Headline!)

6. Write a diary entry from someone in Howard Carter's team

7. Create a leaflet about an exhibit for the museum.

8. Design a job advert for someone to work on a dig.

9. Write a description of entering a tomb for the first time. (It was dark with the chink of light from the opening we had made. The air was stuffy and closed all around us...)

10. Imagine you are member of Howard Carter's team. Write a letter home to your family.

11. Write a short newspaper report announcing the invasion of Britain. (Include a Catchy Headline!) (decide whether you're a Roman or British newspaper first)

How many of them would be vastly improved with a structure checklist, to help students decode the genre?

Let's take the last example to see what this might look like with a structured checklist:

1. Begin with a paragraph that introduces Claudius as a hero due to his past exploits

2. Describe the landing in a way that makes Britain seem hard to invade

3. Write about the first encounter with the British natives to suggest either that they were very easy to defeat by Roman superiority, or show that they were a formidable enemy, defeated by Roman superiority.

4. Write about the decisive battle.

5. Include an interview with a centurion that will show his feelings about the invasion, his opinions of his men, his opinions of the enemy, his opinions of the weather and landscape.

6. Include an interview with a defeated British tribal leader that offers a different perspective. (Remember, a newspaper won't include the interviewer's question, just the answers given by the interviewee). Quotations need to be introduced with a colon, and then speech marks.

7. Conclude with a description of Claudius and a question about the future.

You could differentiate this further by specifying the number of paragraphs, the number or length of quotations. A further trick I'd recommend is insisting on particular vocabulary that you want students to use. This is because it allows you to signal the crucial subject knowledge you want your students to know. Those key words might be:

- Emperor Claudius
- invasion force
- divisions, departure
- Boulogne
- natural harbour
- Catuvellauni resistance
- leaders Togodumnus and Caratacus
- British force met the Romans at a river crossing.
- battle raged for two days.
- Hosidius Geta nearly captured,
- awarded the Roman triumph
- pushed back to the Thames
- Bridge.
- Batavian troops swam
- Togodumnus killed
- war elephants
- surrender of eleven kings
- the final march on Camulodunum

This is crucial to the students' understanding. Combining the checklist with the key words means they must be applying the subject knowledge you want your students to master.

To introduce more complex reasoning and analysis, you could insist on the following connectives – *because, although, however, despite, on the other hand, moreover, most importantly, furthermore.* These will force students to consider more than one point of view.

Will the Writing Checklist Dumb Down or Level Up?

Next, we'll look at a GCSE question that focuses on the same skills.

The question again comes from AQA:
Why was the Spanish Armada defeated? 10 marks
Target: An understanding and evaluation of causation (AO1 & AO2: 5+5 marks)

Answers that recognise and explain several factors to do with reasons for the defeat of the Spanish Armada in specific detail score 6-8 marks, e.g:

1. The Spanish commander had little experience of sailing.

2. After sailing it was difficult for the Armada to get fresh supplies.

3. Some of the huge Spanish galleons were difficult to handle in heavy seas.

4. The English ships did use different tactics, they tried to sink the enemy from a distance.

5. The Spanish tried to grapple and board ships.

6. The English had 54 battle ships. They were light and fast.

7. The 14,000 English sailors were experienced in fighting and sailing.

8. The Spanish had 64 battleships but they included 22 huge galleons which were unsuitable for close manoeuvring.

9. The Spanish stuck together and the English harried the Spanish crescent up the English Channel.

10. The fire ships were a brilliant weapon that destroyed the Spanish formation.

11. The English could re-supply their ship with cannonballs. The Spanish cannon could fire shorter distances.

This answer is worth 6-8 marks out of 10, so roughly B to A grade. It is purely factual, with no discussion of alternative viewpoints. In a question like this, that would be achieved by prioritising which factors were the most significant.

This purports to be a higher order question, testing "evaluation of causation", but as we have just seen, 8 out of 10 marks are available entirely for memory.

Incredible though it may seem, the writing checklist will train your students to perform at least at A grade, without them having to actually think like a historian. It is one of the themes of this book that the difficulty of GCSEs is not in content or skill – students will get B or A grades simply with an excellent memory. However, you need to train students not just to remember, but in how to present what they know in exam questions.

Let's look at the remaining two marks, because the other theme of this book is that we want our students to be able to get 100%. The two marks appear to be given for the conclusion:

Answers that develop ... and evaluate the relative importance of individual factors or come to a summary assessment about the factors involved or provide details of the links between factors e.g.

The weakness of Spanish leadership contrasts with the experience and talent of the English captains and this is shown in their use of the fire ship to destroy the fleet. However, had Parma been more ready to set out they might have invaded. The English commanders simply used their equipment better than the Spanish used their less suited technology.

So, now you can teach the structure of a GCSE conclusion in three simple parts: one key factor was this; a contrasting key factor was that; my related deciding key factor is...

Let me repeat that the final two marks, A+ and A* are awarded for this ability to write a conclusion. This is the ability to evaluate. Now let's go back to our *year 7 checklist*. In the task given to our year 7 students, evaluation is implicit in these parts of the checklist:

- Write about the first encounter with the British natives to suggest *either that* they were very easy to defeat by Roman superiority, *or* show that they were a formidable enemy, defeated by Roman superiority.

- Include an interview with a centurion that will show *his feelings* about the invasion, *his opinions* of his men, his opinions of the enemy, his opinions of the weather and landscape.

- Include an interview with a defeated British tribal leader *that offers a different perspective.*

This is a major reason for the success of the writing frame – it gives students A and A* skills *while they are still in year 7 and 8*. I hope you can see that this is not a gimmick, it is the way exams work. Our terrible mistake in schools is that we decide to teach skills on a journey to year 11, because that is when they are tested. But instead, we could teach those skills in year 7, and then gradually reduce the writing checklist as they move to years 8 and 9. Eventually, we will ask students to write their own checklist first.

Instead we assume the student already has that checklist in their own heads, which is ridiculous. There are nine skills in the writing checklist, and more than ten facts. Even you, the teacher, are not carrying all of that in your head.

We've now seen that the checklist will allow the year 7 students to write at a level that would score 9 out of 10 at GCSE. This didn't happen by accident – it happened because I thought of the demands of the writing task, on its own. It worked because in history, as so many subjects, students are assessed through writing. If they know the conventions of writing well, they cannot fail to access the A and A* grades at GCSE. But the reverse is also true – no matter how much history, or geography, or RE, or PE, or science, or English, or business studies, or drama you have taught them, they cannot get an A* unless you have taught them what writing looks like in your subject. Why wait to teach that in year 11 when it can be taught in year 7?

When I visited Michaela school, I asked Katharine Birbalsingh about the amazing progress her students were making in years 7 and 8. Would she enter them for GCSEs early, when they were ready? In the best possible way, she looked at me as though I were an idiot. No, they would teach a mastery curriculum they value, that would, by implication, go far beyond GCSE by the time students were 16. They'd take the GCSE when they got there, because the end game is a high quality university degree for every student.

It's time to re-examine your year 7 curriculum.

Formal, Rather Than Creative Writing

Let's now look at writing that is actually part of the curriculum, and not therefore dependent on our creativity or management of time. I'll take science as an example, and the scientific method. Here's a very simple guide to the writing structure:

The scientific method consists of six steps:

1. Define purpose (through observation or asking questions)
2. Construct hypothesis
3. Test the hypothesis and data collection
4. Analyze data
5. Draw conclusion
6. Communicate results

That's not bad, because it takes very little effort, and is therefore sustainable. Amazingly, the research suggests that if we break learning down into these steps, it will have a positive effect both on the students' writing, and on their learning of your subject content. But what if students could see what a good written example looked like?

Let's imagine that you have no time to find an example from previous years, or your current classes. You teach in a department which does not routinely share such resources in its schemes of work (in other words, let's assume that you are in an inefficient school, where leadership is focused on the wrong things). Do a Google search for examples of writing up a science experiment.

When I enter "examples of writing up a science experiment" I don't find examples. Instead, I find lots of explanations of how to write up the experiment. This is not Google's fault. It is simply a reflection of how we work as teachers. We explain how to do stuff, instead of just showing. Showing is always much quicker than explaining, both for the teacher and for the learner. And the later explanation will suddenly make much more sense, because your students will be able to see what the explanation refers to.

In other words, when I find a structural checklist of the scientific method, I don't find an example. We need to get to the learning as quickly as possible. Google suggests that we don't do this – instead we default to explanation, rather than showing. How do I infer this from Google? Well, many of these uploads will be by teachers, uploading explanations, not examples.

If I have this conversation with teachers, they become defensive – no, I give examples in my class. But when we observe dozens of lessons, we find this isn't so. Every time, every time, a student writes, they need to think about the model of the piece of writing that will get them 100%. This means you must show that model frequently. Sometimes you will withhold it, to test what your students have remembered, but you would still refer them to it.

This is the gap in teacher's thinking, the gap in planning. The cure is simple – you have all the models you need after every mock or assessment. You can pay for the return of your highest scoring exam papers, to check your understanding of what the writing demands are. Even more importantly, you can call back the papers of those candidates you thought were nailed on certainties for A*, but came away with an A or B. These are the papers that will tell you what you are not teaching. I guarantee, it will almost certainly be something about writing, not their subject knowledge.

Is there any reason why you can't get this organised tomorrow? As usual, do it, and this book will have paid for itself.

The Passive Voice:
(Using Writing to Improve Reading in Your Subject)

Because this is a quicker way to get to the learning, I'll start by trying to persuade you to teach the passive voice. I realise this is a hard sell, as it is not a direct way to teach your subject content. However, most of your text books will be written in the passive voice, so teaching this will make your text book more accessible.

For those many of you who were not properly taught grammar at school, the passive voice is where there is no subject/agent performing the verb, or where the subject/agent is preceded with the word 'by'.

Example:

Active voice

The **boy** *broke* the window – *broke* is the verb, and **boy** is the subject performing the verb.

Passive voice

The window *was broken* – *was broken* has no subject performing the verb. Or

The window *was broken* by the **boy** – the subject **boy** is preceded by the word 'by'.

Nominalisation

Here you take a verb and turn it into a noun (a thing or concept):

The breaking of the window was wrong. My shorthand for this, however, is just to teach the passive.

In the extracts from the science and history texts below, I hope the use of the passive voice jumps out at you as a feature of text book writing – why you should teach it if you want your students to understand what they are reading.

Here's an extract from a science text book: Collins New GCSE Science – Science A Student Book: AQA:

"Ores and economics

Only minerals with enough metal to make it worth extracting *are used* as ores. Unless the metal is very valuable, *it is not economic to process* low-grade ore (rock containing a small amount of metal). However, *economics change*; some metals *become scarcer* or there are new, cheaper methods of extraction.

Metal ores are mined, often on a huge scale, and *transported* all over the world.

Smelting

At the smelter, the *ore is crushed*. It may also *be concentrated*, to remove rock with little or no metal.

Some ores are metal oxides. These *can be smelted* directly. Other ores *are converted* to the metal oxide before or during smelting. To convert the metal oxide to the metal, the oxygen *must be removed*. This is called reduction.

The metal oxide *is reduced by* heating it in a furnace, with carbon. Originally, *the type of carbon used* was charcoal, but *now it is coke* (a nearly pure form of carbon, from coal). The overall reaction is:

metal oxide + carbon → metal + carbon dioxide

The furnace must be hot enough to melt the metal. Other materials, such as limestone, *are added, to remove impurities* in the ore. They form slag."

Now, as a science teacher, you would be right in thinking that students do not have to write in the passive voice to succeed in their exams. However, they will constantly have to *read* in the passive voice – every time they open a science textbook or exam paper. If you want students to go to university, why wouldn't you teach the passive voice, and insist that your students write like that? Wouldn't it make them better scientists?

Moreover, they will need to write in a passive voice should they pursue science to degree level. Even more certainly, they will have to use it in their jobs or careers. This moral purpose might not appeal to you. There is a further carrot. Yes, you will also earn brownie points for using literacy in your subject.

Will your students learn more science from your textbook if they have to transform it? I think they will. However, you will only find out by trying it and testing your students. When I tested staff using DARTs to transform texts, they retained most of the subject knowledge *which I had not taught them*. This is crucial. It is another golden moment I keep referring to, where your students learn more than you teach them.

So, you could ask your students to translate the text into the active voice. It might look like this, with the introduction of the subject performing the verb, 'we':

We only use minerals with enough metal to make it worth extracting to make ores. Unless the metal is very valuable, it is not economic for us to process low-grade ore (rock containing a small amount of metal). However, economics change; some metals become scarcer or we learn cheaper methods to extract them. (You'll see why this is italicized in a minute).

We **mine** metal ores, often on a huge scale, and transport them all over the world. We **crush** the ore at the smelter. **We can also concentrate it,** to remove rock with little or no metal. Some ores are metal oxides. **We can smelt these** directly. **We convert** ores to the metal oxide before or during smelting. **We must remove** the oxygen to convert the metal oxide to the metal. This is called reduction.

We **reduce** the metal oxide by heating it in a furnace, with carbon. **We originally used** charcoal, a type of carbon used, but now **we use coke** (a nearly pure form of carbon, from coal)."

Another way of teaching it is to take the complexity from the active voice:

We only make ores from minerals with enough metal that is easy to extract. Low grade ore is rock that contains only a small amount of metal. We only extract this metal if it is very valuable. This can also happen when some metals become scarcer. Sometimes we learn cheaper methods to extract them.

This has changed the italicised paragraph from 3 sentences to 5 sentences, so it is easier to follow.

Another way of teaching it is to move from this simplified active, to get the students to rewrite it in fewer sentences, in the passive. Again, I would appeal to your sense of moral purpose here.

The Literacy Mat

To help you, here is a resource we prepared at my school for every subject that involves writing. We called it a Literacy Mat because the hook is getting teachers to focus on literacy for those brownie points. It is an easy way to show Ofsted, or indeed your SLT, that you are developing your students' literacy. But remember, this is not why I'm recommending it to you. It is because focusing on student writing leads to improved results in your subject.

Campden Literacy Tips

Peer Marking Symbols

- **Sp** Spelling
- **Gr** Grammatical Error
- **Cap** Capital letter needed or missed
- ~~~ Does not make sense
- **//** Start a paragraph
- **P** Punctuation
- **^** Missing word

Sentences

Common Verbs

Describe
Provide the relevant features or characteristics.

Summarise
Give only the main points.

Compare
Look at two or more situations.
Explain the similarities.
(Note, in English exams, compare also means contrast).

Contrast
Look at two or more situations. Explain the ways they are different from each other.

Analyse
Identify separate factors and say how they are linked together.

Explain
Give reasons for a fact or opinion.

Justify
Explain why one opinion is better than another.

Evaluate
Look at two different ideas and justify which one is best.

Simple Sentence
Must contain a subject and a verb. Most contain an object. The subject does the verb to or with the object.

The cat sat on the mat.
cat = subject
sat = verb
mat = object

Compound sentence
Joins two simple sentences using the conjunctions: for, and, nor, but, or, yet, so (FANBOYS)
All FANBOYS except 'and' need a comma.
Tom likes to read in the library, but Sarah prefers to read at home.

Complex sentence
Contains a conjunction or connective and usually has a comma.
Sarah and Tom went to the cinema, after they had finished their homework.

Ways to OPEN a sentence (START)

With an adjective
Terrible secrets were hidden in his diary.

With a verb
Lying between the pages of his diary were terrible secrets.

With an adverb
Furiously, he accused his sister of reading his secret diary.

With a preposition
Beneath the bed, he hid his diary.

With a pronoun
He realised he should have locked his diary away.

With a connective
Because her brother was careless, Sarah easily found his diary.

With a noun
Sarah gleefully opened her brother's diary and began to read.

CONNECTIVES

Most useful connectives
because, although, however, therefore, consequently, on the other hand

Sequencing
most importantly, secondly, finally, since, next, after, while

Cause and effect
because, therefore, consequently, thus, so

Emphasise
above all, especially, significantly, in particular

Analyse
although, however, unless, except, alternatively, whereas, on the other hand

Compare
similarly, likewise, equally, in the same way

Give examples
for example, such as, as revealed by, in the case of

Adding information
moreover, in addition, furthermore, too (Don't overuse also)

 What are you writing?
Purpose / Audience / Format

 New paragraph when you change
Time / Topic / Talk

Punctuation

Full stop	To end a sentence.
Comma	To join an incomplete idea to a sentence. To separate items in a list.
Parenthesis	Brackets, double commas, dashes – to add extra information to a sentence.
Colon	To introduce an explanation. To introduce a list.
Semi-Colon	To join two related sentences (it works like 'because') To separate long items in a list.
Apostrophe	To show an owner, it goes after the last letter of the name of the owner. To show where letters have been missed out.

 Improve your writing with VCOP for Self and Peer Assessment
Vocabulary **C**onnectives **O**penings **P**unctuation

By far the most popular use from our teachers is getting students to use the connectives. Here are some of their ideas:

- Using the common verbs to support the answering of 6 mark questions
- Using the entire placemat for 6 mark questions – either doing or self/ peer assessing OR grading the quality of written communication.
- To demonstrate effective peer marking using symbols
- Give marks for the person who uses the most connectives in an answer.
- Use the connectives for debates generating interaction
- Make use of compound sentences to add detail to their answer.
- Gapped sentences in MFL
- Giving them a question, giving them the connective and practice sequencing using their connective
- Using the connective words as an evaluation card game.... during verbal evaluations, the cards are handed out at random and students have to add to/complete/expand on their comments. They would also be used when moving on to the written evaluations.
- I liked the swap 6 – each student needs to continue on from another student's work starting with a connective each time
- Practice writing conclusions using connectives.
- Use an article and get students to find connectives or re-write using certain connectives.

So, connectives is where you should start when using the literacy mat.

Is this true, even for maths teachers?

Using Connectives to Improve Writing and Thinking

Remember the impossible Edexcel GCSE maths question of 2015, involving Hannah's sweets?

There are n sweets in a bag. 6 of the sweets are orange. The rest of the sweets are yellow.

Hannah takes a random sweet from the bag. She eats the sweet.

Hannah then takes at random another sweet from the bag. She eats the sweet.

The probability that Hannah eats two orange sweets is 1/3.

Show that $n^2 - n - 90 = 0$.

It's scary because you get a scary-looking equation. However, re-read the question. The question is not asking you to solve the equation. It is asking you to look at probability.

Let's solve it:

Because there are 6 oranges and n sweets, there is a 6/n chance Hannah will pick an orange sweet.

However, the question asks us to consider that the first choice was orange. **Consequently** there are only 5 orange sweets left out of a total of n – 1 sweets.

Therefore, if the first sweet chosen was orange, there is a $\dfrac{5}{n-1}$ chance that the second sweet will be orange.

Consequently, the chance of getting two orange sweets in a row is the first probability multiplied by the second one.

Which is $\dfrac{6}{n} \times \dfrac{5}{n-1}$

The question tells us that the chance of Hannah getting two orange sweets is 1/3.

Therefore, $\dfrac{6}{n} \times \dfrac{5}{n-1} = \dfrac{1}{3}$

Finally, we now have to rearrange this equation.

$$\dfrac{6 \times 5}{n} \times n\text{–}1 = \dfrac{5}{n-1} = \dfrac{1}{3}$$

Or

$$\dfrac{90}{n^2-n} = 1$$

So $(n^2 – n) = 90$

Consequently $n^2 – n – 90 = 0$

The bold connectives come from the literacy mat. I'm not a maths teacher. But, it seems to me that students who are brilliant at maths would have no problem with this question. The many thousands who took to social media, however, were not naturally good at maths.

If they had been taught to use connectives in their maths lessons, would they have done better? I believe they would. They panicked because they had a question where they had no obvious method to fall back on. In other words, they were not used to approaching questions through their understanding of mathematical concepts. They weren't thinking in terms of what *mathematical language* means.

Instead, they were just relying on memory – 'in questions like this, I use this method. And the steps of the method look like this. Repeat for the different maths topics'.

However, if maths teachers taught their students explanations that involved connectives, I think this would change: they would have a much better understanding of what each method *means*, rather than simply seeing what it *does*. Students would have to speak in these explanations.

Using connectives will also help students structure their thinking – here, thinking like a mathematician. Perhaps many of you will have taken none of this example in, because your experience of school taught you not to think like a mathematician. Similarly, many mathematicians will be looking at the connectives, and finding way to dismiss them. Dear maths teacher – what would you lose by trying it with your students' problem solving tomorrow, to find out the effect?

Chapter 11

*"In our society, the women who break down
barriers are those who ignore limits."*
Arnold Schwarzenegger

Self Concept   d = 0.47

This involves getting to know your students so that you understand their sense of self. Hattie tells us "These choices aim to protect, present, preserve and promote our sense of self such that we can 'back ourselves' – that is, maintain a sense of self-esteem. A major purpose of schooling is to enable students to 'back themselves' as learners of what we consider worth knowing."

And "Educating students to have high, challenging, appropriate expectations is among the most powerful influences in enhancing student achievement." Although this is written about self reported grades, it is the kind of self concept to which our students need to aspire.

This seems to me to correspond exactly with the work of Professor Carol Dweck, on growth mindset. These ideas are probably now well known.

1. Establish high expectations
Let students know that you are challenging them *because* you know they can meet your expectations.

Use language that outlines high expectations.

Make clear in written comments that you believe they have the capacity to develop a high level of skill in that area.

2. Value risk and failure

- Show your students that you value challenge by giving them challenge.
- Value and reward effort.
- Measure the progress they make.
- Make this more important than how they compare to others.
- Expect students to make mistakes so we can all learn from them.
- Keep telling students they should expect to find some things confusing and difficult.
- Ask students to share a mistake that helped them to learn this week.

3. Give feedback that focuses on process

- Avoid praising students for being clever.
- Many students think that effort is doing something for a long time. Show them a different form of effort: seeking out challenges, setting goals, being creative, persevering when things are difficult.

4. Introduce students to the concept of the malleable mind

- Share the neuroscience which shows that brains develop through effort and learning, and that they are more malleable than previously thought. When practising challenges, their brains form new connections, making them smarter.
- Share examples of when you learned from mistakes, or changed your view from a fixed to a growth mindset.

Chapter 12

Early Intervention   d = 0.47

The first thing we might notice is there is no data for late intervention. In 2009, was it even a thing? I point this out because the word "intervention" is overwhelmingly associated in our schools with year 11. Our thinking about intervention might be very different if we simply called it "teaching". It would then be obvious that early is best. We would start in year 7.

Year 11 style intervention isn't in the revised *Visible Learning for Teachers*, and it isn't in the EEF Toolkit. That's not to say it is ineffective, but just that it appears to be unstudied. Leading the field in the UK is probably PiXL, a group of over 1000 schools dedicated to improving exam results. Several schools are now following the David Brailsford model of 'marginal gains', or the Clive Woodward model of making 100 things 1% better, in the hope of improving performance. Schools are becoming performance cultures. But what if we got our intervention in early – would this minimise the number of students we would need to support in exam years?

The Times today (2016) reports that three times more men than women are asked to repeat a year at university. The increase has been dramatic since 2009. Does our performance culture favour the quick fix, the quick burst of revision, the last minute exam practice, the reward of instant results – do this work now, and get this result next week, or tomorrow?

I think it does.

I'm not going to denigrate these here – if we get students to learn their subject so that they only retain that knowledge for a few weeks, we are not failing them. They benefit from the increased opportunities that passing exams gives them. These days, the school's reputation benefits just as much. But, in the same breath, we must admit, there ought to be a better way – creating lifelong learners, a learning community in which people want to know more. This is where we really want to be – making a difference.

John Green, author of *The Fault in Our Stars*, describes education in a series of metaphors, in his TED lecture on *Why Learning is Awesome*. Schools and exams present a series of hurdles over which students must jump. However, many students are not interested in the hurdle. To a twelve year old boy, a shirt and tie looks a lot like a shirt and noose. Instead he would like schools to treat education as a different metaphor, making cartographers of us, so that we are curious about seeing a little more coast, a little more of a mountain range. We build a map, linking our learning, and crucially, a community of learners.

Early intervention does this, focusing on skills and knowledge that children need in order to become successful learners, not in order to pass an exam. If it is correct, why is its effect only slightly bigger than average? Why is it not brilliant? One reason is that early intervention research often centres on early years, indeed the best time appears to be the first 18 months of a child's life. So, the effect is actually quite powerful if it is measuring progress many years, even decades later.

But there is another possibility: passing an exam is as much about the exam skill as subject knowledge. The GCSE process asks a student:

Do you plan your time well; do you underline the key and command words so that you are answering the question; do you show your workings; do you double check for spelling and punctuation; have you used the right vocabulary that will be in the mark scheme; have you remembered to evaluate rather than just describe or analyse; did you check which questions you needed to answer; did you practice stamina, so that you could keep going in the last half hour; did you do the maths questions a second time, to see if you got the same result; did you use any time at the end to check your answer; did you practise having neat handwriting, like a girl: if you are a girl, did you make sure it had no decorative circles or hearts above the i's, and wasn't as big as the gap between lines?

I could make this list bigger – for an English exam it would be much bigger – four times the length at least. So, I really mean it when I say at least 50% of a student's score can be their ability to do this particular exam, rather than their knowledge of your subject.

A lot of these are based on a growth mindset: I will put in effort; I will challenge myself with personal bests; I will practise past papers and seek out my mistakes; I will not give up until I am told to put my pen down; I will aim for 100% and see how close I get.

One intervention will be to model this much earlier – whenever students have an exam. We can teach them to use mind-maps to link their learning across different domains in our subject. We can teach them how to revise, and then get them doing it.

This would have a more lasting impact than many of the interventions in school.

So, does it make more sense to intervene in year 7, or in year 11?

If Most Students Who Struggle Do So With Reading and Writing, What Should We Do?

15 years ago, the National Strategies produced a brilliant resource called Literacy Progress Units, for year 7 catch up. These were brilliant. They were aimed at students who had achieved a level 3 at KS2, and diagnosed their problems in phonics, sentence level, organising writing, or reading between the lines. Then the strategies provided a series of lessons which targeted each kind of weakness, in a series of 20 minute lessons. These folders are still lurking in SEN departments across the country, largely ignored. This is a shame – if you have any desire to improve literacy in your school, get hold of these.

Many schools abandoned these because of low average effects.

The Problem With Averaging Effects

Consider the situation where 10 students out of 40 make 8 months extra progress. The other 30 make no months extra progress. The overall value of the intervention will be 10 x 8/40 = 2 months on average. And it has cost you quite a lot of money in wages. Doesn't seem worth it, when judged on the average of 2 months progress. But that average masks the fact that a quarter of your cohort has had their life chances permanently changed for the better. It would certainly be worth doing for them, even if you couldn't predict in advance which students will benefit. Those 10 students will fly, leaving10 fewer students needing intervention in year 11.

The worst thing that can be said about early intervention is that it will clearly show you which students have shown a response – you will have names who you know are likely to keep responding if their progress slows again. We don't use data this way – we look at discrete year groups. Perhaps we should be more interested in the child's journey over time? It seems wrong to decide on helping this way – shouldn't we help everyone? I'd argue that the situation in year 11 is that at that stage we will do so. But, if we intervene in year 7 we can at least discover who the good responders are. It is them we should be throwing further support at in years 8 and 9.

Assertive Mentoring

I achieved a much greater impact with assertive mentoring. I introduced this in February of year 11. 31 students who were in danger of missing their target grades, especially at the C grade, across a range of subjects were selected. I launched it with high profile mentors: the SLT, strong heads of department and teachers with the right reputation with students. Meetings were at least weekly. The assertive part was a no excuses culture – "you haven't finished that history essay. Ok, let's go to see your teacher now, and find out exactly what has to be done by nine o'clock tomorrow. Will it help you if I phone home to let your parents know?" Etc.

If you are going to run such a scheme, it is worth putting in time training the mentors, so that actions don't just follow the meetings, but happen *during* the meeting.

In some ways it was spectacularly successful. 16 of the students matched their FFTD target grades, and so had made a grade progress in many of their GCSEs. 15 had averaged a grade worse; the mentoring had made no difference to them. So, overall, value added was neutral, therefore not a significant impact, (although still in line with FFTD predictions – so in the top 25% for progress). On the other hand, 16 lives had been changed – at least for now.

But let's return now to what education should be about: creating curious learners who are able to connect ideas and disciplines, ask and answer questions, and develop techniques of good memory. The earlier our intervention, the more likely we are to create that kind of learner.

Intervention Through Curriculum

I worked with a consultant on some interventions who paused for dramatic effect one day and asked about intervention, "remember the good old days when we just used to call it teaching?"

Teaching as intervention. Imagine that. Well I do. Are you in a school that is looking to remap the key stage three curriculum? Are you a cartographer of learning? You will see later in the chapter on acceleration, that the curriculum is your best intervention. And it begins early: whatever your school context, it is at the start.

What if you simply had a really ambitious curriculum, that everyone would follow? The chances are that most students would excel. Do it while you can. There is zero risk in this, because your students won't learn less than they did with your old curriculum. If the curriculum is too challenging, you will find ways to make it accessible. What's more, so will your students. There are numerous studies to show this is so. My favourite involves Bohunt school that teaches other subjects, like science, maths or drama to a cohort of students entirely in a foreign language. Yes, they get brilliant at the language. But, better still, they excel in the other subjects. This is the concept of desirable difficulties introduced to us by Robert Bjork's research, allied to the concept of challenge, which is an early intervention.

An Anecdote You Can Ignore, But it Influenced my Thinking

There is one other experience I think is relevant to early intervention. When my daughter took her KS1 mock before Easter, aged 7, her teacher made an interesting discovery. Jess knew hardly any maths, and had probably learned little new maths in the preceding eighteen months. An ear infection had led to her missing some days from school as a five year old. This happened with disappointing regularity. We overcame her hearing problems because we constantly read to her, and there was no need to have her diagnosed as dyslexic – she may be, but I am convinced that a diagnosis would hold her back – even though her spelling at 20 is still a relative weakness. But we knew nothing of her difficulty in maths, because she sat next to one of the most academic girls in the class. What she didn't know herself, she was prompted to do by her friend, or she simply copied. And what was a short term coping strategy became engrained. Maths became a mystery.

So we met with a very concerned and apologetic deputy head, and I asked questions about how four year olds learned maths. From the back of a cupboard, she produced some dienes blocks. You might remember these, strips of wood carved with notches in batches of 10, single cubes, a giant cube notched with 100. Everything I needed to show why we count in tens, and how the numbers fit together. The blocks taught addition and subtraction, but also multiplication: you could literally see how many tens formed the cube of 100. And this led naturally to division. Numbers would just make sense.

A normal intervention would involve my sitting down with some SAT questions, and trying to teach the easiest problems, and then working our way through the harder ones. "Here's the method Jess. Do what I do. Good, now do it again with a similar example. Good, now some more examples, so that it becomes a habit. Well done. Right, now let's move to another type of question, with another method..."

Well yes. But that is just a series of methods. Would she use it to solve a more complex problem if she is away for the next step in teaching? Unlikely. So I ignored method, and instead got her to see how numbers work.

As I said, there was no chance she was going to get worse. I was also reassured, knowing that many European countries did not even begin teaching formal maths till the age of 7.

As we sat down to our first 20 minute session, Jess began by crying, smacking herself in the face, bashing her head against the kitchen table, and then literally pulling out her hair. (This was far worse than any avoidance behaviour I've had in class).

I ensured our sessions lasted no more than twenty minutes, no matter how little she had learned, and I remained patient and persistent. She quickly saw that I was not interested in performance – we were starting right at the beginning, after all. All she needed to do was make an effort for those 20 minutes. This went on for about a month until her SATs, where she got the level three she wanted.

But this has reinforced my conviction that your ambitious curriculum needs to begin with the very basics, the fundamental concepts of your subject. Only when your teaching fills in these blanks will your students have the foundations to build success.

Jess worked her way up the sets every year, so that by the end of year 8 she was in the top set for maths. She also gained a first in the statistics element of her psychology degree.

Our interventions in year 7 desperately need to focus on literacy and numeracy, and we should be relentless in pursuing this, 20 minutes for each, every day. Not to do this is to fail our students. There are a hundred objections to this, but they are all about making time. There are no objections to having a literate and numerate student by the end of year 7. And so there can be no real reason not to do this, only pretend reasons. Don't pretend – we are keeping it real.

Chapter 13

"The better you get, the less you run around showing off as a muscle guy. You know, you wear regular shirts – not always trying to show off what you have. You talk less about it. It's like you have a little BMW – you want to race the hell out of this car, because you know it's just going 110. But if you see guys driving a Ferrari or a Lamborghini, they slide around at 60 on the freeway because they know if they press on that accelerator they are going to go 170. These things are the same in every field."

Arnold Schwarzenegger

Quality of Teaching   d = 0.48

How can the quality of teaching have such a low effect size, where 0.4 is average? We would expect it to be top wouldn't we? Well, no. The success of your students is affected by what you do. But it is much more affected by what you get your students to do, and more importantly, what you get your students to think about. It is quality of learning that makes the difference, much more than quality of teaching.

There are lots of ideas in this book about the quality of teaching, and even more in any list of courses by training providers. However, these are just different ways of telling you that you need to be an awesome human being, impressively in charge of everything you do at all times. However, by focusing on learning, you only have to be slightly awesome.

How Do You Judge Your Quality of Teaching?

The Bill and Melinda Gates Foundation have invested millions in trying to find an answer to this question. You may have read their research, showing how unreliable lesson observations are. Where a lesson is outstanding, there is only a 60% chance that two observers will agree. Similarly, where teaching is inadequate, there is only a 10% chance that two observers will agree. These rather miss the point of the research, which instead tried to find solutions to the problems of lesson observation.

Once observers are trained in a method of observation (admittedly from a checklist), there is a positive correlation between what observers see, and the results of students:

Observing Lessons

"Based on observation results alone, students who had the top 25% of teachers gained 1.2 months of learning on state math tests (relative to the average teacher), while students who had the bottom 25% lost 1.4 months — a gap of 2.6 months."

Observing Lessons and Using Student Surveys

The top 25% of teachers identified using lesson observation and student surveys were more successful, with 2.8 months, and the bottom 25% were even less successful who lost 2 months, a gap of 4.8 months.

Observing Lessons, Student Surveys and Value Added Results

"Combined measures, however, were better able to distinguish among teachers with different student achievement gains. Using a measure that included observation, student survey, and value-added results, students taught by top 25% of teachers gained about 4.5 months of schooling, while those taught by teachers in the bottom 25% lost 3.1 months — a gap of 7.6 months."

The observations themselves should be frequent, rather than long, in order to improve their reliability:

"Additional shorter observations can increase reliability. Our analysis suggests that having additional observers watch just part of a lesson may be a cost effective way to boost reliability by including additional perspectives."

The Met Project then tried to discover what weighting should be applied to each of these three components. This is a complex picture, especially as there are two kinds of tests it took into account, none of which look that like our GCSEs. However, they recommend no single weighting, but suggest there are two that look most promising:

33% for each or 50% for past value added results, 25% for observations, and 25% for student survey

However, these are based on one year's data. In order to be more predictive, the Met project recommends average information over all the years where such data is available:

"Still, it is fair to ask, what might be done to reduce error? Many steps have been discussed in this and other reports from the project:

First, if any type of student data is to be used—either from tests or from student surveys—school systems should give teachers a chance to correct errors in their student rosters.

Second, classroom observers should not only be trained on the instrument. They should first demonstrate their accuracy by scoring videos or observing a class with a master observer.

Third, observations should be done by more than one observer. A principal's observation is not enough. To ensure reliability, it is important to involve at least one other observer, either from inside or outside the school.

Fourth, if multiple years of data on student achievement gains, observations, and student surveys are available, they should be used. We have demonstrated that a single year contains information worth acting on. But the information would be even better if it included multiple years. When multiple years of data are available they should be averaged (although some systems may choose to weight recent years more heavily)."

Danny Hilditch and I at Chipping Campden School have tried to turn this into a way for teachers to audit their teaching, to work out what changes would have greatest impact on results. *Each category comes from What Makes Great Teaching?* This is the spreadsheet with our weightings. Time will tell how accurate these are, but the principles are accurate. Some things really are more important than others, and will give you more bang for your teaching buck.

Please try it yourself and see whether it helps your students to improve.

What makes great teaching		
Pedagogy points 25	**Total**	**Adjusted**
		25
1. Knowing why students fail in your subject	0	0.00
2. Knowing student misconceptions	0	0.00
3. Knowing how students think about their learning	0	0.00
4. In depth knowledge of the syllabus	0	0.00
5. In depth knowledge of the mark scheme of the exam	0	0.00
		0.00
Quality of Instruction points 25	**Total**	**Adjusted**
		25
1. Powerful questioning	0	0.00
2. Meaningful Assessment and feedback	0	0.00
3. Review and practice of old learning	0	0.00
4. Practice of new learning	0	0.00
5. Modelling new learning	0	0.00
		0.00
Class Climate points 15	**Total**	**Adjusted**
		15
1. Relationships with students	0	0.00
2. Expectations of students' progress	0	0.00
3. Encouraging self esteem, worth, confidence	0	0.00
4. Valuing failure	0	0.00
5. Valuing grit, resilience	0	0.00
6. Valuing effort rather than ability	0	0.00
		0.00
Classroom Management points 15	**Total**	**Adjusted**
		15
1. Good use of time	0	0.00
2. Clear, consistent rules, sanctions	0	0.00
3. Physical environment enables learning	0	0.00
		0.00
Teacher Beliefs points 10	**Total**	**Adjusted**
		10
1. Have clear beliefs about how students learn	0	0.00
2. Focus on teaching practices that enable learning	0	0.00
		0.00
Professional Behaviours points 10	**Total**	**Adjusted**
		10
1. Engaged in CPD	0	0.00
2. Reflecting on their own teaching practice	0	0.00
3. Supporting colleagues	0	0.00
4. Liaising with parents	0	0.00
		0.00
This gives a score out of 100		**0.00**

Chapter 14

*"The success I have achieved in bodybuilding, motion pictures, and
business would not have been possible without the generosity of the
American people and the freedom here to pursue your dreams."*

Arnold Schwarzenegger

Concentration, Persistence, Engagement   d = 0.48

"Plant, Ericson, Hill and Asberg (2005) have shown that students with higher achievement scores can attain the same or better grades with less study time." Practice should be on tasks which "are initially outside their current realm of dependable performance which can be mastered within hours of practice... hence, the requirement for *concentration* sets deliberate practice apart from both mindless, routine performance, and playful engagement."

Persistence and motivation are improved by getting students to focus on personal bests.

Deliberate Practice.

As a tutor I became fascinated by students, who appeared to have the same ability, getting very different results. This was made very visible when students all sat modular science exams. So I interviewed those who had performed well in excess of their FFTD predictions, regardless of their ability. I wanted to know how they studied. Then I asked them to present this to the parents of all the incoming year 10. There were three types of deliberate practice.

1. Students who organised their learning as mind maps. Here they isolated key concepts, key vocabulary, and showed how each piece fit with the

rest. Typically these were on permanent display on bedroom walls and bedroom furniture.

2. Students who wrote revision cards, so that they and others could keep testing them.

3. Students who used past papers relentlessly, retesting themselves on any questions they found difficult.

That's it.

I've repeated this several times, and students recommend web based routines that essentially do those three things. Some students, at the very top of the ability range also do the following:

4. Go through the published syllabus, cross off what they already know, and highlight what they don't know, or **what the teacher has not yet taught**. Interestingly, it is quite common for such students to find that teachers have not taught the full syllabus.

Your students need to be doing this every few weeks from the moment they arrive. Does your curriculum do this?

Look how closely these match the definition not just of practice, but of deliberate practice. My son also demonstrated it to me like this. Geography and the sciences are a progression of discrete and sometimes related facts. So the key to these is a good working memory. The best way to develop this is to pay attention in class, and never leave a lesson if you have not understood something. With a good memory, he was able to score 100% at these in GCSE.

What if homework simply tested what had been taught in the lesson or series of lessons? Which subjects might we view as over 90% memory? All the humanities. MFL? That's most of the eBacc. At GCSE, where would you rank science? English Literature? If you ask the question, "could a student with a photographic memory gain an A* in my subject?" you will have a measure of how powerful memory is. For my money, a student with a photographic memory would gain an A* in all subjects that weren't practically based, even maths, where the recall of method is probably enough for an A*, at least before problem solving is introduced post 2016.

Do you therefore teach students how to remember? Should you? The easiest way to start is with deliberate practice, where students practise what they don't know.

Your most valuable way of doing this is to use a free online site called Brainscape. Write short questions and answers, or concepts and definitions.

Brainscape presents these as revision cards. You test yourself, then report your level of expertise or confidence. The site keeps testing you, but far fewer times on questions that you knew well, and far more frequently on questions you were less secure on. This is the very definition of deliberate practice. There is no excuse for you not trying this site now. Really, put the book down and have a go. Get the app. Again, this book will have paid for itself.

This becomes even more powerful later when we look at spaced learning and interleaving. Another site is Memrise. This uses the findings of Robert Bjork and others into how memory works in an even more precise way. No doubt other sites will also begin to use this research – however, the point of this chapter is emphasising the importance of deliberate practice in developing memory.

Chapter 15

"I've heard all of your questions, and now I have three questions for you. Let's put climate change aside for a minute. In fact, let's assume you're right. First – do you believe it is acceptable that 7 million people die every year from pollution? That's more than murders, suicides, and car accidents – combined. Every day, 19,000 people die from pollution from fossil fuels. Do you accept those deaths? Do you accept that children all over the world have to grow up breathing with inhalers?

I have a final question, and it will take some imagination. There are two doors. Behind door number one is a completely sealed room, with a regular, gasoline-fueled car. Behind door number two is an identical, completely sealed room, with an electric car. Both engines are running full blast. I want you to pick a door to open, and enter the room and shut the door behind you. You have to stay in the room you choose for one hour. You cannot turn off the engine. You do not get a gas mask.

I'm guessing you chose the door number two, with the electric car, right? Door number one is a fatal choice – who would ever want to breathe those fumes? This is the choice the world is making right now. To use one of the four-letter words all of you commenters love, I don't give a damn if you believe in climate change. I couldn't care less if you're concerned about temperatures rising or melting glaciers. It doesn't matter to me which of us is right about the science. I just hope that you'll join me in opening door number two, to a smarter, cleaner, healthier, more profitable energy future."

Arnold Schwarzenegger

Questioning   d = 0.48

Questioning is the most misunderstood skill in teaching. We all question, probably in every lesson, and because we always question, we naturally assume we do it well.

But we tend to use questioning to get the right answer, so that we can move on. Hattie adds "the majority of questions are about 'the facts, just give me the facts', and the students all know that the teacher knows the answer." There is merit in asking these, but you would be far better doing this by actually testing students on the facts; "here's a test. You have 20 minutes". That way you would know exactly what *each* of your students does and doesn't know. And so would they.

The questioning I usually see, looking for *correct* factual answers, is the opposite of what questioning is for. We should be aiming to find out what students and the whole class *don't know*, so that we can work out where to go next. This is not a show of thumbs or green, amber, red self-assessment which is subject to peer pressure, and a lack of honesty in students. Remember how the election was too close to call in the polls? Remember the Labour landslide we were expecting? Because self-reporting is inaccurate.

So, the most frequent purpose in asking factual questions is to find error; "mistakes are the essence of learning". It isn't to get right answers. This means that you have to sample your class without using volunteers. Volunteers are the wrong sample, because they self select – they usually know the answer. They give you the *wrong* information.

Another reason to avoid always seeking right answers, is that your questioning will tend to be too easy. The second kinds of question need to extend students' thinking. This will obviously involve giving them thinking time. The easiest way to do this is to give them a partner, and 20 seconds to a minute to discuss your question.

You can insist others comment on what they hear from their fellow students. You may have heard this called, "Pause, Pounce, Bounce", or Tigger (Paws, Pounce, Bounce – geddit?). Nevertheless, discussion that you control, but require students to develop will force them to think deeper, and allow you some time to reward volunteers, by allowing them to self select. If you take this route, remember to get students to take notes, and remember to have one at the computer, typing their notes, to compare to others in the class, and to give you something live to teach note taking from.

Why Questioning Needs to Discover
What Students Don't Know

Imagine a student who arrives with three level 5s. What would happen if you gave them a textbook, revision guide and link to a YouTube video, and told them to get on with the lesson you were going to teach your class? I predict they would learn your whole lesson in the first half hour.

What I am really asking is, what extra do we give these students, which they couldn't otherwise do for themselves? What's the point of being in your class? I think there are two things: engagement and challenge. Here challenge means finding out what the students don't know, and making them learn it.

The most powerful way of achieving engagement and challenge is questioning. This is our main way of making a difference.

Sampling

Questioning is at its most engaging (by which I mean all students believe they might be picked) when students are selected at random: all students are likely to concentrate, knowing that they could be picked at any time.

The most effective and efficient way to do this is with lollipop sticks, each with a student's name. Here transitions are much faster than an IT based sampler.

Question the whole class. Then pause while they think. Then pull out the named stick. This wastes no time. It helps to have the sticks (or pot or cup of sticks), in your hand, so you don't have to delay finding it. In theory, it forces everyone in the class to think of the answer, and in theory this means they will be learning.

Another advantage of the sticks is that you put to one side the names who got an answer wrong, or could not answer. This means you *always* come back to them, and there is less opportunity for them not to learn. This means students are more likely to make progress.

A further advantage is in building class relationships – although paradoxically students don't like this, because they are always accountable. However, you never get a student asking you why you are picking on them. They can't imagine that you are asking them a question because you don't like them (which many will if your questioning pretends to be random).

Compare this to typical questioning which is directed at students to check that they were listening – subtext – "I'm asking this because you are a lazy toad". We've all done it, but many teachers do it every lesson. It will almost never happen with sticks.

If you sample five students, and one makes a mistake, perhaps 20% of your students don't know. If this is key learning, get others in the class to teach them, in a maximum of two minutes, and then sample those that did not, or seemed not to know. Not to do this is to signal to your students that it is acceptable not to learn in your lesson. And indeed, in that part of your lesson, they won't have learned if you don't get others to reteach for you.

A valid objection I get to sticks is the desire for volunteers to share ideas, and thereby develop class discussion. That is what volunteers are for. But when you are checking for understanding or memory, you are sampling, not fishing. And for sampling, use sticks. This should also happen during class discussion, because you want everyone in the class to think about what a volunteer is saying to them.

Questioning Speed

It should not be unusual for you to sample 6 students in a minute, especially if your questions have a right answer. Early in the lesson, questioning speed is vital.

To maximise engagement, ask everyone the question, and only then pick your stick. This means all students try to answer it in their heads first. (Doug Lemov in *Teach Like a Champion* calls this 'At Bats', forcing the students to practise thinking and learning).

There is much mention of the short amount of time teachers give students to think of answers. However, 2 – 3 seconds for examples of recall may not be unreasonable. You are, after all, trying to find out what students don't know.

Going Deeper

The most important phrase in your vocabulary, whatever your subject area, is, "what happens if..?" Once a concept is mastered, dig deeper. What happens if X has a minus value? What happens if rainfall declines by 30%? What happens if Lenin does not die? What happens if Lady Macbeth doesn't tell Macbeth to kill Duncan? What happens if the level of oxygen rises to 30%? What if I change it from the past to the past imperfect? What if you had to use oil paint? What if I want every player to touch the ball before you score?

The key to the "what happens if" question is that it demands that the student applies knowledge in a new context, and also links it to previous knowledge. For this to work, you must allow thinking time, often as much as 15 seconds. (Studies suggest most teachers allow fewer than 2 seconds).

To promote listening, ask other students to comment on the reply they have just heard.

There is also a class ethos advantage to the "what if question". You are actually asking a question to which the teacher might not know the answer, and the student is not expected to know the right answer. Instead they have to show you *how they think*. This asks students to think like an artist, like a mathematician, like a geographer, like a scientist etc.

Going deeper will reveal where students cannot apply concepts. This is time to stop the lesson and focus on the skills you want to develop.

You will have to deviate from your lesson plan. For example, students may be able to tell you 5 effects of populations moving into cities, but not be able to link them in terms of cause and effect. Here you stop the lesson and look at how connectives might build a reasoned sequence or argument about the positive or negative effects.

The most common mistake teachers make is to stick to the lesson plan. A lesson plan is always provisional, and sampling should always invite you to question whether you should deviate from it. This does not indicate bad planning, it illustrates expert teaching.

No Way Out

A student should never get away with "I don't know" to a question that isn't simply about recall. Your answer must be, "show me your thinking, then I'll know how to help you."

If the question is about recall, the stick is kept aside. You might ask that student to repeat three correct answers they have heard others give. I often ask my students to stand until they can remember three answers other students have given. Because this is routine, it reminds students that they have to listen in the listening parts of my lesson.

If this still proves difficult because you feel it will lead to confrontation, or because the answers themselves are not straightforward, you can ask to "phone a friend". This works very well if answers are at least two sentences long. The original student then has to repeat the answer back to you in their own words. No exceptions; everybody answers.

Volunteers

Most teachers want to reward the enthusiastic. They feel allowing volunteers helps the more-able. They secretly want to hear interesting or correct answers which they feel, incorrectly, represents the whole class, so they can move on. They secretly want to hear this so they can feel good about their teaching. (This is often secret, even from themselves).

This is counterproductive for a number of reasons.

- Certain students dominate your teaching.
- The rest of the class can become passive, knowing you will focus on the volunteers.
- You get incorrect feedback from the class – four students give you good answers and you judge it safe to move on to a new concept.

Instead

- Questioning speed and going deeper will ensure that you hit many of your volunteers every lesson, so you have no fear of disappointing your volunteers or dampening their enthusiasm.
- The role of the volunteer is to answer a question that you can have no reasonable expectation that everyone else should know – this is often a "what happens if" question. Volunteers are only used to offer something new to the class. Anything else is indulgence, giving the advantaged more of what they already have, and depriving those in your class who do not.

The Learning Pit

Questioning must become difficult. This makes learning uncomfortable. It must be a condition of your lessons that students make mistakes. If students don't, the pace of learning is too slow, the degree of challenge is too low.

If you use the sentence starter, "what if..." you will always have this kind of questioning.

The learning pit is a metaphor to describe that state of being outside your comfort zone, and questioning should reassure students that this is the natural place to be. I've picked it up from Barry Hymer. Initially, this may also be a good metaphor for your state while you are developing questioning skills.

Exit Slip

How often do we set learning objectives at the beginning of the lesson, and never refer to them again?

The exit slip finds three questions to ask students at the end of the lesson. The answers to these questions should fully meet your learning objectives. They are a great discipline for you , as they focus your lesson on a maximum of three key things you want your students to understand. (These three things might still form one learning objective). For example, your objective might be:

To understand how and why the force of gravity acts on objects at rest and objects in motion.

Your exit slip might be:

1. Why does an astronaut's mass stay the same in space, but their weight changes?

2. Why are tall things more likely to topple over?

3. Why does a spacecraft approaching the moon only need to use its thrusters for part of the journey?

These answers are written and allow you to see what your students need to learn next. Crucially, they also tell you if there is something they have not yet learned. Even more crucially, they tell you who will also be able to teach as a starter next lesson, perhaps explaining the concepts in a way different to yours. This increases the chance that the other students will learn what you want them to know.

Common Mistakes When Questioning

- Looking for agreement: "So, are we all agreed that..?" The answer is always "no", but with this question you pretend the answer is "yes". Instead, sample.

- Your intonation when presenting two alternative answers clearly signals which answer you are looking for. A false sample is created. "So, do we think the first answer is right, or do we think the second answer is right?"

- Asking the class a question that has only two possible answers. "Will the current run clockwise or anti-clockwise?" This reveals little information – use the exit slip, or be specific – "what is voltage measured in?"

- Looking for hands up. Seeing 5 of these will make you think the class are engaged. They are not, 20 are deliberately telling you they are unengaged, and you will ignore the message.

- Only remembering to question like this when you are being observed. It will feel and look clunky. You are not questioning to satisfy the SLT or HOD, but to make students engaged and challenged.

- Allowing the student to answer a different question to the one you asked. Be pedantic about this, because you had a reason for asking your question. They can always follow up afterwards.

- Ignoring a logical answer that doesn't fit what you wanted. Usually you will simply have to say, "Yes, well done, that does answer the question I asked. I should have worded it like this..." and ask your question again. This should happen nearly every lesson, because that's how often a student will give you this kind of answer.

- Getting a poor answer and rephrasing what the student has said, so that you are now giving the correct answer. Often this is even done with the pretence that this is indeed the correct answer that the student gave.

    Teacher: What caused the rocks to crack when ice was formed?

    George: The ice was cold.

    Teacher: Yes, the ice was cold, which caused the water to expand, which gradually cracked the rocks. Well done George.

- Guess what is in the teacher's head. Many questions are like this. Avoid them at all cost, as it is not real questioning. Why? Because the student will learn nothing from it.

    Teacher: What's the most important thing the Romans introduced?

    Student A: Sanitation

    Teacher: Yes, sanitation was good but...

    Student B: Medicine

    Teacher: Yes, medicine was helpful, but...

    Student C: Education

    Teacher: Ok, I should agree about education, but...

    Student D: Aquaducts

    Teacher: Good, yes water, but...

    Student E: Irrigation, that's water Miss

    Teacher: Yes, it is water, quite right, but...

    Student F: Is it public baths miss?

    Teacher: Yes, very good, but I didn't say the answer had to be about water.

    Student G: Is it roads miss?

    Teacher: Yes, its public order and peace from warring tribes. Well done.

And this of course is the best case scenario, where the students have rehearsed lots of facts, but no one guessed what was in the teacher's head, and no one answered the question – and you haven't taught why it is the most important.

- Allowing a good answer from someone who is calling out. Quite apart from the way this undermines your class rules, it also gives you a false sample.

Why teachers don't use random questioning and why they should change their mind.

1. It stops the buzz.

Often this is because you like hearing from volunteers with exciting ideas. Those four, five or six people you regularly call on are doing most of the work. The unspoken, but very real, contract that you are making with the rest of your class is that they can opt out.

2. I like to aim my questions at specific individuals.

Fair enough. A lollipop stick has a name on it, but that doesn't mean you have to call out that name. There is room for you to cheat a little.

3. It's too much faff.

Really? Organisation wouldn't rank in my top ten skills . I teach *each class* in an average of six rooms per fortnight. I have three separate logins just to get ready for a lesson as soon as I arrive. Slightly organised is my middle name. I have to carry all my resources with me. But I don't tend to forget my sticks.

4. I already use a random name generator.

That's pretty good. But how much time does it take you to go over to the computer. And then how long does it whirr, building up the suspense? 5 seconds, 10? That seems inconsequential, but add it up over 20 questions, and you realise that with sticks you could have asked about ten more questions that lesson. So each student might have had ten more goes answering in their heads. If you teach that class three times a week, that's thirty more things they might have learned or made more likely to remember. In 39 weeks, that's over 1000 goes your students aren't getting. All because you like technology and a bit of bling. I'm sticking to the sticks.

Multiple Choice Questions

There are many online ways of getting multiple choice tests marked for you. Time saver number one: no marking! A few I have used are Socrative, GCSEpod, Show my Homework and Moodle. Socrative and Moodle are both free. A well constructed multiple choice question offers answers that are nearly right, but contain a typical misconception. They are brilliant at working out what students don't know.

You can also download results in a spreadsheet. Discover what subject knowledge your class as a whole are missing. Now you know what to teach next, or to set for homework. I can't overestimate the importance of this.

The research from neuroscience and psychology around spaced learning and forgetting encourages this approach. Leave the multiple choice test for two weeks, then make the class do it again. Do it again a month or six weeks after that. Testing, in this activity, is teaching. Repeating the test – because it covers subject knowledge you want your students to have – automatically leads to them acquiring that knowledge.

Moreover, if you use peer teachers, you already have a spreadsheet of results that tells you which students are knowledgeable enough to teach others in the class.

All the subject content for an exam could be treated this way, with a multiple choice for each section or topic. If you want students to improve over time, each multiple choice test would include some questions from previous tests. Logically, these extra questions would be on the topics that students did least well on in those tests, so that they get more practice at them.

Eliciting

A recent trend I have seen, especially in NQTs, is the belief that teachers should draw out knowledge from the student. Often this involves trying to elicit something that is not even there:

"What causes were there of the flooding in New Orleans, Nina?"

"Rain, sir."

"Yes, well, it must have rained quite a bit, but it wasn't like Noah, Nina, not the rain."

"Poverty and violence, sir."

"Thank you Declan, yes there was poverty, and many of the victims were poor, and the flooding did lead to violence."

Etc.

If you want your students to know something, show it to them.

One reason many teachers do not like giving a model in advance of learning is the unspoken, often unacknowledged belief that eliciting information from the student is the best way forward. However, even in the best case scenario, this involves the teacher waiting for a student to give a correct answer. This may involve several students getting the answers wrong. I would suggest that it is best to teach students the right answer as soon as you can. Then test them on it.

In the worst case scenario, however, eliciting turns into a "Guess what is in my head" exercise, where the teacher waits endlessly for a student to give them the answer they had anticipated.

If you want to elicit information, let's call it a test. Give the whole class the test, and find out what they don't know, so that you can alter your teaching later. But don't do it as a series of verbal questions: that is a waste of time.

Chapter 16

"Someone you trust wants to talk to you."

"Who is it this time, my Mother?!"

Douglas Quaid, 'Total Recall'

Parental Involvement   d = 0.49

Hattie defines this as teaching parents about "the language of learning" and "the language of schooling".

Parents evenings? Check. Reports? Check. After school detentions? Check. Letters of commendation? Maybe. Drop in sessions for parents? Maybe. Introduction to GCSE for parents? Probably. Revision skills? Maybe. A better questionnaire than Parentview? Probably.

Does any of this make a difference of more than 2% to students' progress? Probably not.

If you want a litmus test for how your partnership with parents actually makes a positive difference, look at how you spend your pupil premium money.

How do you use your pupil premium money?

Do you recycle your old school computers, to make sure that they can all word process, and make it more likely that they will get online? Many will have online capability through the use of mobile phones. If your school has an excellent VLE, or uses online platforms like GCSEpod or Show My Homework, do you make sure they have an online capability? Why not, it can cost less than £10 per month, and the school receives £935, or £1900 for a looked after child.

Do you ask your parents of pupil premium students how they would like you to spend a proportion of the money outside school? Wouldn't they be in a very good position to decide what would help their child's learning?

Do you buy textbooks for these students to take home?

Do you invite parents of EAL students in to school to learn English with their children? Imagine how much more quickly the children would learn if they were also teaching their parents. And imagine how the parents' life chances in the UK might change with a greater grasp of English.

Do you invite disadvantaged parents in and train them in the language of your school – target setting, assessment, setting, the dozen or so acronyms you always use etc? Do you show them how to navigate your school website for learning resources, or contact with the school? Do you meet them once a term, to find out what you and they could do better? Do you buddy them up with other parents or teachers who succeeded academically despite receiving free school meals when they were students? (Do you know if any of your teachers fall in this category?)

Do you make sure that these parents are taken to universities? How are you raising their aspirations?

Do you offer real life maths lessons to these parents, so that they can see university fees do not act as a debt, but as a tax – in other words, are better for poorer students than they've been since the introduction of loans? Or so that they can choose the right mortgage deals, or card finance, or current account or overdraft facility?

Better still, do you give them a qualification, paying for parents to take maths GCSE if they don't have it? What about GCSE English? Would this help their children's development? Almost definitely. And it will probably help their employment prospects, and to understand APR, so they hold on to more of the money they have. Do you use your sixth formers or retired teachers to teach this?

If they play sport, do you pay for them to join a club outside school? Do you subsidise their musical instrument lessons? Do you download all of GCSEpod on a £40 tablet and give it to these students?

Do you ask the Virtual Head Teacher to liaise with parents of your students in care, to ask what they would most benefit from in terms of links between them and the school, or resources they should provide?

I imagine the answer to most of these questions is no. I understand that. We are subtly obsessed with class in the UK. Political correctness forces us to turn away from anything that might label someone disadvantaged to their face. We believe it is a great offence to tell someone they need help, even though we may be offering real help that might improve their lives.

So don't label. Communicate. Ask questions and listen. Find out how we can change lives. Then go out and do it.

The Problem of Teaching Assistants

How many thousands of pounds are you wasting in TAs, where your own school data will tell you the bang for your buck needs a hearing aid to register? How much of your pupil premium money does this represent? 80%? 90%? Is this morally justifiable?

Imagine this was your money, to be spent on your child. And the government said, "listen, we are going to take this money from you, out of your wages. We are not going to let you decide how to spend it on your child. But we are going to give it to your school to spend however they like, because your school will make far better decisions than you will."

"Your school doesn't have to measure whether any of the ways they spend that money help your child, or ask you for your opinion about whether it helped, or ask you if you could think of any better way to spend it. In fact, your school does not have to tell you anything personally. If you want to find anything out, you can check on the school website, where schools have to publish how they spend the money."

It's worse than that though, because what the government actually says is this, "........."

This is not a thought experiment. This is what is really happening. This really is your money. Just because your student is not related to you, in this scenario, is the moral imperative not the same? Your school is in loco parentis. That should mean something. Yes, we teachers are well meaning people, but our actions, rather our inactions, are deplorable. We do not intend to be arrogant and dismissive, but our actions are. This should be an emotive issue – don't think like a teacher. Bring to the issue your emotion as a parent: your money; your child. How should it be spent?

Chapter 17

"You'll get more from being a peacemaker than a warrior."

"It's not what you get out of life that counts. Break your mirrors! In our society that is so self-absorbed, begin to look less at yourself and more at each other. You'll get more satisfaction from having improved your neighborhood, your town, your state, your country, and your fellow human beings than you'll ever get from your muscles, your figure, your automobile, your house, or your credit rating."

Arnold Schwarzenegger

This section looks at the increasingly powerful effects of students working together. That doesn't need to mean group work.

Co-operative Learning   d = 0.42

"When students become teachers of others, they learn as much as those they are teaching." *Visible Learning for Teachers*, by Professor John Hattie.

This chapter is not about group work. Your whole class is a group, and will benefit from cooperating, and so is a pair.

Students learn more if they teach, than if you teach them. This is a bit worrying, and clearly wrong, says the voice in our heads. They have no training – how could they possibly have more impact than we do?

Well, let's consider how it might work in a lesson. Let's use a maths lesson to dramatise what happens in your subject. Every student in every maths lesson has to work on a problem, often a dozen such problems in a lesson. Whether the maths teacher has set this up or not, students always help each other.

We simply can't stop students cooperating – they do it all the time. However, in how many maths lessons do I see students regularly called to the front, to talk through how they solved a problem? Not so much. Even if I set the bar low – one student in every lesson, still not so much. Well, obviously, what student could possibly give an explanation that is better than our own? None.

But let's define 'better' as 'more useful'. Your brilliant explanation didn't work for Judith, who is still getting surds wrong. But Justine comes to the board and explains why she didn't do 'this' and instead did 'that'. This is much more useful – it had never occurred to you that, after your brilliant explanation, anyone would think to do 'this' – but because Judith and and Justine had very different starting points to you, they did.

The trick is therefore for you to create opportunities where students have to help each other. One tactic, luckily dictated by the new maths curriculum, is to give students a problem to solve. This is just as applicable in your subject. Would Ghandi stay in the EU? Would Churchill have invaded Vietnam? What is the right amount of chilli to put in this brownie recipe? How could we live on a planet with 50% carbon dioxide?

You can also increase the responsibility of your students. Set them specific topics to research. You might guide them to websites, books, YouTube videos, so they have to return with a 5 minute lesson that delivers that content in a memorable way. First you will have modeled it. But once you have done it with one class, there will be many models from different students, and ways of teaching that you would not have tried yourself, but which you can now steal – have you made a YouTube video for example? Now, the four students in a group may teach the content no better than you would. But, in learning to teach it, they will have mastered it much better than they would in your lesson.

What's more, they will tap into some resources that you will never have considered. Google Thug Notes, 4 minute summaries of novels, delivered by an African American PHD in Literature, in the dialect and accent of a street gang member. Or try Dan Cottie for amazing science, or 'squirrels in my pants' by Phineas and Ferb in French and German. The goal is for your students to become experts in ways that you cannot always generate in class.

Our head of English calls it this – See, Do, Teach, which comes from Grey's Anatomy. You model what you want the students to do. They do it alone, in pairs, or groups. They return to class and teach it to individuals, pairs, groups or the class. I favour the latter, because I learn more this way, stealing ideas from the students. By seeing what is not taught well, you will realise what your class are likely to have found difficult. You now know what to revisit. Stuff that helps you work out what to teach next is gold, and you should always dig for it.

Small group learning   d = 0.49

Hattie observes 'Roseth, Fang, Johnson and Johnson (2006: 7) concluded "if you want to increase student academic achievement, give each student a friend."'

This means giving a task to a small group of students trained in group work skills, and instruction is tailored to the group. Peers need to be with students who have made different progress so they can "mediate", e.g. teach each other. This does not mean students have to be in a group, by the way, and are usually better off not being in a group. It is also a clue as to why mixed ability teaching can be so effective.

In a mixed ability class you can sit students in pairs who will "mediate" in this way. The difference in students' abilities actually helps. Moreover, paired seating then becomes differentiation. The less able student has an immediate source of help – again, teaching more than you can teach. If this 'teaching' student is more-able, there is a greater chance that more than 50% of their teaching will be correct. Similarly, in having to explain and teach, this student also learns more.

Peer and self-assessment   d = 0.53

Hattie warns that peer assessment is wrong in 50% of cases. This, however, is a glass half full moment. In the worst case scenario, it reduces your mark load by up to 50%, because half of the work will simply be agreed by you. This allows you more time to teach those who are not assessing themselves or each other correctly. Your instinct may well be to focus on what is wrong, and so dismiss peer assessment as useless. But if you look calmly at the percentage above you'll see that this is an emotional reaction. Persevere. After all, if your workload is reduced, what is to be gained by not using peer assessment?

To make peer assessment work, you must be clear about what you ask students to assess. Let's look in detail at the Personal Learning Checklist (PLC). This is an idea I've adapted from Pixl, to be both more explicit, and more in tune with my own moral purpose. Pixl Learning Checklists seem to concentrate fully on exam skills – while this has merit, as students will be measured through an exam – I also want to focus on wider skills that are applicable to more than one question in the exam, and to my subject, English, in general.

There are some key principles in making this useful to peer assessment:

1. Translate the knowledge and skills into language students can readily understand.

2. Design activities that make students use it, both to write something first, and to assess afterwards.

3. Apply it to your models of A* answers or work.

4. Test students on it, so they memorise it.

This is for the Cambridge IGCSE English Language GCSE:

	Personal Learning Checklist for IGCSE Question 1	Yes/No
1	I can **infer** (work things out) from the passage	
2	I can write about the thoughts **and** feelings of a character	
3	I can find points from **all** parts of the text	
4	I highlight them in **three** different colours for each of the bullet points	
5	I group them in a **different** order than they appear in the text	
6	I write an opening sentence to introduce the situation and the **purpose** of my writing	
7	I **analyse** (offer two different points of view, or question an opinion in the text)	
8	I **evaluate** (say why one opinion or point of view is better than the other)	
9	I am persuasive, using **AHFASTERCROCH**	
10	I sequence ideas logically in **paragraphs**	
11	I know the best **vocabulary** to use for the particular audience of my writing	
12	I know vocabulary is more important than **spelling** (choose the best word, even if you can't spell it)	
13	I know the **audience** is the examiner and the person named in the question	
14	I write **formally**, not colloquially, unless it is for a specific effect	
15	I put myself into **role** in my writing	
16	I write an **ending** that is definite and satisfying	
17	I know the words I **often spell wrongly**, and I have made sure to learn these before the mock	
18	I **check for spelling** by reading my writing from the end, and read right to left	
19	I know the **punctuation mistakes** I normally make and I have learned these before the mock. The most common are: • Wrong or random use of **capital letters** • The **comma splice** • **Apostrophes** to show an owner (not just because the word ends in S) • Not **paragraphing** for changes of Time, Topic, Talk	

| 20 | I highlight commas and **check for the comma splice** by checking to see if what comes before it and after it both make sense on their own. | |
| 21 | The examiner and other students in my class can read my handwriting done under exam conditions | |

This is a checklist for a question paper that has three questions. This checklist for Question 1 comes from the mark scheme, the examiner's report, and from my experience. This is so much more powerful than simply giving students the specification, or the mark scheme. This one checklist contains everything they will need for one sixth of their whole GCSE.

It also teaches me and the student skills that will count at least twice – skills that will be assessed in other questions.

You might be appalled at this – your students will not be able to concentrate on so many skills in each question. However, out of these 21 skills, only numbers 4 and 5 are specific to this question. All the other 19 criteria are relevant to at least one other question.

4 and 5 are also the only ones related to exam technique. This is important because the PLC will force you to practise that technique with your class.

Students use this to set their own learning goals or for their peers. A student identifies their own weakness, requesting help from a peer. Or you see what areas need re-teaching to the class.

Only three of these suffice for students to answer all the questions on the reading paper, which is 50% of their exam marks. Consequently, the effort you put in to students' peer assessing will always be worth it.

Students' attitude to peer assessment is often negative. This happens where it is sporadic, and replaces the teacher comment. This easiest way round this is to keep your grade secret, and only reveal it after the work has been peer assessed. Using the checklist, the peer highlights the skills attained, leaving the blank ones as targets for the student to meet on a redraft. Then they grade it.

The student can then challenge this, as can you. You will easily see who is applying the criteria very wrongly, and intervene.

The point is to make students think hard about what quality is in your subject. This necessarily means they will make mistakes in assessment. Mistakes are valuable, revealing to you what your students still don't understand. So you have to persevere, as these indicate what you need to reteach.

So, what does this mean for your teaching?

You simply cannot get round a group of 30 students quickly enough to ensure that they are making progress. All of your teaching and assessment is therefore a compromise. With peer assessment, and self-assessment, your students can suddenly progress more quickly. It is a moment when students learn more than you can teach them.

Hattie notes that self-reported grades have the highest d measure of value-added. Although it is not clear why from, *Visible Learning, Visible Teaching*, it is clearly beneficial for students to see what skills or knowledge they are missing. Indeed, most students are very harsh on themselves, and usually on each other. The more explicit you can be about the skills and knowledge that students need to demonstrate, the more likely they are to see deficiencies in those skills.

With checklist peer assessment, students who fear failure can't pretend they don't understand. They have to acknowledge skills they've achieved. Then they acknowledge specific areas they need to improve on. It is impossible for them to simply give up, because they can see that they have already found their way through part of the difficulty of the question. They become much more optimistic about finding their way through the other parts.

Fear of difficulty is also a reason students don't like self assessment. To get round this problem, train them; display the work they are assessing, and assess it together.

I use an iPad, photographing the work, and displaying it on the board. Much more frequently, if the work is writing, I get a student to type theirs on my computer, ready to display.

It is highly likely, if you have no iPad, that your phone will do. Displaying students' work is probably the most powerful technique you can use. Your photograph is powerful, helping students see what high standards, or mediocre standards, look like. I've visited a school where every teacher had an iPad, and none of them had used it to display the students' work. Madness, you'd agree. But, in every school you visit, 90% of teachers will have a phone that could do the same job, wouldn't they? So get snapping.

Peer influences   d = 0.53

"Friendships can play an important part in the classroom environment, as they often involve learning opportunities ... enhancing academic achievement". This suggests that rigid seating plans, where students are separated from friends, are a hindrance to learning. Rather than banning friendship pairing, it may be worth simply moving those friendships that do not work. Many of the top interventions depend on the influence of peers, so we need to teach our classes what good paired work looks like.

The easiest way is your seating plan, where one student is the teacher. Friends are also a useful resource as teachers. Often you can identify the, say, 12 students who have scored brilliantly on a topic or skill. Then allow those who struggled to spend 5 minutes, or shorter, with one of these students to be re-taught.

Similarly, if you have all your students in rows it is easy to number them 1 and 2 and get the 2s to move to make a new pair. Getting students to work with new partners will also add to classroom cohesion in the next section.

Peer Tutoring   d = 0.55

Hattie reminds us "peer tutoring has many academic and social benefits for both those tutoring *and* those being tutored". The effects are even higher when the peer tutor is older.

Now, we must sit the more-able with the less able, because the tutor gains as much as the tutored. Moreover, if the less able have a peer tutor, they are much less dependent on your reaching them – their partner will always reach them in time. Yes, sometimes they will be taught incorrectly, but even this is more efficient than waiting for you. You'll still spot misconceptions later when you look at books, or randomly question, or set tests and you can change teaching accordingly.

But many of you will teach an option subject, where the class has a wide range of abilities. We are conditioned to see this as a problem. It isn't – it is a blessing – seize the opportunity for peer tutoring, and your students will work harder than you.

Cooperative v individualistic learning   d = 0.59

Again, this emphasizes the importance of peers. It is more successful once "surface knowledge" has been learned, and then moves into discussion. Once again, this is not group work. It means students cooperating toward a common goal. If the goal is to learn new information, cooperative learning is a poor method, as you will see when we look at direct instruction.

Hattie is making a value judgement when he talks about the facts of your subject as "surface knowledge". The thought experiment about photographic memory will help you here – memory alone will give your students an A grade. It is the analytic and evaluative skills that are so important to cooperative learning, and you should use it to teach these A to A* skills. It is only at these tasks that it is worth using group work.

How Can Peer Tutoring Beat Individualised Instruction?

I once asked my head teacher to observe a lesson, in a series of three, where 7 experts taught the rest of the class in groups of 3. The experts had to go beyond A* in order to teach. The other students took notes and asked questions to clarify their thinking. Instead of asking students what they had learned, he asked them how they felt. Naturally, some felt anxious at my lack of input.

'How do you feel about your learning?' is a good question to ask students, but it is never the best way to assess their learning. Ask students about what they have learned, how it relates to what they learned before, what questions it might raise about what they are going to learn next. My head did not trust peer teaching – it didn't feel right to him. And it felt alien to some of the students, a feeling they expressed and he graded my lesson 'good'.

(This no complaint – I have had classes where I have almost never taught an outstanding lesson, and there are occasions where I give myself an 'inadequate' rating for my planning or teaching, and many which I'd say 'require improvement. After all, if I'm not honest with myself, my teaching can't improve).

I'm sharing this to illustrate the barriers you might have in trusting the students, and why they are the wrong barriers. It is not about how you or your students feel – none of us would risk failure if we gave in to that. Without failure, we limit the speed of learning, and repeat things we already know, because it feels safe. This example highlights our problems with peer teaching. It feels wrong to us, and to the students. Shouldn't we be teaching? Isn't that our job?

No, student learning is our job.

Chapter 18

"I have always been a huge fan of The Celebrity Apprentice and the way it showcases the challenges and triumphs of business and teamwork. I am thrilled to bring my experience to the boardroom and to continue to raise millions for charity. Let's get started!"

Arnold Schwarzenegger

The Dangers of Group Work

When observing lessons I keep seeing group work. These lessons usually flounder and often fail. Many of us feel that group work is a true test of our skills, showing off peer learning, our control of discipline and pace, and achieving the ultimate aim of being the guide on the side, rather than the sage on the stage. Phil Beadle, in *How to Teach*, a book I love, even recommends seating your students in tables of six. But, when you're not awesome like Beadle, film the lesson. Chances are you won't like the lack of learning that you see when you re-watch it.

So What's the Problem with Group Work?

Professor John Hattie's *Visible Learning* is particularly scathing about the teacher as "facilitator", claiming that all the data points to this kind of teaching as low in value.

Doug Lemov, in *Teach Like a Champion 2.0,* details 62 techniques used by the most successful teachers in his schools. Group work is not even mentioned. Like marking, it is a British fashion. The closest he gets to group work is paired discussion. But Lemov names his techniques after studying his teachers with highest value added. This should give us confidence that our students can excel without group work.

There are two questions to ask yourself:

1. What do I want the students to learn?
2. How will they best learn it?

Usually the answer is "not through group work".

If the answer is "through discussion", would more be achieved in a pair? If they need more ideas, you can seamlessly introduce a new pairing. In a group of four, by contrast, two students are all that is needed to complete a task, so two can opt out. If you choose students at random to feed back, each of the four group members will feel they have a 3 in 4 chance of not being picked. These feel like good odds.

However, in a pair, it is much more obvious that you are not contributing. The probability of being caught is much higher. If you select students to feedback at random, the odds feel like 1 in 2. This is much less comfortable, so as a student I am much more likely to wish to stay on task.

A further problem is your positioning – it is very difficult to monitor each group. Once you move in to assist or question a group, you will probably leave half the class unsighted, and it doesn't take a genius to take advantage of this. It simply takes opportunity. In most group work lessons I see, the teacher provides opportunity again and again.

A final problem is the inordinate amount of time group work takes, eating up time in planning, and then more as you get drawn to particular groups. A good rule of thumb is to ask how fast a single motivated student would get through your tasks working on their own. Now you can see how much time the group work potentially wastes. If the individual will do better with another's ideas, then pairing is usually a better solution.

To Summarise:

1. Is group work the best way to teach what you want the students to learn?
2. Have you modelled the group work skills and told the students you will assess them?
3. Can you avoid getting sucked in to the discussion?
4. Are you in charge of short time limits that you can then choose to extend if you need to?
5. Have you thought through how to force students to keep learning during the plenary?

Classroom Cohesion   d = 0.53

Classroom cohesion is a positive atmosphere in the classroom, not connected to group pride, but to commitment to task.

After I had visited a school that taught Pythagoras to a top set at the end of year 8, I asked in my report, "At this stage in the year, is Pythagoras theorem well placed? The students grasped the concept very quickly, and found it easy." They were simply learning a method: $a^2 + b^2 = c^2$. What if they dealt with Pythagoras algebraically, i.e. $a^2 + b^2 + 2ab - c^2$, so that they could understand the mathematical proof rather than simply following a method?

The proof is illustrated brilliantly with one square rotated at 45 degrees within another square, so that its corners meet the other's sides. Understanding the proof is so much more exciting than just understanding a method. I didn't know the answer, but if algebra is the language of maths, when should students be exposed to it regularly? The Chinese do know the answer – one of the teachers who taught maths at Bohunt school in a televised 'experiment' with year 9 observed: "When I first introduced Pythagoras's theorem, I decided to let the students find the proposition, prove and apply the theorem. That process is an important feature of maths teaching in China. But a lot of students said they found it unnecessary to prove Pythagoras's theorem – knowing how to apply it was enough.'

In terms of classroom cohesion, the proof demands that students together accept a level of challenge. Simply working through the method fails to do this – each student will work through at their own pace, or the pace of their partner. They could be in anybody's class. However, if you frequently team students up with different partners, or groups, and then make them rely on each other to solve problems, the cohesion of your class will improve dramatically.

Share your assessment data so that the whole class can see their improvement over time. Even sharing a visual display of who has completed, or not completed homework over the last 6 weeks has a powerful impact on those who haven't. I also mark homework out of 100%, which has also led to more students trying to gain higher percentages – because I publish them.

Carol Dweck also urges us to use the word 'yet', thereby banning the use of 'I can't'. So, what students say instead is, "I can't do it yet..." This is more than a gimmick – it needs to be the condition of how you set work, not just a mantra you offer students when they struggle. By that, I mean you need to present students with work that makes them struggle.

For example, in creative writing, I might typically ask each student to write for one minute in response to a title. Then write for one more minute, but start a sentence with an adverb. After each minute they get a new instruction, always adding to the original text, so that it continues to make sense. Start with a verb. Start with a connective. Write a sentence no longer than four words. Write a one sentence paragraph. Use a metaphor. Include alliteration. Start with 'surprisingly'. Include a texture. Use a colon. Write a 30 word sentence. Revisit an idea from the beginning, but in a new way.

My choices are not arbitrary, but the sequence is. Consequently, it becomes increasingly difficult. And yet, my students do not write gibberish. Most of them write something that requires only a little editing. Most also write something which is far more accomplished than if I had simply given them the title and got them to write for 12 minutes.

Accepting Challenge and Learning From Failure to Create Classroom Cohesion

Acceptance of challenge is therefore the best way to create classroom cohesion. The weak link is likely to be you. Teachers are the most reluctant to challenge students, because we don't want to damage the students' self esteem.

The balance of research, however, does not establish a causal relationship between self esteem and academic progress. "However, while self-efficacy and self-esteem are often found to be related, the increasing evidence revealing the positive effect from student self-efficacy for academic success does not likewise demonstrate a direct positive influence from self-esteem on school achievement (*Ross and Broh 2000*)."

Albert Bandura describes self efficacy: "*People with high assurance in their capabilities approach difficult tasks as challenges to be mastered rather than as threats to be avoided.* They set themselves challenging goals and maintain strong commitment to them. *They heighten and sustain their efforts in the face of failure. They quickly recover their sense of efficacy after failures or setbacks. They attribute failure to insufficient effort or deficient knowledge and skills which are acquirable.* They approach threatening situations with assurance that they can exercise control over them. Such an efficacious outlook produces personal accomplishments, reduces stress and lowers vulnerability to depression."

My italics are to highlight the importance of failure to your students. Your skill is in helping them find a way through that failure – but before this, failure is necessary.

I've practiced this with my own students, but also my own children. My daughter, in common with most teenagers, could think of nothing worse than standing in front of her English class, and giving a 5-minute Desert Island Discs talk, featuring 5 objects that revealed important aspects of herself. Her talk counted towards her GCSE grade. She confided that her teacher had invited her and a few other girls to give their talks to her in private, at a lunch time. "That seems really kind Jess. You can do that if you want. I'm just going to tell you why I never let students do that. When you've left school, it would be a tragedy if you had not got over this fear. If you ever want to succeed later in life, you will need to be able to stand up in public and speak confidently. Sometimes my students cry, and fail, and I let them practise with me later. But they always have to come back and do it to the class."

She took the risk, overcame her fear, and got an A* in the speaking component. Last year, as coach of the ladies rugby second team of Loughborough University, she had to deliver 5 speeches at awards night. She rang me to tell me how well it had gone, and to remind me of how I had pushed her to speak to the class in year 10. It had been a breakthrough moment for her. Her 'kind' teacher would have deprived her of it.

If you don't have children, imagine the child you'd like. Would Bandura's words describe them? Would you like them to describe you? Then you have to challenge. In summary, classroom cohesion happens when students accept challenge.

Developing Teamwork or Leadership

Teamwork is an essential life skill. For those of us who believe that education should be about more than exams, teaching group work is a vital part of our job. So there is a moral imperative to get group work right.

Modelling.

In order for students to see effective group work, you have to model this, so that they *see* it.

Outline your success criteria, keeping it simple:

Group Work Success Criteria

1. Each member of the team has to ask every other member to contribute;
2. The most effective members challenge ideas or build on those of others (challenge or extend should be your mantra);
3. There is turn taking;

4. Ideas have to be captured, probably on paper;

5. Everyone in the group needs to be able to articulate these.

Place a group in the centre of the class, and give them a problem to solve or a discussion to have. Everyone else has a person in the group to assess against your criteria. Develop this by getting them to focus on the kinds of questions that their person asks, and the body language they use. Ask them to note the effects these have on the others in the group. It never fails to surprise, and therefore educate.

You could film it to show in later lessons – as a model, or to show progress. Only once your students have seen how successful group work operates, are your class ready to try it.

Roles in the Group

It is fashionable in books on teaching to recommend roles in a group, e.g. chairperson, recorder, reporter, questioner etc. This is an attempt to make sure that everyone is accountable, rather than building on any real skills of leadership or teamwork. For this reason, I would encourage you to avoid assigning roles.

If you are still wedded to the idea, ask yourself if any successful group you have been a part of has ever been constructed in this way? Would a department meeting work better this way? A family discussion? No!

Managing Group Work

Give everyone a number in the group at the beginning of the group task. Use only numbers 1-4. When calling on anyone to report back, make it clear that you will choose a number at random – every group member will want to grasp what the group has learned, as they may have to report back.

Your most important rule is not to get drawn in to the groups. Standing between two groups, you can monitor discussion without intervening. To intervene is to reduce their problem solving. Don't think you have to earn your money by teaching here – your job is to listen and be alert to common misconceptions, or spot examples of great teamwork that you may want to share later.

If you must intervene, do it with a question that the group can solve. Move away. I'm serious about this – this is usually where group work goes wrong. The teacher loses control of the time because they get sucked in to discussions. There is a law in all schools that states that as soon as the teacher talks to any individual or group, it is compulsory for other students to go off task.

Plan time checks that don't give students enough time, so they will stay on task. Tell them that they will need to report back in 4 minutes. You can add extra time after this to the discussions if they need it – you always control the pace. This also allows students to feel a paradoxical sense of control: "I've noticed two groups have nearly got a solution, but the other six need more time. I'm adding two more minutes".

If your class are not yet brilliant at goupwork, have student observers assess the teamwork of groups – 1 per group, using criteria this particular class need to work on. Give them time to report back to you, to the group, to the class – this will focus students on the team working skills, and also reward them for it.

The presence of your student observers also encourages students to stay on task, because they know that they will be assessed in public.

Then the golden rule of managing group work is, when one group has finished, you all finish – at least to review the learning so far. If not, you have allowed 4 students to go off task, which will spread to other groups like a forest fire.

Chapter 19

"This isn't a plane, this is a canoe with wings!"
"Then get in and start paddling."
John Matrix, 'Commando'

Problem Solving   d = 0.61

There are occasions when students will learn more from investigating something in a group. Often this is best done by giving each pair in a group a different part of the topic or problem. They will then report back to the other pair in the group, who accept or question what they are taught. New topics can then be introduced, with new pairings within the group, or new groupings.

This is especially useful when students are required to solve genuine problems in your subject: – a flow chart to remember how to construct French verb tenses; a mind map to show the links between division, percentages, fractions and algebra; an investigation on data and sources to decide if Hitler could only have risen to power in Germany, or could have done so in Russia, or the UK; how to recycle 80% of school litter; how to teach the similarities between the world's major religions; how to improve homework in your subject; design an exam where questions combine more than one domain of knowledge; write a 500 word story in German etc. These tasks become much more creative and motivating, both for the students and for you. They are dependent on students having covered subject knowledge already, but will still involve a degree of new knowledge.

The teacher sets up problems where the teacher and students:

1. Define the causes
2. Identify alternative solutions
3. Prioritise these
4. Plan what to do
5. Evaluate the outcome.

However, most teachers do not use problem solving as a regular part of their teaching. There are two main reasons for this:

1. The curriculum problem.

You need to plan a series of lessons to teach content. Students need to have mastered a sufficient range of resources so that they can debate their relative merits. In many departments this planning is left to the individual teacher. And this time pressure is unsustainable. Again, this is a powerful argument for making sure that your department plans schemes of work at the level of individual lessons, so that teachers don't have to plan their own.

2. The expectation problem.

Teachers need to feel they are in control. If you set up a meaningful problem for students to solve, they are very likely to go wrong in parts, miss the significance of some evidence, not allocate their time wisely, etc. They will make mistakes, which feels instinctively wrong to us.

But the root cause of our desire for control is actually a lack of expectation. We think that students will struggle to live up to this high level of responsibility. We don't want to put them in situations where they might fail. But, as we keep seeing, students need to make mistakes in order to improve. Once we have structured things, we then need to let go. It will be messier in the short term, but better over time: they'll learn more.

There are many possible reasons why problem solving works:

- The question is a real question, where different solutions may be possible, even in maths.
- This leads to intrinsic motivation.
- Learning is essentially a social activity – we learn from each other.
- The task is challenging, but with no pass or fail answer, difficulties are less painful.

- Instead the process of learning becomes important. Failure becomes a signal to do something different, not an attack on our sense of self.
- There is a sense of play involved.
- An element of drama is built in – conflict, at least at the level of explanation or ideas, is required by the task.
- You don't have to listen unless you want to.

Don't confuse this with PBL, or Problem Based Learning, which has d 0.15. Numerous studies place direct instruction far ahead of this. PBL assumes this is how students should *gain* knowledge, and therefore fails. With problem **solving**, *you have already taught your students the subject content.* The purpose of the problem is to get them to think harder about what they already know, thereby learning to apply it in different contexts.

Let me explain what problem solving should look like, using an example question from an AQA Geography question:

"Global warming is perhaps the most serious environmental issue of our time. This is because the world's population is growing rapidly. The graph above illustrates carbon dioxide (CO_2) levels measured annually. Furthermore, methane levels have already doubled, so thickening the 'chemical blanket'.

With the help of Figure 7, explain possible causes of global warming."

This is the *advice for the examiner*:

"The extract refers to the increasing population worldwide which leads to an increase in demand for energy – including fossil fuels – compounded by the development of industry and in poorer areas such as China as they try to get richer and use a lot of coal to generate electricity. This increases carbon dioxide levels in the atmosphere – they have gone up by about 20% in 40 years on the graph and this means that the short wave radiation can enter but less of the long wave radiation can escape leading to a build-up of heat and an increase of temperatures."

But, the candidate needs *less* knowledge than this to answer the question, and a lower level of skill in using the graph – in fact there are no numbers referred to at all in the examiner's model answer. *The examiner's full 4-mark answer* is:

"World population is going up so there is a growing demand for energy. Countries are also developing manufacturing industries and these too demand electricity – usually from fossil fuels. This leads to more carbon dioxide in the atmosphere and an increase in temperatures as the gas acts like a blanket and prevents heat from escaping so warming the earth up."

Your job is to make them better geographers than this.

Compare this to a problem solving question you might set: *If we can't lower carbon emissions, what other cures are there for global warming?*

How much more would students learn from this? Remember, this isn't a PBL question, because you don't mind what cures they study, they are not looking for an answer you already know. The prior learning you are reinforcing is what they know about carbon dioxide, because all the suggested cures will have to interact with, or remove carbon dioxide. The new learning is a bonus, learning for learning's sake. But also, reinforcing old learning, because it creates new links. The cartographer gets to draw a larger, or more detailed map.

A conventional search on Google will provide these sorts of answers to the question:

1. Reduced reliance on cars
2. Improved fuel economy
3. More efficient buildings
4. Improved power plant efficiency
5. Substituting natural gas for coal
6. Storage of carbon captured in power plants
7. Storage of carbon captured in hydrogen plants
8. Storage of carbon captured in synthetic fuels plants
9. Nuclear power
10. Wind power
11. Solar photovoltaic power
12. Renewable hydrogen
13. Biofuels
14. Forest management
15. Agricultural soils management

But these only partly answer the question, as many of them look at reducing emissions, whereas the question asks students to think about solutions where emissions can't be reduced. Some interesting alternatives:

We could introduce sulphuric acid to the stratosphere in a globally affordable way:

"According to (Harvard Professor David) Keith's calculations, if operations were begun in 2020, it would take 25,000 metric tons of sulfuric acid to cut global warming in half after one year. Once under way, the injection of sulfuric acid would proceed continuously. By 2040, 11 or so jets delivering roughly 250,000 metric tons of it each year, at an annual cost of $700 million, would be required to compensate for the increased warming caused by rising levels of carbon dioxide."

www.technologyreview.com/featuredstory/511016/a-cheap-and-easy-plan-to-stop-global-warming/

Alternative ways of doing this are being explored in Britain:

"The Stratospheric Particle Injection for Climate Engineering project, or SPICE, is a British academic consortium that seeks to mimic the actions of volcanoes like Pinatubo by pumping particles of sulfur dioxide, or similar reflective chemicals, into the stratosphere through a twelve-mile-long pipe held aloft by a balloon at one end and tethered, at the other, to a boat anchored at sea."

www.newyorker.com/magazine/2012/05/14/the-climate-fixers

Further avenues students could pursue are suggested in the same article:

"There have been proposals to send mirrors, sunshades, and parasols into space. Recently, the scientific entrepreneur Nathan Myhrvold… has proposed deploying a million plastic tubes, each about a hundred metres long, to roil the water, which would help it trap more CO_2 … (This is not as crazy as it sounds. In the center of the ocean, wind-driven currents bring fresh water to the surface, so stirring the ocean could transform it into a well-organised storage depot. The new water would absorb more carbon while the old water carried the carbon it has already captured into the deep.)

The Harvard physicist Russell Seitz wants to create what amounts to a giant oceanic bubble bath: bubbles trap air, which brightens them enough to reflect sunlight away from the surface of the earth. Another tactic would require maintaining a fine spray of seawater—the world's biggest fountain—which would mix with salt to help clouds block sunlight."

This isn't a project – this research took me under 15 minutes, it is the type of problem that could be looked at within a lesson, or for homework in preparation for a lesson. It would lead to a much greater engagement with the subject knowledge, and a much more profound understanding of how climate change might be halted.

They might learn about the rate of climate change, the likelihood of reducing emissions, whether alternative energy sources will ever do enough, whether cars or industry are greater keys to the solution, which countries are the major players, what are the implications of Britain going it alone etc. This is another golden moment when your students will learn much more than you can teach them, making them expert geographers who incidentally take a GCSE exam.

Teaching Students How to Use Google

If you do try this approach, you will also need to model some key aspects of using Google:

1. Using – before a word, phrase or website to exclude it from your search

2. Using quotation marks to get the exact words you want included in the exact order, "solving climate change"

3. Use OR and quotation marks to search for more than one thing at the same time: "climate change" OR "sulphur"

4. Google's "What Do You Love?" search, wdyl for short, which puts all your searches on one page, like an online newspaper – you just have to try it to see what I mean. Go to *www.wdyl.com*

5. You'll also need to show students how to choose which site to click on, by reading the description, instead of clicking on the first site at the top of the list.

Chapter 20

"For me life is continuously being hungry. The meaning of life is not simply to exist, to survive, but to move ahead, to go up, to achieve, to conquer."

Arnold Schwarzenegger

Goals Setting   d = 0.50

Hattie writes about communicating the "learning intentions". This isn't just a lesson objective. It is about the big picture, so that students can see the shape of the thing – a unit, or a whole course. It is, if you like, a map. It is also the teacher and the student knowing the different starting points for all the individuals in the class. Do not pretend that they all start at the same place.

Then it involves showing "what success will look like". "Learning does not happen in neat, linear sequences." Again, we will see the importance of this in the chapter on modeling. Another key advantage of modeling is that "They may also learn other things not planned for", that golden moment when students learn more than you teach them.

What About The Teacher's Goals?

So how do you set goals in your teaching?

Much of our time is spent working out what to teach, the order in which to teach it, what and when to mark. In other words, our goals are largely about workload and time management – getting through the curriculum.

What if we had different goals?

- You want students to become independent, so you give them a research problem, two YouTube videos and two websites to consult. Then they have to teach the class.

- You want students to learn to work collaboratively, so you construct problems that they must solve together. You get them to set a new problem that will test the learning of another group.

- You want students to become better at questioning, so you present them nothing unless they ask you a question. You prepare a series of question stems (there are plenty on the internet based around Bloom's Taxonomy) and ask them to apply this to a topic.

- You want students to remember what you cover in the lesson, so you find ways to make the learning memorable – students relate it to their lives, draw mind maps, create mnemonics, use absurd narrative, visit the memory palace, and you keep testing through multiple choice, or Quizlet, or Socrative, or Brainscape, or Show My Homework etc.

- You want students to accept challenge, so you use random questioning, personal bests, and make questions increasingly difficult until they get stuck.

I've approached this backwards, thinking of myself as the learner first. This often helps me apply the research, as it stops me from being defensive about my experience, which might contradict the research. When I do this, I notice my goals are centred on my students' behaviour as learners first, and on subject content second. Why?

At the back of my mind, I always worry that a motivated student could learn the whole content of most lessons from a book in 20 – 30 minutes. When trainee teachers do learning walks, I always ask them how long their student spent visibly engaged with what they had to learn. Vary rarely is their answer longer than "20 minutes".

But what if students set their own learning goals?

I want to:

- learn how atoms work.
- be able to solve quadratic equations.
- know the best way to revise chemistry.
- know how knowing Macbeth will affect my future.
- get an A on my next assessment.
- know how to pronounce Spanish correctly.

These goals can be transformative, because they make the student and the teacher think differently about learning.

For example, let's look again at the PLC. Here, every student will have a different starting point. Because they might all have different lesson objectives, I can't efficiently get to them all in a lesson. So I will use students who have mastered much of the PLC to teach a partner, or test a partner. I'll think carefully about my follow up test, or tests, so we can all measure how far we have come in mastering the PLC.

Once I have considered learning with goal setting in mind, I have to make decisions about the way I teach. The most profound one here is that I have reversed the normal teaching sequence – teach, teach, teach, and test at the end. I've begun with testing, then taught and tested much more frequently. Research will also shows that this leads to more progress.

Student Goal Setting

Let's look at the students' goals. How will I become better at pronouncing Spanish? I can record myself on my phone, computer or tablet. I can try Duolingo, where I can dictate. Dragon Dictation, or iAWriter allow me to dictate in Spanish. I can get my teacher to make me read a text out loud, and then re-read it until I am accurate. I can find a Spanish speaking student in school and practise with them at lunch.

To revise chemistry I will do one past paper a week. After three papers I'll just take past questions on the subjects I get wrong. I'll ask Gemma to remind me how to balance the equations. I'll make flash cards with key definitions, and get my brother to test me. Go over questions in the text book on any topic I don't know really well.

Goal setting now becomes true personalised learning. Some students will flounder, but that shouldn't deter you. Students who struggle to set goals are the same students who struggle with homework, or to stay on task. They would be a challenge, however you taught them. But with goal setting, you'll have more role models to help those students who do struggle.

Chapter 21

"You gotta be shitting me!"

"No. I am not shitting you."

Terminator, 'Terminator 3: Rise of the Machines'

"Can you hurry up. My horse is getting tired."

Harry Tasker, 'True Lies'

Professional Development   d = 0.51

Let me declare an interest here.

I am in charge of CPD, and so far, I may have been wasting my time with whole school staff training. Why? Because one size rarely fits all. I can see how a teaching and learning idea can be used for any subject, because that is the way my mind works. Subject specialists find this understandably hard to do, because the majority of their day is spent thinking about how to teach their subject.

I recently taught 90 student teachers in literacy and modelling. One activity involved them all having the Campden literacy mat. I asked them, in departments, to use it to develop something that they could have, taped to their students' desks, so students would be able to refer to it throughout the lesson. To my horror, the English students started to simplify it and redesign the literacy mat, a completely wasted effort – the mat is good to go. They could have prepared a literature mat, showing how to select, integrate and analyse quotations. Or one for persuasive or narrative writing. But they didn't. This is not their fault – the problem is me:

I couldn't think myself into their starting points, even though I am an English teacher. And this is the problem with most CPD.

Another problem is our disposition as subject experts. We are the experts, so we know much better than the whole school trainer, so we see no reason to change our behaviour.

Therefore, take ownership of your CPD.

What does the research suggest we should do? The MET project from the Bill and Melinda Gates foundation is quite clear. Marry the progress results to lesson observation.

How would you develop teachers with CPD in your department?

Start with the curriculum. Are you teaching the right content? It is an obvious maxim that a brilliant teacher with an average curriculum will do worse than an average teacher with a brilliant curriculum. If this is not obvious to you, visit some MFL classrooms, and you will likely see brilliant teaching married to a curriculum that is the same as every other school's, the very definitinition of a McDonald's curriculum.

Film the lesson unobtrusively. I use my iPad. Give the video to the teacher, and watch. I've refined this so I also film my thoughts at key points in the lesson, so that my questions are specific to specific parts. I will also usually interview a student, or a pair, outside the room, about their learning during the lesson. This minimises the impact of my opinion, and maximises the teacher's opportunity to change their own opinions.

Not to film the lesson is the worst kind of dishonesty – it is the kind that lets us tell lies to ourselves:

Teacher: I am the subject specialist, the observer therefore does not know what they are looking for, they probably spoke to the wrong students, they don't understand how the learning will translate over time into other lessons.

Observer: I have seen a fair sample of the lesson, I am not biaised towards specific features of a lesson that I am looking for, I only look for things that make a difference, I have spoken to a fair sample of the class or looked at their books.

These are lies because they are default positions. Any part of them might be right at any one time, but we, teachers and observers, tend to believe in them at all times.

A video cuts through all this – this is what I saw, says the observer, and as a result, this is what I think. Now, you look at the same thing, and tell me what you think. What should we share to help others? What do you need to change most in order to get even better? To me, this is the opposite of threat. However, you probably have to experience it first before you will agree.

This is a measure of how poor we are, in schools everywhere, at improving teaching and learning. Consider how, if we pay to learn a sport, or to drive, or to dance, or to do an evening class in art, maths, a language, we require the person we are paying to watch us as much as possible, and then to correct us as soon as they see a fault. We would take our money elsewhere if the tennis coach took our money, then spent all their time with the weakest member of the group, and ignored the rest of us. Isn't this exactly opposite to what happens in schools with lesson observation?

Use the audit from *What Makes Good Teaching?* to decide what needs most attention.

Use the 7Cs (find these in chapter 37) with all classes to self diagnose – according to a large proportion of your students, what aspect of your teaching should you develop?

There is something incredibly satisfying about becoming an expert in any area, especially in your own professional life. So also concentrate on something the 7Cs say you do well and try to develop this so it becomes excellent. You will then become a valuable resource in your department, and your school – an expert others turn to.

The principle is clear. Look at your impact. Find out what you do less well, and get help to improve. This is not the process in schools, where we wait to be told our impact, told what is wrong with our teaching, told to improve. And which of us likes to do what we are told?

Chapter 22

"They're six year olds... how much trouble can they be?"
John Kimble, 'Kindergarten Cop'

"No more complaining. No more 'Mr. Kimble, I have to go the bathroom'. Nothing! There is no bathroom!"
John Kimble, 'Kindergarten Cop'

Classroom Management   d = 0.52

We might expect this research to be about managing student behaviour. However, this is more about relationships than classroom management. Hattie states: "The teachers' role is not to decide on the challenge and then break it down into manageable bits so that it is easier for students: instead, his or her role is to decide on how to engage students in the challenge of learning."

Think about your department schemes of work, or the lessons that your colleagues teach. When you look at differentiation in your school isn't it the opposite of this?

This over reliance on scaffolding is another reason perhaps why having a TA is so damaging to student progress in so many schools. Students become risk averse and deskilled – they do not see how to accept challenge, but instead fear it.

Classroom management needs to change this fear: "The primary purpose is to allow students to feel okay about making mistakes and not knowing, and to establish a climate on which we welcome error as opportunities. Learning thrives on error." To create this feeling of safety, students need to feel that the teacher cares.

Hattie talks about "with-it-ness", the ability to see problems or triggers before they develop. This is not just a behaviour management technique. It is allied to the skill of learning "what not to attend to", so you can focus on the barriers to learning.

I also like his advice to focus on the ambivalent disengaged, rather than the disruptive, as they are the greater number of problem students, at 20% of all students. They are also the easiest to change. These are the students you need to build relationships with. However, an even more interesting perspective was given to me by Andy Williams, a maths teacher in my school. He advises to ignore the two worst offenders in your lesson – they are likely to remain a problem, even if you give them lots of attention. Instead, pick the next four students. These are the four students who work much better when either of those two worst attention seekers are not in your lesson. If you focus on these four, you will dramatically improve their behaviour, and also starve your two attention seekers of attention. These four, most likely, will be your "ambivalent disengaged", and where you will make most gains.

Classroom Management of Behaviour

Managing the behaviour of students has only a moderate impact on learning. This is counterintuitive, and would probably challenge the experience of every teacher you know.

However, *What Makes Great Teaching?* describes it like this:

"Classroom management (Moderate evidence of impact on student outcomes)

A teacher's abilities to make efficient use of lesson time, to coordinate classroom resources and space, and to manage students' behaviour with clear rules that are consistently enforced, are all relevant to maximising the learning that can take place. *These environmental factors are necessary for good learning rather than its direct components.*" (My italics)

How often do we mistake good behaviour for learning itself? If you watched the 2015 BBC documentary on Bohunt school teaching 50 of its year 9 sudents the Chinese way, you will have been horrified at the appalling behaviour of the students towards their Chinese teachers, only to reach the payoff – after only 4 weeks they were already 10% ahead of the control group. I'm not recommending a Chinese system here, only pointing out how unimportant even very unfocused behaviour can be to eventual progress. Yes, this was a small sample, and yes, careful editing had contributed to the impression of very poor behaviour. However, many of you could go a whole year and still find it difficult to compile this number of clips of poor behaviour with all your classes, never mind one. And yet, learning still triumphed, because the curriculum was so well thought through.

Would the students learn even better with perfect behaviour? Yes, that's probably what happens in the Shanghai school. The solution to this is cultural – you really can have a whole school culture of amazing behaviour. Visit Michaela school to see what I mean. But for the rest of us, how do we get 'good enough' behaviour that still leads to excellent learning from our classes?

I am not an expert in behaviour. These methods may therefore be useful to you – they are what I have tried, usually with great success. There are, in any school, teachers with a reputation that students dare not cross. You will learn a lot by simply watching them. In my experience, however, I would also need a personality change – I am simply not that relentless, or consistent. I am in awe of these teachers because I know I could never be them. Instead, I offer these ideas for those of you not blessed with the right persona that makes misbehaviour so unlikely:

Strategies for Classroom Management of Behaviour

You may be learning the hard way, as I did. Every teacher meets students with whom they don't succeed: don't take it personally.

You will have met teachers who are expert at being in control, exude confidence and presence, and who constantly sweat the small stuff – uniform, sitting up straight, pens down, please and thank you, good morning and good afternoon.

Usually, we assume that it is their force of personality, their constant need to be in control that delivers excellent behaviour. But there is another way of looking at this. Sweat the small stuff. The best advice I received as a parent was about rules. Have as few rules as possible, but stick to them absolutely. The more rules you have, the easier it is not to enforce them, the easier it is to cede control. This is also true in teaching. The fewer rules you have, the more you will enforce them, the more you will send the message that you have control, and yet the more freedom you can allow your students.

The smaller your stuff, the more productive your sweat.

In teaching, choose only the rules that make a difference to learning.

The rules for students are few.

1.   No one talks over anyone else.

2.   Pens are put down in order to listen.

3. No coats are worn, uniform is correct.

4. Only what the students need for learning appears on desks.

5. The seating plan is the seating plan.

6. Bring all your equipment.

That's it. That's the small stuff – 6 inviolable rules.

Teacher Talk

How you present yourself has a dramatic effect.

If you have your own room, greet students as they enter. If possible, know something about each student; their interests, something they did in another lesson etc. Comment on it. If a student does not make eye contact or is out of uniform, send them to the back of the line.

Doug Lemov writes about 'positive framing'. It helps me to think of my talk as descriptive. Narrate the successes in learning behaviour – "just waiting for one bag to come off the table, thank you. James has already underlined his title and written the date...20 seconds till learning begins."

Never talk over a student while they are speaking. "I'm talking," is usually enough to silence them and make them realise they are interrupting you.

Describe the behaviour, rather than give a negative instruction. "Jessica, stop turning round, and stop talking please," invites Jessica to disagree – "I wasn't talking. Everyone else is talking." etc.

However, "Jessica, you are turning around," is clearly true, she can't tell if others are turning around, and she is most likely to comply.

Use "thank you" rather than "please", as it encourages reciprocal behaviour. "You're tapping the desk. I need you to stop. Thank you." Please creates wiggle room.

Avoid warnings if you can. A warning says, "I will put up with your misbehaviour for a while longer. You got away with it this time." Instead, deal with any non-compliance by keeping the student behind. This is not to punish you – 2-5 minutes is usually enough. The student, however, is accountable to you.

Use positive framing – "I need you to listen" is much easier to comply with than "stop talking."

But you can do better. Be specific. How does a student know what listening looks like? "I need you to put your pens down. I am going to pick on two students to tell us what they think. Then I am going to select one of you to say whether you agree or not."

Never negotiate in a lesson. If a student comes to you before a class, negotiation can be vital – "Can you move me away from Jason, Miss? I know he will distract me, but he's my friend, so I can't move myself away."

In a lesson it is different, as public negotiation makes all your rules conditional. "Sir, can I sit with Georgia today, we worked brilliantly together yesterday." The response is "I've asked you to sit here." You might add "I'm willing to discuss it after the lesson" if you want to appear reasonable. Students are rarely keen to discuss it after the lesson, because it was just a negotiating ploy. If it is real, they'll stay, and you can negotiate.

However, you can pretend to negotiate, using "maybe" or "perhaps". "Maybe you did work well with Georgia yesterday, but today I need you to move. See me after the lesson to discuss working with her tomorrow."

Avoid shouting at all costs.

In italics are the techniques I see most often got wrong by teachers when I observe lessons. They are also the ones I feel will have most impact if got right.

Dealing With Off Task Behaviour

- Have a seating plan. It tells everyone that you are in charge. This is your room. Don't let students move because someone is away, unless you choose to make a new pairing.

- If a student persists in being slow at things e.g. putting up hands, writing notes from the board, getting to class etc, call them on it. Talk to them at their desk. Make sure you stay taller than them.

- Never give a detention to punish yourself for a students' misbehaviour: 10 minutes of your break or lunch is more than enough. Usually 5 minutes makes the point just as clearly. Instead, if things persist, phone home, see the tutor, see the bigger picture with a head of year.

- If your head of department runs detentions for homework, use it. If it is a behaviour problem, do not pass it on until all other avenues have been exhausted. Giving the student a head of department detention simply tells the student that you can't control them.

- Use your school's Attitude to Learning descriptors to get students to grade each other. It is consequently very powerful peer assessment, because you are not picking on them.

- Ring home – don't write, unless it is to praise. Ask for the parent's advice, which will bring the parent onside.

- Bell Work. If you are lucky enough to have your own room, have on the board some work that students can immediately get on with. If you are pressed for time, have an open ended question. 'Is it better to live in a city or in the country?' 'What is the most useful mathematical formula for a builder to use?' 'Should each village have a wind turbine?' 'In French, how would you give directions from here to the Co-op?' 'Who would win in a fight, Ghandi or Martin Luther King?' 'Who is more evil, J B Priestley or William Golding?'

- Transitions. The best way to improve these is to practise and time them. Two minutes saved in a lesson is 6 minutes saved in a week, or one whole lesson every ten weeks.

The Strategies That I Think Most Often go Wrong, and Have the Greatest Impact

1. *Equipment. Is there ever a reason why a student should not have a pen, or an exercise book? If they don't, keep them behind – 5 minutes is enough to punish them and not you.*

2. *Do not talk when students are talking and hope that they will gradually tune into what you have to say. Wait. Demand that they listen through your pause, and though your narration – "just waiting for three people to stop talking, thank you".*

3. *Resources. If you give them out, learning cannot begin. See transitions. If you give them out, your back is turned on anyone who wants to misbehave. Choose who hands out resources and who collects them in.*

4. *Listening to students – do not turn your back on the class. Position yourself with your back to the nearest wall, so that you get the widest view.*

5. *Call attention to off task behaviour with a gesture, using your hands or eyes. If you have to use words, narrate what you see.*

Questioning

Use the questioning skills in the questioning section. A challenged and engaged student is rarely disruptive. If they are, it is likely that you have not taught them that failure is important.

- *Make learning public. Students who have had a one minute, or thirty second discussion, report back to the class. They are chosen at random.*

- *If students have had to learn something, bring them at random to the front of the class to demonstrate it.*
- *Use random questioning.*

Feedback

- Assess what you value all the time: do the verb, adjectives and subject agree? Has she applied the formula correctly? Did this team create space for their team-mates? Does the design take account of all of the user's needs? What would be better in the choice of ingredients? By all the time, I mean every lesson, unless you are lecturing them. (But if you are lecturing them, video it, and put it on YouTube, so they can study it again).
- Test their memories – making them remember things helps learning, and disrupts misbehavior.
- *Assess stuff all the time. Display students' work in real time, by getting them to type directly, or use the interactive white board pens, or by photographing and projecting.*

Writing

All the techniques in the early section on 'managing writing' will help you here.

The Strategies That I Think Most Often go Wrong, and Have the Greatest Impact

1. *Board = Book, says Doug Lemov. Learning does not happen when students copy from the board, but when this writing is reviewed. For this reason, it needs to be 100% accurate – no missing words, nothing spelt incorrectly. It is a great way for you to be heard monitoring high standards by the rest of the class as you patrol the room.*

2. *When students are writing, you patrol the room. As you read over the students' shoulder, "This needs underlining; you need to back up that point; that sentence doesn't make sense: this is excellent because; I like the way that..." If students know you are looking, they are more likely to do their best. If you give a reason why you like it, they are more likely to understand it as a learning activity, rather than a desire to please you.*

3. *Many, lessons will have time for writing. There is no multi-tasking while a student writes. Consequently, there must be silence. Give yourself permission not to teach at this stage. When students write, they find out what they know and don't know. If you teach now, they will learn less, so*

step back. Watch for what they don't know, and plan what you will do in response later – don't respond now.

Body Language

- Have a signal for getting quiet, and time your class. Set them challenges to beat or match a previous time.

- Vary where you teach from. No part of the room should be out of bounds to you. Break the fifth wall – the one 5 feet from your board that many teachers refuse to cross.

- Pause a little longer than is necessary before you speak – it suggests you have something important to say.

- Use palms up gestures to invite ideas or get students to contribute.

- Use palm down gestures to invite calm or quiet.

- Adopt a thinking pose to model thinking when you ask students to think.

- Use power poses, making yourself wide.

- Every child chews gum every day in every lesson. You know what I mean. A signal from you – perhaps a finger pointing at the bin, is enough for them to deposit their gum. There does not need to be any discussion along the lines of "I wasn't chewing" because everyone knows they were – see the beginning of this point.

- Have different voices. Teaching is becoming a female profession, and many women have naturally higher pitched voices. When speaking in a higher pitch, it is much easier to convey nervousness or panic when you feel under pressure. Listen for the moments where you use a lower pitch – you will probably find that you also speak more slowly, and students are calmer. Film yourself to see what I mean.

The Strategies That I Think Most Often go Wrong, and Have the Greatest Impact

1. *Every time you write on the board, you invite misbehaviour. Type, or get a student to type at the computer.*

2. *When you stop to talk to students, position yourself with your back to the nearest wall, and sight of the rest of the room.*

3. *Intervene as soon as you spot anything. This is "withitness", the ability to predict what will escalate, and get involved with minimum fuss, as early as possible.*

4. *Have non-verbal cues to call attention to ways that students do not treat your room as a learning environment. A student using fewer than 4 legs of a chair, a head on the table, pen tapping, drumming, coats off, bags off the table...etc.*

5. *Stand still to deliver instructions. Anything that distracts students from what you are saying is counter productive – watch the teacher who delivers the best assemblies if you want to see how it is done.*

This chapter could run and run. I've included, I imagine, techniques which other expert teachers might disagree with – we all have our own style. This is why I won't keep adding to it. However, if you focus on the italicised techniques, most of your lessons will have behaviour that enables excellent learning.

Chapter 23

"You'd let me die here?"

"No. That's the last thing that will happen to you. First, the air's gonna heat up in here to 451 degrees. Then your pass will explode like a Roman candle, your socks will ignite, and your fingernails will melt."

Gordy Brewer, 'Collateral Damage'

Direct Instruction   d = 0.58

Ok don't get excited. This does not mean lots of teaching from the front, teacher talk, copying from the board. It doesn't mean a return to the good old days.

It begins with explicit success criteria, modelling what success looks like. It involves a guide as to how the teacher should present the lesson. Yes, it tells you how to teach. In other words, it is teachers working together on a series of lessons or scheme of work, so your own colleagues are showing you how to teach, and vice versa.

Then, with modelling of successful work, there is guided practice. This is very much the same as worked examples that has a d 0.57. Significantly the research favours giving the answer first, sharing it "up front" in a worked example.

Teachers often dislike direct instruction as a method of working. Results be damned, research be damned, what about my personal freedoms? I'm a professional, dammit, stop interfering in what I do.

Let's Look at Direct Instruction Another Way

Imagine a conversation in your department about workload. When will I have time to mark every two weeks? And how can I find the time to make sure that I set the right amount of homework? How do the SLT expect me to follow this marking policy? My kids always do well, why should I have to change what I do? If I do X, when am I going to be able to plan lessons? Why should I keep students behind if they don't do their homework?

The complaints are nearly always about time, and you feel the SLT are to blame. They set the policies and expectations, after all. And you'd be right, the SLT are to blame, but not in the way you think.

Direct Instruction tells you what to teach, and how. Imagine now a scheme of work that tells you exactly what to teach, the order in which to teach it, and your methods of instruction. Your homeworks and assessments are already predetermined

Many of you would feel aggrieved that you could not teach the way you wanted. You'd feel belittled, not treated as a professional, lacking autonomy. To hear that it is a superior intervention wouldn't make you exactly predisposed to accept it.

But what freedom, or autonomy, are you actually being denied? The freedom of not having enough time. Because your current scheme of work only sets out the subject matter you must cover, you are forever planning lessons and getting resources together. That freedom to plan good lessons is hampered by the lack of time to make them as good as you like. Those resources need to be photocopied. Because you are responsible for the homework you set, you are forever trying to think up something useful. Often you'll just ask your class to finish what you thought you were going to get through in class.

Your professional freedom is therefore partly illusory. You are always trading one priority against another, reinventing the wheel.

And what if that describes everyone in your department? All classes will suffer. Nor will the teacher improve quickly, because there won't be enough time for reflection or sharing good practice.

Yet, if just one GCSE class gets bad results, it affects the whole department's results. Your freedom has brought extra stress to the whole department. If you teach English or maths, your class will affect the whole school's results, probably an Ofsted grading. So what are you getting freedom from? Stress? No. Workload? Nuh uh. Responsibility? No way.

This is why I believe it is an SLT fault. It should be the role of the SLT to insist on direct instruction, in such a way that professional freedoms are guaranteed, reducing workload and improving progress.

How Direct Instruction Gives You Greater Freedom

What if you all had the same lesson plan, but could choose to deviate from it according to your class or energy levels?

Here was my process as a head of department:

- Plan in pairs or threes. Now the strongest teachers have an input in every part of the curriculum. Planning together reinvigorates everyone. "Why would you teach it that way? Wow, that resource is amazing, let's use it. How will we model that concept? What's the best way to assess that if we want to improve progress, rather than just decide on a grade?" This is the best CPD, because it is always 100% relevant.

- Start with the assessment criteria at A and A*, and work backwards. Ensure students at C and above can access top grades, and many will master them. At the very least several predicted a C will gain an A if you have done this correctly.

- Do not plan individual lessons to be kept as different files. Instead, place the whole learning journey in one document, using PowerPoint (or equivalent). All your texts, videos, photos should be included in the PowerPoint at the place you want to use them.

- Because the PowerPoint covers the whole unit, you can easily use part of a previous lesson as a starter, to test what has been retained.

- Colour code your slides: e.g. yellow headings for students tasks, blue headings for advice from the examiner's report, green headings for translated criteria from the mark scheme, orange for homeworks, purple are models from previous students, etc. Navigate easily using slide sorter view.

- Keep a version of annotatable texts in Word.

- Importantly, they can be altered live, on the board, by students.

- Now you never have to plan a lesson.

- At any point, you can adapt the lesson, but only because you have planned something even better.

- Because everyone teaches the same scheme of work, sharing happens constantly. At the end of the unit, improvements are pulled together in department meeting time, and added in 'live'.

To see how to directly instruct your students, read the sections on modelling and worked examples.

Chapter 24

"I'm addicted to exercising and I have to do something every day."
Arnold Schwarzenegger

Mastery Learning   d = 0.58

Mastery learning involves very clear explanations of what students have to master. Students work through short tasks that are carefully sequenced. They get regular feedback by working with peers, teacher correction and frequent assessment. Testing is designed to find out what students can't do, and appropriate interventions are subsequently made. *Each unit is preceded by a diagnostic test, so that interventions can be planned from the start.* I've italicized this to emphasise its importance, but also to highlight how unusual it is in teachers' practice.

The EEF Toolkit defines mastery learning:

"Mastery learning breaks subject matter and learning content into units with clearly specified. Learners work through each block of content in a series of sequential steps. Students must demonstrate a high level of success on tests, typically at about the 80% level, before progressing. Those who do not reach the required level are provided with additional tuition, peer support, small group discussions, or homework so that they meet the expected level.

Mastery learning appears to be particularly effective when students work in groups or teams and take responsibility for supporting each other's progress (see also collaborative learning and peer tutoring). It also appears to be important that a high-level of success is set. When students work at their own pace, as opposed to working as a part of the group or whole class, it appears to be much less effective (see also individualised instruction)."

Apparently it is even more effective with lower attaining students.

Test students before teaching, to find out what they already know. Organise the questions in your test around discrete topics, so that you know what topics students will have to return to.

You must lead intervention, using TAs, other students, and parents. Catch up sessions would be compulsory. However, is extra work sustainable?

Test using online quizzes, which are marked automatically.

Maths, art, music, drama, all DT and MFL are all mastery curriculums, where everything is related to everything else. Structuring that curriculum is paramount, because one set of knowledge builds so clearly on prior learning. If 80% mastery is demanded, each unit becomes progressively quicker to teach because so much of what is needed has already been mastered.

The easiest way for you to envisage this is to imagine learning a language. What would you want to use a language for? On holiday, to ask for directions, visit attractions, buy gifts and order food. In conversation, you'd want to express preferences, talk about what you would like to do tomorrow, or the future, and talk about what you have done, using the past tense.

Yet in a whole year of Spanish, using Listos, you never learn how to talk about tomorrow, or yesterday, only the present tense. Of the 54 topics, only 28 are useful to you in this way. The rest are arbitrary – naming things in your bag, giving nationalities, describing pets, talking about school...

Now consider what the curriculum leaves out. There are three verb endings – er, ar, and ir. Their conjugations are not explicitly taught, nor tested. Worse, nearly all verbs are in the I or he/she form.

Consequently, the language to talk about this – first person, second person, third person singular, first person plural, third person plural, second person plural are never taught in the first year. This is bizarre, because it is relevant to every single sentence a student hears, reads or writes.

My own languages department is filled with extremely skilled teachers. They are brilliant at teaching mastery. But the curriculum mainly demands mastery of vocabulary, nearly 50% of which is arbitrary. Year 7s are not asked to master the structure of Spanish, so it is very hard to connect their knowledge. But, if we changed our curriculum, so that one skill or set of knowledge is built on by the next, what a learning journey we could create.

Now, if you are not a language teacher, you can see the issue is the curriculum. A language teacher is likely to disagree, because their experience is that students find languages hard. Our classrooms are mirrors, reflecting back to us ourselves. This Spanish curriculum is exactly analogous to your subject.

Chapter 25

"WHEREAS an ICT Digital Literacy Policy would be consistent with the Administration's goal to strengthen the economy, expand the skilled workforce...

I, ARNOLD SCHWARZENEGGER, Governor of the State of California, by virtue of the power and authority vested in me by the Constitution and laws of the State of California, do hereby order effective immediately"

'She taught Schwarzenegger to speak English and encouraged him to read books. "He'd never actually read a book before he came to us. Quite often I would send him books that I thought he might find interesting."'

Diane Bennet, in an interview in The Telegraph.

Worked Examples and Whole School Literacy   d = 0.57

Before we consider worked examples, or modelling, especially of writing, we should first consider that darling of Ofsted and SLTs, literacy. We should see literacy as modelling, and not as we do at present, subject specific vocabulary, key words, a bit of etymology or word root, some PEE paragraphing, spelling, and marking for SPAG.

Whole School Literacy

Listen, there is no Santa, and there is no literacy. Yes, Ofsted, teaching schools, governments, and more pressingly SLTs say there is, but it ain't so. Just as we roll out Santa, and tell our children he'll come present-laden down the chimney if they're good, so those seasonal visitors to your classrooms will give you a big fat (not-grading-really-outstanding-sorry-slip-of-the-tongue) tick for literacy, if you too are good.

But you don't really believe in it. You believe in your subject. What are power crazed visitors asking you to do anyway: teach spelling, subject specific vocabulary, punctuation, and the small matter of how to read and how to write? Hello, I have a curriculum to get through. So yes, you roll it out for an observation and then move discretely on.

Let's put Santa and 'literacy' away and try a different tack. Do your students learn your subject through writing, reading or talk? Yes? For many this will not be merely what they do *while* they learn, but also *how* they learn.

So literacy in most subjects is actually learning. This isn't a cheap semantic trick – when we read, we encounter new knowledge; when we write we try to remember that knowledge; when we re-write in a new context or genre, we understand it; when we explain it to someone else, we begin to master it.

For teachers of practical subjects and maths literacy really kicks off with modelling. This is the chapter you should read to show your SLT you are 'doing' literacy, and help your students make excellent progress.

The new Ofsted framework (2015) no longer names it 'literacy' but instead teaching is described as outstanding when "Teachers embed reading, writing and communication ... exceptionally well across the curriculum". So far so good. However, the Ofsted approach to evidence is woeful.

HMI reviewed their evidence in 2013: *Improving literacy in secondary schools: a shared responsibility*. It features seven case studies of schools with exceptional literacy.

At the time of writing, schools aren't gaming the progress of students entering year 7 at levels 3, 4, and 5. It is also a surprisingly stubborn figure. If your level 4s average a C-, they probably will perform similarly every year, and so on with level 5 and 3, despite wide fluctuations in the ability of your cohort.

Four of the case study schools are distinctly average in this measure during the years where the Ofsted report comments on them.

School A			
Entering at	**Level 3**	**Level 4**	**Level 5**
2014	F+	D-	B-
2013	F-	D+	B
2012	F+	C-	B

184

School B			
Entering at	Level 3	Level 4	Level 5
2014	F+	C-	B
2013	E-	D+	B-
2012	E-	D	C+

School C			
Entering at	Level 3	Level 4	Level 5
2014	E-	D+	B
2013	F+	D	B-
2012	F+	D	C+

School D			
Entering at	Level 3	Level 4	Level 5
2014	F+	C-	B
2013	E	C-	B
2012	E	C-	B
2011	D	C	B+

- Should we equate literacy with progress in exams? I am an English teacher, I care passionately about reading books for pleasure – I am in love with Orwell's idea that books "become part of the furniture of one's mind and alter one's whole attitude to life". But literacy can't do that, and 'drop everything and read' or unguided reading during tutor time will only signal our values about reading, but it will not engender a love of books in any student who doesn't love books already.

- So yes, if students get better at literacy, at reading and writing, I would expect this to result in higher progress at GCSEs generally. Sit down with a science paper, and calculate its reading age. You will quickly see how demanding of a student's literacy exams are. Ditto MFL and humanities, PE, drama and, most of all, maths.

- Should we value improvements in our students' reading, writing and communication if it doesn't improve their exam results? No. Just as if your SLT judged 70% of lessons to be outstanding, but results were as the four schools above, I'd argue that the observations were judging something else, other than learning. The improvements would not really be real, but a bias in our observation.

With this in mind, go back over the results of schools A, B, C and D. There is probably only 2011 for school D that you would be happy for your child to attend, confident that they would make at least good progress. Look at the average grade for their level 5 students. B grade? Would you be satisfied with that for your child?

One of those schools has a Head Teacher who is an expert in literacy. Here is another with a head who is an expert in literacy.

School E			
Entering at	Level 3	Level 4	Level 5
2014	E	C-	B
2013	E	C-	B+
2012	D-	C-	B+
2011	E+	C	B+

They're good, but they are not outstanding results that say "we're doing something special with literacy that really has an impact on results." The slightly awesome teacher always asks, "show me the impact."

Given the paucity of Ofsted's evidence, it comes as no shock to read their conclusion: "Recognising that there's no one way to get it right", because they have incorrectly included schools where literacy has little impact.

But there are three schools in its report that do show excellent progress, and these do show a very common approach – there really is one way to get it right (three bullet points anyway).

Getting Literacy Right

Woolwich Polytechnic School			
Entering at	Level 3	Level 4	Level 5
2014	D	C+	B
2013	D	C	B+
2012	D	C+	B+

These results are pretty good, especially so when a large proportion of students have English as a second language.

Their approach included this:

"For writing:

- *provide a structure students can use when planning their own writing*

186

- introduce the task with discussion of key words and phrases, ensuring that students build up a reservoir of relevant vocabulary
- *model the activity, inviting students to discuss how the teacher's model meets the task's objectives or how it might be improved*
- reassure students in the very early stages of English acquisition that they may write in their own language and then, with help, discuss in English what they were trying to communicate."

I've placed in italics the activities that are not specific to learning English as a second language, and so are likely to pay dividends in all schools.

Because so many students speak English as a second language, great emphasis is placed on talk for writing:

"For speaking and listening:

- *plan 'talk' into all lessons, ensuring that it engages all students, is purposeful and structured and that individual contributions are monitored and developed*
- *encourage students to draw on their own experiences and to use their own language if they are struggling to convey an idea or feeling in English*
- *give students time to rehearse their contributions, so that they are less anxious*
- *systematically introduce key vocabulary and phrases*
- *model good speaking and listening, demonstrating high expectations.*"

Springfield School			
Entering at	Level 3	Level 4	Level 5
2014	E+	C	A-
2013	E	C-	B
2012	E+	C	B+

Their approach was:

- "Departments met to write a teaching sequence for a piece of extended writing in their own subject and to display key words.
- Departments also came together to identify common errors of spelling and grammar in students' work that they wished to highlight and correct.
- The school followed this up by producing lists for all teachers of students' most common spelling mistakes.

- The English department also made available lists of spellings grouped according to particular linguistic structures, such as words with unstressed vowels or double consonants.
- A literacy marking policy was agreed.
- The next step was for individual departments to ensure that extended writing had a secure place in all their schemes of work."

The dominant technique appears to be the focus on extended writing, particularly with the more-able, and it is level 5 students who are making most progress compared to other schools.

Our final school is unique. It is a school designed by the architect Norman Foster, and it is a school that has started from scratch. Their first results are excellent, by any measure. Their results are exceptional, and would stack up against St John the Baptist. Only 10 schools in the country will consistently get their students achieving these grades.

The City Academy			
Entering at	Level 3	Level 4	Level 5
2014	C-	B	A
2013	No data	No data	No data
2012	No data	No data	No data
2011	No data	No data	No data

"The key, according to the principal, is that systems, including those for literacy, must be simple, straightforward and consistently applied.

Starting with literacy

The school has established a literacy policy with five strands that guide the work of all teachers.

- Students in lessons should always speak in sentences.
- There should be a consistent policy on marking and feedback (a 'green pen' approach).
- Students should always have a 'book on every table'.
- Teachers in all subjects should model writing for their students.
- Students should be taught to organise their extended writing into well-structured paragraphs.

Teachers modelled the appropriate language, for example:

In full sentences, please. 'In the first place, we should get rid of fractions and then...'

Can you explain that in a full sentence? 'I know that magnesium is more reactive than copper because...'

Marking in all subjects has a literacy focus, as do success criteria and learning objectives. There was an equally explicit and shared expectation that students' writing would be carefully structured, using paragraphs, capital letters and full stops. There was a sharp focus on students' literacy skills, quality of writing, technical proficiency and pace of working."

The best school in this Ofsted cohort would therefore seem to agree with my very simplistic approach – get your students to read and write more in your subject.

The Secret of Literacy

1. Model the texts you want students to write.
2. Two schools also emphasise how talk is a preparation for writing.
3. Mark for literacy, insisting on basic standards.

Now, I wouldn't suggest such a small sample size of schools could justify that this is what successful literacy should look like in your school. However, it coincides very precisely with the much more robust data about worked examples and modeling. If you do nothing else, change the word 'literacy' to 'modelling', and you will have a focus that teachers of all subjects will find relevant and useful.

Chapter 26

"My name is Julius and I'm your TWIN brother."
"Oh obviously! The moment I sat down I though I was looking into a mirror."
"We're not identical twins."

Julius Benedict, 'Twins'

Worked Examples   d = 0.57

Modelling

The importance of modelling can't be overstated. To show students how to succeed, you actually need to show them, modelling exactly what success looks like. It is astonishing how often this simple fact is overlooked.

Many teachers think they're teaching a particular subject or topic, and consequently teach what they think is important or interesting or engaging, in that topic. This is usually a mistake, because it misses exactly what the examiner is looking for. Start with the mark scheme.

Let's pause a moment and deal with the justified accusation that this is teaching toward the exam. For the defence, what have you gained if, after all your brilliant teaching, the student has not done well in the exam? Nothing, and your student less. Also, for the defence, the A* grade is a proper grade – examiners at least as passionate about your subject as you have tried to construct an exam and assessment criteria that reflects excellence. In most cases, to teach to the A* offers content and skills that you value in your subject.

I have just begun teaching the new AQA English Language exam. I sat the sample paper, without looking at the mark scheme, having experience and an English degree. Did I get 100%? No chance. Perhaps A* on every every question? Again no. This is because the exam is full of examiner's assumptions that you simply can't guess from the question. Only once you sit the exam for yourself, are you able to teach students to get 100%.

For example, in an OCR English Literature exam, on *Lord of the Flies*, the examiners reward:

- Sophisticated, *critical* perception in response to and interpretation of text(s)
- Cogent and precise *evaluation* of relevant detail from the text(s)
- Sensitive understanding of the significance and *effects of writers'* choices of language, *structure* and form

Translate this with the students, to explore what they don't know, rather than anticipate it. Thus, I quickly discovered they did not know how to decode the word 'critical'. To them 'critical' meant 'crucial', or 'dangerous', and they did not associate it with criticism.

They decided that it meant 'to judge'. The next criteria looked at 'evaluation'. They knew to evaluate they might look at two different possibilities, or interpretations. Here I offered them a mime, standing, raising each hand alternately at my side, mimicking weighing scales. When I moved both hands and eventually settled into a prose, with one hand significantly higher than the other, they were able to see that evaluation also means reaching a conclusion as to which possibility or interpretation is best. The mime was simply a visual way to help the students remember what evaluation meant in later lessons.

Now students could go beyond what I had assumed they could do. For example, they simplified both of the criteria, being 'critical', and 'evaluative', to 'reaching a judgement'. To offer two interpretations, they decided to use a single connective, "however", then added "although".

So far so good. Next I had to write a model answer, typing part of it live, so I could explain my choices as an exam candidate. Here it is:

"Question: How is this a powerful ending to the novel?"

My two key words are **"powerful"** and **"ending"**, and so I will make sure that I include these at the beginning of my answer.

I am also going to make sure that I include this quotation, which will fit any *Lord of the Flies* question, because, if I am going to write about the **"structure"** of the passage, it will always be relevant to relate it to the ending, the "**structure**" of the novel as a whole.

"Ralph wept for the end of innocence, the darkness of man's heart, and the fall through the air of the true, wise friend called Piggy."

The Start of My Answer

Golding's ending brings together the conflict between the adult world and that of the "innocence" of the boys in a powerful way. Most powerful is the contrast between the "naval officer" and Ralph. *The boys have lost their "innocence",* as they are about to murder Ralph. Ralph realises this, which brings him to feel pity, so that he "wept": he has understood that all men are capable of great evil. *When Golding calls it "the darkness of man's heart" he implies that we are all capable of evil, and perhaps that this is our natural state.*

The opposite of darkness is light, and Golding deliberately makes the naval officer appear in white, "a white topped cap" and "white drill". This *contrasts* immediately with the murderous Jack, who symbolically wears his old choir hat, described as "the remains of an extraordinary black cap". *The word "remains" is a reminder of death, as is the colour of the hat, as it reminds 1950's readers of the hat put on by a judge passing a death sentence. One reading of this is that the officer, despite being at war, has managed to retain his innocence, symbolised by the "white".* His "British" values are emphasised, and this civilization has allowed him to remain good.

However, Golding might also be using this ironically. Perhaps the adult world is merely a disguise for the "darkness of man's heart". Consequently, the officers first thought is to shoot the boys if they are not British, as implied by his first action: "the officer looked at Ralph doubtfully for a moment, then took his hand away from the butt of the revolver." Before we can say that Golding wishes us to attack the British feeling of moral superiority, however, it is significant that the officer ignores his "heart". *He moves his hand away from the gun **before** he finds out Ralph is British.* This might also show the morality of civilization saving him from savagery, even during a nuclear war. So we must look for other clues as to Golding's purpose in introducing the naval officer."

Students told me what to italicise. These had nothing to do with the above criteria I was explicitly teaching. I was teaching what 'critical' meant, and what it means to 'evaluate. I also explicitly wanted them to see how the ending of the novel could be quoted for any question, even though the question would always be on an extract.

However, because I presented them with a 100% model, they were, individually, able to learn so much more. I can infer from the italics that they were concerned with how to write about the author's ideas, how to develop ideas about irony, how to signal a change in viewpoint, which words would force them to do this. They realised the importance of authorial tone, and use of irony. They were more likely to remember these because they are based on what they already knew.

What to do With Your Model

You could simply annotate your model, to exemplify the criteria. This is what a worked example does, and it has a d 0.57.

However, you should get students applying the criteria themselves. Ask them in pairs to look at one part of the criteria each. For example, one row of the class would look at how the model explored Golding's language, another Golding's use of structure, another how the answer evaluated, and the final row at how the answer reached that judgement. Yes, this is teaching towards the exam. But these are also skills that would still stand up to scrutiny in a degree.

I watch countless lessons where detailed modelling is not done. I raised this at one senior leadership team meeting. One of my colleagues reasonably pointed out that teachers would want to produce an excellent lesson for their observation, and would therefore not want to model writing, but to do something more exciting, through which they could demonstrate their skills.

But is this reasonable? In most subjects, your students will need to demonstrate their learning through their writing. Surely, a more logical choice for those teachers would have been to showcase how they teach this? What you need to showcase in your observations is what you need to get great progress from your students. Learning. Worked examples show students, exactly and precisely, what to learn.

Teaching to the Test

You don't have to override your passion for your subject, and the passion that you want to engender in your students. But when you get down to the business end, how they will be assessed, you must help them succeed in every part of that assessment. Not to do so is negligent, not a sign of your passion.

I would add that I think most intervention in schools is misguided, indeed morally wrong. The idea we should simply do more is immoral. The best way to intervene is to give the students the big picture first, the model they are working towards, and an understanding of how their skills will be assessed. This happens in the classroom. It is called teaching. It's not the constant demands for mentoring, extra lessons, revision plans, holiday clubs etc which have become commonplace in our schools.

My Ten Point Plan for Modelling, On a Scale of 1 – 10, Where 1 is Effective and 10 is Most Effective

1. The Quickest Way to Do Literacy

Focus on spelling, capitals, full stops, and subject specific vocabulary.

Ok, this is only number one because it doesn't fully promote understanding of your subject. But it's also the easiest one to achieve, to get right with some of your students, all of the time. It will still have a significant impact on the quality of writing of many students.

Give subject specific vocabulary. Then patrol the room to insist these are correctly spelled. Use a highlighter where they go wrong. Probably 80% of spelling mistakes are simply careless – students can correct them without further help from you.

Next, if you were similarly alert to capitals and full stops, you'll improve the writing in most average students' exercise books. You don't have to teach them this, you simply patrol the room and make sure your students are accurate. You are changing their habits, with a highlighter.

Genuinely, if most of your students did all of these, and you were rigorous about introducing the subject vocabulary and making sure that it was spelled correctly all the time, your books would be better than most other teachers in the school.

You'll need to patrol the room every lesson. However, patrolling the room, pink highlighter at the ready to highlight mistakes, really will work. But only if you make it a habit.

To improve this further, be alert to the comma splice, where students use a comma instead of a full stop. You should also provide any other adult in the room with a highlighter and ask them to do the same. With the help of a TA, you can see 20 books in under 5 minutes. It is also a great way to make sure they have a positive impact on your whole class, rather than simply the individual they are supporting.

2. The Quickest Way to Develop Student Talk

Do your students always speak in sentences? The more you insist on this, the better your students will become in your subject. Often students get away with simply giving one or two word answers. You can understand this when you watch teachers trying to get through the subject content and questioning is often just a case of checking understanding. However, over time this doesn't develop the students' language. So, speaking in sentences has to come first. Only then can we move to speaking in paragraphs.

This will change the way you teach. You'll start asking questions that need to be answered in sentences and there will be fewer questions which are simply recall. You will necessarily start asking students to explain. "So, why is 3x greater than 3y?" or "why does heat change the state of a property?" or "why does the verb ending need to change when we are changing the person from "I" to "we"?" They will only think more deeply if you do, when framing your questions. Then it's a short step to getting them to link sentences together in paragraphs. If they can do that orally, they'll do it brilliantly in writing, and succeed spectacularly in your subject.

3. Connectives

Simply focus on six connectives: **because, therefore, however, although, consequently, furthermore.** Enlarge and display them.

This technique works with any subject, even one in which students don't write. Give your students these six connectives and you will dramatically improve, not just the way they write, but the way they think. You can do this as a starter activity, or with written work, or with speaking and listening.

For example:

"**Because** the heat was applied to the metal, the molecules began to move faster, and the metal expanded. **Therefore**, when we heated a ball of steel that fit through a ring, we found it could no longer fit through the same ring once heated.

However, once it had been cooled down in water, it reverted to its original size. **Furthermore**, this was accomplished very quickly, so we can see that molecules change their state very quickly. **Consequently**, metal can expand and contract very quickly, because it is a solid.

Although this works very well for metal, it is much more difficult to control with gasses".

This level of detail from a student can only be retrieved orally through very advanced teacher questioning – either by your continually probing deeper (probably one question for each new connective), or bouncing the question round the room – again 5 more times – to get others to develop the answer. This takes time, and might still only involve a maximum of 6 students. But in pairs, all students can do it, simply moving to the next connective.

In pairs, they would also prompt each other, filling in gaps in their learning. Then you could listen to one or two individuals, to recheck learning. How much more efficient is this than the expert questioning described above?

Moreover, that expert level of questioning rarely happens. However, if you have a routine with connectives, it will fit appropriately in your teaching every week. It will always be worth the few minutes you give the task, because everyone benefits, every time.

Whatever your subject, students will have to think in incredible detail to link facts or concepts together. And if they can do that, they're speaking in paragraphs. Anything that a child can speak, they can therefore do in writing. Obviously the reverse is also true: if they can't do it in speech, they probably can't do it in writing. Consequently, you must teach connectives, mustn't you?

4. How to Improve Student Writing

Paragraphing

There are three things to teach about paragraphs, the three Ts. Change paragraph for a change of Topic, a change of Time, and a change of Talk. Your hinge question will always be to get students to look at a published text, and ask them to decide which of the three Ts accurately describes the reason for the paragraph.

Students often find it very difficult to see how different elements of their knowledge link together. You'll have noticed this if you have tried to get them to apply anything in a cross curricular way.

If I use the example of connectives in my heat example above, it may be easier for you to see what I mean. Students will assume that all the ideas expressed are about the same subject – heat – and therefore each sentence should be part of the same paragraph. However, looking at each paragraphed section, you can show how each one marks a subtle change in thinking, a slightly different Topic.

This allows you to be much more explicit about what thinking looks like in your subject. For example, as a science teacher, I might tell my class, "whenever you express a full idea in science, you will need to do it in three paragraphs. Anything less than that cannot be the full idea." I am not after an empirical truth here (sorry scientists), I am after a rule that I and my students can apply consistently and, as a consequence of the rule, nearly always be very good at thinking or writing like a scientist.

You increase sophistication if you tell them to start sentences with connectives, as this forces them to use complex ideas at the beginning of their sentence, and they find imaginative ways to finish it.

And then finally, if you're educating your students to be literate, they need to be writing in different genres. So a typical history task might be, " Write a newspaper article about the Battle of Hastings". That's nearly useless, unless you've taught the actual genre to the students.

So you'd have to talk about headlines, and bylines, how journalists quote to give both facts and opinions, to control our reactions; how quotations are introduced with a colon; how a writer will try to include quotations from different points of view; how they build towards a climax; how names, occupation and sometimes ages are introduced in noun phrases; how the writing never has a conclusion; how it might end by quoting a view from a person the newspaper most agrees with; how in newspaper articles you never put the reporter at the scene. Many students write as though it is a live news report on TV – "I'm at the scene, and I ask Mrs. James, to tell me what she saw. She said..."

I didn't learn to identify any of those features because I am an English teacher – I just looked at three different newspaper articles. Arguably, 'noun phrase' might be part of my specialist subject knowledge, but it is knowledge many of your students bring from primary school. Anyway, you would spot the convention, even without being able to name it.

But, if you truly wanted your students to be brilliant in your subject, they would have to write in different and interesting ways: discussions, arguments, persuasive pieces, newspaper articles, diaries, stories. All kinds of different ways of writing. If you do that, students will become better writers and better learners of your subject.

The National Strategies produced some brilliant literacy resources on the conventions of different text types. These were largely ignored in schools because we are teachers of our subject, and it is very difficult to justify the time spent on writing when you are under pressure to get through the curriculum. I might not convince you, but go back to The City Academy's data, and think again.

Harness the Power of Storytelling on Memory

Knowledge is so much easier to remember and sequence in a story. If you need evidence of this, try to translate this retelling of the beginning of Little Red Riding Hood in Spanish. It is an extract from Easy Spanish Storybook: Little Red Riding Hood by Ana Lomba.

Caperucita Roja

"Caperucita Roja vivía con su mamá en una casa muy bonita.

Un día su mamá le dijo a Caperucita Roja, "Caperucita Roja, la abuelita está enferma. Por favor, llévale esta cesta."

"Muy bien mamá," dijo Caperucita Roja.

Caperucita Roja caminaba por el bosque cuando, de repente, salió un lobo malo de detrás de un árbol.

"¿Caperucita Roja, adonde vas?" dijo el lobo.

"Voy a casa de mi abuelita," respondió Caperucita Roja."

If you read it through three times you will become aware of how story allows you to organise and understand knowledge. For example, after re-reading, try to answer these questions:

1. What is the word for 'red'?
2. What is the word for 'Little Riding Hood'?
3. What is the phrase for 'one day'?
4. 'House'
5. 'Very well'?
6. 'Forest'?
7. 'Grandmother'?
8. 'Wolf'?
9. 'Said'?
10. 'Asked'?

Stories automatically sequence information *in a context we already know.* This part is really important, as it lessens the cognitive demands placed on memory and understanding. In short, because the brain already knows stuff, the new stuff has a handy place to go, a hook to hang on.

You can see how easy this storytelling technique might be in getting students to remember:

- The water cycle in the adventures of a raindrop from birth to reincarnation.
- The strange love affair of the positively and negatively charged electrons in their neutron home.

- The miracles performed by Jesus retold by Jamie Oliver, or other chef.
- The causes of WW1 as an autobiography of a main character called 'War'.
- The transfer of energy from oxygen to muscle as a Star Wars style mission.

Here it will be easy for you to proscribe conventions – key vocabulary that must be included, number of paragraphs (at least one for each event), some key characters to be included, a word limit. The key here is memory will be enhanced – effectively, you will be teaching revision. Understanding will be enhanced, because each fact will have another two facts to relate to – the one that preceded, and the one that followed, in your plot.

Now, let's delve a little deeper into what that would mean for you as a languages teacher. Here's the translation of Caperucita Roja:

Little Red Riding Hood

'Little Red Riding Hood lived with her mother in a very beautiful little house.

One day her mother said to Little Red Riding Hood, "Little Red Riding Hood, grandma is sick. Please take this basket to her."

"Very well, mother," said Little Red Riding Hood.

Little Red Riding Hood was walking in the forest when, all of a sudden, a bad wolf came out from behind a tree.

"Little Red Riding Hood, where are you going?" said the wolf.

"I am going to my grandma's house," answered Little Red Riding Hood.'

High frequency words, obviously crop up again and again. Only "riding hood", "wolf" and perhaps "forest" are extraneous. The rest are words you really need your students to know. How much easier will learning be for them if you teach them the language through stories that they already know?

Because many of these are fairy stories, they already deal in high frequency words, because these are the very words that young children learn first.

How to get Students to Proofread

David Didau tells us practice does not make perfect, "practice makes permanent". Most students simply don't bother checking their work, so they repeat inaccurate spelling, random capitals, full stops only when they can be bothered, and string sentences together, separated by commas.

You've already met the pink highlighter. Another powerful technique to use at the same time is to narrate what you want.

"Jacob has underlined his title. Jacob, you haven't spelt 'diffusion' correctly. It's on the board, please make sure that you get it right." And by narrating what you want from the students, they'll tune in to what you're saying, and correct themselves.

"Jasminda has already finished the first paragraph. She's started a new line for the next paragraph. Well done Jasminda, thank you very much. Jo has started her new paragraph with a connective. Well done, she's got 'therefore' and she's used a comma after it."

"Abid has crossed out two words and put their correct spellings in the margin. Thank you Abid. He's used a comma instead of a full stop in his first five lines though. Can you find it Abid?"

It doesn't have to be English; you could be narrating what you want in maths. "Ingaborg has shown her working really clearly. Well done, thank you Inga." Just narrate what you want.

(As an aside, you can also see why it is so important to use lollipop sticks in your questioning. One reason is that they prevent bias. On proof reading this section of the book, I suddenly noticed my own bias. Moreover, this is a bias I would hotly have denied had you 'accused' me of it.

Did you spot the gender bias? The girls got work right, while the boys were only partly right. Revealing, isn't it?)

The pink highlighter pen creates a routine. Students know they have to correct everything in pink. Sometimes this does not lead to improvement – yes, they correct everything that you pink, but each time you visit the book, there are just as many pinks per line.

One solution is to set the class, or individual a target. "If there are more than two pinks in six lines, I won't mark it"; If there are more than 4 mistakes in 10 lines, I'll make you do it again." You decide on the appropriate level of challenge.

And if there are a number of students making the same mistake, which they haven't been able to correct, you know that you must stop the lesson straight away and reteach that bit. The final advantage is that it is feedback that comes to the student at exactly the right time, when they are making the mistakes.

It takes no lesson preparation and you could legitimately do this every single lesson, as soon as the students are engaged in any kind of work. Make the students proofread, and proofread the work yourself. Because it takes up no more of your time, and is therefore only a change of habit. Arnie's words come ritualistically to mind. Do it. Do it now.

5. The Quickest Way to Develop Student Reading

It isn't difficult to teach reading in your subject, in the same way that it is not difficult to teach someone to run. "Look," you would say, "you just need to go out and run." You don't really concern yourself with technique – think of the thousands of people who complete a marathon every year. No one says to them, "relax your shoulders, don't bring your hands across your body, move them forwards and backwards. You would be more efficient if your knees came up an extra ten degrees. Breathe in through your nose and not your mouth." They just get better by running.

But we overcomplicate reading. We say: It should have been done in primary school. I am not an English teacher. I am an English teacher, but what the hell is synthetic phonics, dotting and dashing? So we abdicate our responsibility to teach reading. The lesson of my analogy here is very simple – to get better at reading, you simply have to do lots of it. To get better at running, you simply run.

Insist that all students have a book, and therefore they might read it at any time where you don't want to differentiate by giving extension tasks, (after all, what kind of reward is that to the more-able student?) Or you might think about spaced learning – giving students time to forget – teach new content for half an hour, have a five minute reading break, and test or review what you've learned.

The more times that you find ways of getting them to use the book, the easier it is. This will scare many of you, afraid of losing curriculum time, so I won't push it.

But we can all do this:

It astonishes me how few students are required to read out loud. More typically, we scaffold the work for our classes by reading out loud to them, because we perceive two advantages – we get through the text quicker in order to get to the curriculum content, and we differentiate for those who can't read the words by showing them what the words are.

But the secret message to them is, "the teacher will read out loud, so I can sit and think about whatever I want, I don't actually have to follow what the teacher is saying anyway. When I have to do some sort of activity, I'll put my hand up and say, "please miss, can you help me?" Or, ask the person sitting next to me."

Don't be that teacher. Don't create that student. Get students to read out loud *in every lesson* where a text appears. If it's a particularly long text, you might alternate with them, reading at most a paragraph yourself. As your students practise reading, you can work out what their problems are and intervene. So they might stumble over a word. Nominate someone as the word expert, and that struggling student can call upon that expert. Crucially, they must then read the word out correctly. Don't let them skip this stage, because many of them will try to.

If a student doesn't know what a word means, simply blank it out and ask them to put a word in its place. This needs to be modelled. Usually, simply reading to the end of the sentence will provide **ample** clues for a sensible **decoding**. Sometimes they should re-read the **preceding** sentence, and perhaps then read forward. This isn't a **technique** that always gives the right meaning. You are teaching a technique which means your students will never be stuck – they will always be able to use an **approximation** that makes sense of the text. Very occasionally, this will result in misunderstanding– I **vividly** remember thinking 'opaque' was another word for transparent using this method, but I remember it, because it is probably the only occasion where it went so dramatically wrong.

To see how effective this is, imagine the preceding paragraph in a text book. You might think, "I really need to read this paragraph out and explain the vocabulary in it to my class – look at the number of words they might struggle with" (these are the ones I've placed in bold). However, if you asked students to follow the blanking technique, logic would lead them to get words that had very similar meanings. The exception would be 'opaque', but they would be able to substitute 'not transparent', using the clue that 'transparent' was 'dramatically wrong'.

It should go without saying that when you are reading in class, you should always have the text on the screen. But I'll say it anyway, because in at least 50% of lessons I see, teachers don't do this. Why would I put it on screen, they think, the students have it in their text books? Firstly, because the blanking and guessing I've discussed above will only be explicit if you can get everyone looking at the text at the same time – that means you at the board, with hands on the words. Then it means a student at the board – "come and show me how you would decode".

The second reason is to do with behaviour. You can teach from anywhere in the room. All students become part of your domain. If you are behind someone, they will be less likely to go off task, because they don't know when you are watching them. Indeed, it is almost impossible for you to read any of the text on the board if you are standing at the front – having it displayed will force you to break the fifth wall, and own your room.

Specialist Vocabulary

Without subject specific vocabulary students can't express themselves like a historian, like a mathematician, like an artist, etc. At the time of writing, the best way I know to do this is through a two websites, Brainscape and Memrise. Check them out now, unless you already use a better one.

Whatever your subject, there are always specialist terms you need students to know. Start by making a list of 50, or be lazy and Google them, with definitions. Memrise differs from Brainscape in that it uses cognitive science to work out when to retest you – an algorithm predicts when you are beginning to forget. It also has several different ways of testing you, including testing your spelling. I've learned over 1300 words and sentences in German, starting from scratch, in three months.

The final reason to do this is your students' exam literacy. Even maths questions demand a high level of literacy. Here's the first three questions of an AQA paper:

1. Which sequence is a geometric progression?

2. Which of these is not used to prove that triangles are congruent?

3. Circle the expression that is equivalent to $2a + 5a \times 4a - a$

These are the easy, one mark questions, to get students off to a confident start! Your exam is likely to contain just as many problematic words. Your job is to go through the exam paper, make a list of these, then their definitions, then visit Brainscape and make a revision deck, or a revision course on Memrise.

6. Show and Tell

Show and tell guarantees success, even if everything else in the lesson is falling apart. To introduce a personal note, there are plenty of teachers in my school who do lots of teachery things much better than I do. Even if I confine myself to the English department, this is true. Great relationships with students? A and B are much better than me, B especially with difficult students. Great lesson preparation with PowerPoints? Probably everyone in the department but one – I'm the second worst at this. Great written feedback? C, E, and F. Organisation of resources? C, F, and G. Now let's factor in these limitations on my teaching: I don't have my own room, so always lose time setting up the lesson – at least 5% of my teaching time. I miss lots of lessons through delivering outside courses like the Outstanding Teacher Programme, or through visiting other schools.

Last year, that was about 7 hours I missed with my year 11 class, or two weeks' worth of teaching, that other teachers didn't lose. I have lots of other priorities in my role as assistant head, which take energy away from my teaching. I teach 70 minutes away from my home, so my time to plan, mark and prepare is more limited.

Yet my classes make excellent progress every year. This year 57% of my students made 5 levels of progress, the highest of any class in the school. It doesn't happen because I am brilliant at the teachery things. But I am a little bit awesome at modelling. In particular at the aspects numbered 7-10 here. This is why I urge you to change your practice and take them on.

Each and every time, without exception, that you get students writing, put one of them at the computer as a typist. That means you will always have an example of students' work to assess. Often the best example is a middle ability student who will make typical mistakes that ten other classmates also make. Because you are experts in your subject, you can never write as badly as your students. It's really difficult for you to anticipate the mistakes they will make. However, you don't have to. On the projector, it's simply there. Now what you teach will be directly relevant to your students' state of mind – they will more readily see that this learning is directly relevant to them.

This means you feedback every lesson; it is live. It arrives exactly at the time that students need it. In other subjects where you might not be writing, you have a camera or visualiser. Probably 95% of you own a camera phone, or an iPad, already with you in school.

It takes no effort to photograph a student's work and email it to yourself. If it's a successful example (by which I mean you don't have to quality assure it before photographing it), then you get to model what success looks like. Where it isn't successful, you get to model how to improve it. This has another huge advantage: because they are always accountable, and they always know that you are going to potentially put their work up, your students will always want to do well.

A middle ability student will often write two or three times as much as they would in their exercise book, because they are desperate not to be seen to underachieve in front of their class. It changes the ethos of your lesson. So, show and tell is the best way to assess, the best way to make students accountable, and the best way to work out what it is they don't know. Three bests, requiring no planning, no lesson preparation, no extra resources.

But the greatest advantage is that you can change the text – edit in class to make it better, so that it moves from being an B/A or A* to getting 100%. And then editing it further so that, instead of being 300 words long, it is 200-250 words long, so a grade B student could write it in the same time as a grade A* student.

If you have an android phone or tablet you will be able to use a dictation app that quickly allows you to dictate student writing, and convert to Word. Dragon Dictation is probably the most famous, and it is free.

If your subject is practical, photographs or short video are even more important. Got a projector in the gym? Play a thirty second clip of two students performing the skill well – talk through the elements of mastery in the skill while students warm up. Do the same with a 20 second clip of students who have nearly mastered the skill, showing it to your class while they stretch. I'll deal with video in section 10.

7. Teach Students to Get 100%

This is the skill I see done least well in school. When I talk about modelling, this is what I mean. When teachers talk about modelling they often mean show an example, or be really specific about four features of the text which, even in an English lesson, is done through an example of three paragraphs, or fewer. This scratches the surface of modelling, in the same way that showing someone the gears, brake, clutch, accelerator, mirrors and steering wheel scratches the surface of modelling how to drive. This works as a pretty exact analogy of most of the modelling I see in class – none of it is wrong, and none of it can be skipped, but it is no preparation for skill at the whole thing – driving on the road.

When I talk to teachers, they all believe that they do model. However, I'd like to suggest that teachers come at it with expectations which are too low. None of us holds deliberately low expectations, but it is built into the DNA of school systems.

For example, everyone takes GCSEs at 16, therefore GCSE A* is the highest any student should aim for and even then, what, only the top 25% should do so? What if they could do the GCSE a year early, or two years? You'll be familiar with one example already – year 9 students taking GCSE media studies in one year, and beating their FFTD predictions.

This is true even in my own school, where a large class of year 11 students take AS Philosophy and Ethics every year, one year early, with great success. Nor are these students the top 25 on ability in the year, though some of them will be. They simply aim high, as do their teachers, and they succeed spectacularly. Has this spread to other subjects? No. Which is a kind of wilful blindness – ah, no, it wouldn't work in my subject, because … (insert numerous reasons that equally applied to the RE teachers, but which they so clearly overcame).

How many linguists would take A2 in a language if they had already gained an AS in year 11? How many scientists would thrive taking AS English literature in year 11, knowing there would be no room for it in their sixth form choices? How many would be intellectually capable of taking AS geography in year 11, having taken the GCSE in year 10, or indeed, not bothered with the GCSE, but starting the AS course in year 10? What if we trained year 8 students who loved cooking to be chefs by the time they reached GCSE – they'd get the GCSE at year 11, but incidentally. I could go on and on here, pointing out changes which to me seem eminently possible, but to you might seem like blue sky thinking. I'm positing it this way, so that you will see that my next suggesting, teaching students to *only* get 100%, and not beyond it, is the *least* we can do.

Your model needs to aim really high, to get 100%. Let's imagine a GCSE class. Your model is A*: be explicit about what makes it A*. It's no good writing something of 500 words, when your students only have time to write 250 words in the exam. So it has to match what the students actually can do. Once they become proficient, they might reach 300, or 350, in which case you can change the model.

Being explicit, you'll find an incredible number of skills in the model. Here is an AS history plan written with our head of humanities, who had already written a model answer. In other words, she was already modelling. She had four things she wished to focus on. This, though, is the plan we came up with, with at least 17 areas to focus on:

History Paper 2 – Italy AS Question C (20 Marks)

Factors Questions

Before Writing

1. Chop up the question to:

    - Find the factor.

    - Find if it is a cause or a result.

    - Find the focus; is it the event or period?

    - Find four or five factors that answer the question.

Writing Your Essay

Paragraph 1

2. Your first two sentences will **make a statement** about the question.

3. Those two sentences work as your introduction; there is no other introduction.

4. Your first paragraph must have the factor from the question. (If you miss this in your essay, you lose 50% of the marks).

5. Explain how this factor is related to the question.

6. This paragraph, like each of the next paragraphs, must contain three facts.

7. A fact tells us – **who, what, when, where**. You will need to write about **two** of these in order to explain a full fact.

Paragraphs 2 – 4

8. Deal with each additional factor in a separate paragraph.

9. Each of your paragraphs must have three facts in support of your factor.

10. A fact tells us – **who, what, when, where**. You will need to write about **two** of these in order to explain a full fact.

11. Each of the next paragraphs should say why this other factor also caused whatever is in the question.

12. Each of the next paragraphs should end with a comparison to the factor in the question, saying whether it is more or less important than that factor.

13. To make this comparison, use the connective "**however**".

Paragraph 5

14. **Only if you have time**, you can write about a fifth factor.

Conclusion

15. Write about the relative importance of the factor in different **places**, or at different **times**, or with different **classes**.

16. Use the phrase "**even if**": this will make you write about the relative importance.

17. End your paragraph with a final sentence which gives the main cause or result.

Because I approached this with no subject expertise, we proceeded with the mark scheme, the model answer, and my questions. These were helpful because I asked them as an innocent, a student if you like. Take nothing for granted. You might think you know what a fact is, but what qualifies as a fact in a history AS exam? The answer was, it depends on the context. Ok, let's look at three contexts to see if we can work out some rules. Yes, it will be who, what, where, when, but not just one of these. Ok, how many? I'm not sure. Ok let's try finding some facts in your model. Having done that, are there any facts that contain any more than two of who, what, where, when? No, ok, we'll have a limit of two. This state of innocence in your questions, or looking at it from the student's perspective, is essential, because as an expert in your subject you will instinctively know why you do something. Finding ways to explain that instinct is hard.

This process becomes incredibly explicit, and hopefully incredibly helpful. Once we'd done it, we dramatically changed the model. Out went the introduction. Out went the extra facts which were not necessary to get 100% (we only got rid of these because the answer was too long for students to reproduce in exam conditions). It had been 1600 words long, but in their exam time, the ablest students had only managed to write about 1000 words. So the model had to be simplified, and shortened. Of course, we also kept the 1600 word model, so she could later teach beyond 100%.

Now, when I showed this checklist to trainee history teachers they were shocked at its length. Instinctively, perhaps like you, they felt it was too explicit. This, however, is not the proper test. The proper test is to try it with the students, and see the effect on learning. Our head of humanities tried it in her next lesson. Her students loved it, apart from some of the most able. The challenge for them is then to do it better – these students can clearly see the standard they are trying to match or, by choosing their own method, beat.

There is another instinct we have as teachers that makes our modelling less successful: teachers typically in my experience (you might be different) tend to give students the model *after* they've attempted the question, or exam and after they've already made mistakes. Then we give them the model and say "oh, by the way, this is what you should have done." This is a costly, not to say demoralising, use of time.

Instead, give them a 100% model first. Explore why it is 100%, then get them to redo that question, with that exact model, so they must try to reproduce it. You'll find for many students that's very difficult, even though they've had the answer first. It becomes clear to them what they do not yet know. This is a much narrower focus than it would be without having seen the model first.

It's not cheating to teach the model in this way, because by the time they get into the exam, it's the 100% answer you want them to give. Then, as they become increasingly good, change the context. "So, this is what we wrote about about the Battle of Hastings. Now let's see what made that 100%. Good. I'm going to give you a similar question, but this time it's going to be on the Battle of Agincourt. Apply the same principles, show me what you can do."

The Mark Scheme

With the model must come the mark scheme. This has to be in language that the students understand. You should simplify it, using language even your grade C students can understand. Focus on the key differences between the grade boundaries, because they need to be able to assess B and A grade answers in order to fully understand the journey to A*. Remember, if they can't understand every word of the mark scheme, then they can't properly aim for 100%.

Now the mark scheme can be used with the model answer, so you can be explicit about how it meets every part of the criteria.

And then, finally, this bit I hardly ever see teachers do. There are lots of rules that aren't in the mark scheme. However, they are in your understanding of what makes a good answer. You'll spot this for your yourself if you write an exam answer that you think should score 100%, then compare it to the mark scheme. You'll find there's lots of stuff you're doing that isn't in the mark scheme, but nevertheless you value. If we go back to the AS history example, the mark scheme is explicit about requiring a conclusion:

"a relevant conclusion/judgement, incorporating well developed understanding of historical interpretations and debate"

However, this is entirely undefined. How does the student know if their conclusion qualifies? You will instinctively know. So, from the teacher's model we were able to draw out the unwritten, hidden skills of the mark scheme. That's how we identified the three skills in the example above, 15, 16 and 17.

8. How to Use a Model Answer

There are lots of ways to teach from the model. My top four:

1. Reconstruct it from the key vocabulary. Call students up, highlight a particular word, maybe one per line, or two per sentence. This is the key vocabulary, that they think is the most important. Once that's up, **get rid of the rest of the answer**, and they just have that key vocabulary. Can they reconstruct the model in the order in which the vocabulary appeared?

2. If you have interactive software, rather than just Word, you can tap each word to change its colour – let's say yellow – **then at the end change the background to black, which will swallow up your black words**, leaving only the yellow on display. This keeps the overall shape of the text, so students can more easily picture the original, even once the other **words have vanished**.

You'll find **reconstructing what is missing** has a profound effect on the way they write, and how they think. They won't reproduce your exact example, but something that scores very highly because of the key vocabulary they recognise makes up the answer. Similarly, they will learn implicitly about the **structure of the answer, the sequence of ideas.**

3. Model **the sequence** by keeping only the topic sentences of each paragraph, perhaps with a bit of key vocabulary within the paragraph. These will help them structure the answer and hopefully remember what went in each paragraph after the topic sentence.

    Wondering about the words in bold? Key vocabulary in the topic sentence refers back to an idea, typically in the last sentence of the preceding paragraph. This feature is what I have tried to demonstrate with my words in bold in the previous paragraphs. To get students to understand this, model it. Reread the bold bits in sequence; see how visual a method of teaching this is, and how easy it is to be explicit once you have the text on the board. Initially, you might show the way the topic sentences link. Next, get a new text, and ask students to do this for you.

4. You can reconstruct from a picture of the structure. Imagine it's a newspaper article, where you can draw in the columns, draw a space for each paragraph, which delineates both its position and size; draw a space for the picture or for pictures; you might stick in say ten words, one for each paragraph, and then they appreciate how the structure works.

    Or it might be an argument piece, in which case highlight the first word of each paragraph, each connective, and each bit of punctuation.

5. You might expect me to recommend cloze exercises or the DARTs activity of chopping up the paragraphs, getting students to rearrange them in the right order. These are perfectly valid, but they suffer from being much less explicit than the activities I've detailed above. They also involve more planning for less effect, which is another reason to consider the first four ideas first.

6. So far I've asked students to reconstruct an existing answer. This is because the goal is not just that they will make progress, it is that they will score 100%. It isn't a real 100%, but it is very close. Firstly, it is a real 100% if they get the same question in the exam – so a top tip is not to do the model on last year's exam question, as that is the only question guaranteed not to come up again this year. Secondly, it is a very high score on the skills of a written answer. Now have them practise the same

structure of answer, with similar vocabulary, for a new question. And then another new question.

9. Film Your Explanations

This is an advanced technique. Partly this is because you are a teacher, and therefore either a perfectionist, a control freak or painfully embarrassed about being photographed. I qualify as the third of these, but let's face it, I'm wholly visible all day to over 1000 people, all of whom can tell exactly what I look like. So, I got over it ("build a bridge, dad, and get over it", my daughter used to say). The same goes for your objections to the sound of your own voice. To see how ridiculous this is, ask any class if you like the sound of your voice, and the chances are they'll think they can never shut you up – you are a teacher, after all.

Then there is the fear of technology. But you can point a phone and touch the video icon, and that's all you need. You don't even need to edit it, in the same way that you don't edit what you explain in class. You just get on with the explanation. You can edit, of course, if you want to. iMovie, YouTube editor and any other app you want to use takes minutes to learn. This will dramatically improve your explanations. (Many of us use 100 words when 25 will do – for example, I've already deleted 60,000 words of this book).

Film your models, explanations, and teaching. There are so many advantages. It will make you very precise in your explanations, and it will allow you to edit so that it tells your students exactly what you want it to.

Film not just the model, but your explanation for how it is constructed, which is very valuable to your students. They get to see how you think, where reading the model only gives the end point of your thoughts. If they can see how you think, they will learn that much more from the model.

Obviously, you should get a YouTube account. The more videos you put up, the more your students will watch them, and the more you will force them to use the advice you're giving them. It will discipline you, not to make a beautiful video, but to give perfect explanations. The easiest videos on YouTube are screen capture ones – Screencast-o-matic for example records your voice over whatever is on the screen. See any Mr Bruff English video if you want to see how easy it is, and how a less than attractive voice is no barrier to excellent communication.

Trust me – I didn't even start till I was 47.

How many resources have you rediscovered, and wondered why you stopped using them? However, if you have made a video, your best teaching, your best explanations, are preserved for all time.

If you've had a bad day, or a bad week, students can still get 100% because they have access to your films on YouTube and they can teach themselves. Look back over the last term. How many bad weeks did you have with reports, parents' evenings, mock exam marking? Exactly, at least one week in four. That's 25% of your teaching time when students aren't getting you at your best. With video, you can change that. More importantly, when you've been a bit rubbish, your students can change that for themselves – YouTube is always there.

Over time, your planning is reduced, and your impact on student progress increases. You will receive lots of positive feedback from all over the world, because the whole world watches YouTube. It means you'll probably invest in the 30 minutes it takes to make that 5 minute video on photosynthesis, because it will matter to your students.

Now, let's talk about your retirement. Let's say you retire at 59, instead of 60. That's about £1000 to £1500 off your annual pension. You could keep tutoring for a while, say at £25 per hour. Or you could allow adverts on your videos. 30 minutes a week will give you a video a week, or 52 per year. This will give you 500 videos in 10 years, if you put almost no effort into it. I began by making four videos in my first year. Now I make two a week. It is simply a case of filming what I am already delivering to my students. Within ten years, these videos will be earning over £1000 a year. It is a little vulgar to talk about money, but it will have the same impact on my pension as another 12 months in work. For me, it's an extra snowboarding holiday a year while my knees still work, or one gourmet lunch a week at Le Champignon Sauvage.

Chapter 27

Nine Techniques To Model Writing

"Writing out my goals became second nature, and so did the conviction that there are no shortcuts. It took hundreds and even thousands of repetitions for me to learn to hit a great three-quarter back pose, deliver a punchline, dance the tango in "True Lies", paint a beautiful birthday card, and say "I'll be back" just the right way."

Arnold Schwarzenegger

1. How To Use the Exam Criteria and Mark Scheme to Model Writing

Teach Complex Sentences

Let's look at an 8 Mark question:

"18 (d) Explain how Miss Tears could help Westshore Netball Club attract junior membership through her role as a physical education teacher at the local secondary school.

[8 marks]"

The full mark answer is:

"Miss Tears could make sure netball is on the curriculum so students are playing it. This will allow them to develop their basic skills which will hopefully motivate them to participate in netball outside of school. In addition to this Miss Tears may arrange for some coaches from Westshore Netball Club to come into school and run some taster sessions for students to encourage them to attend the club on an evening. To help with this they will distribute flyers to promote the club. This will enable the students to become familiar with the coaches at the cub which will help integrate them if they attend the club. Miss Tears could arrange for the club to move its training and matches to the school site. As this venue is familiar with students it could encourage them to join the club as they will not be going somewhere they are uncomfortable with."

This is a genuine quotation of the whole answer from the examiner, completely devoid of commas. This is bizarre when we look at part of the marking criteria:

"Students spell, punctuate and use the rules of grammar accurately and use a wide range of specialist terms precisely". The model answer should fail this test!

Here is the same answer, with the requirement that every sentence must be a complex sentence with **one** comma in it. There are 8 marks, so there must be 8 sentences, unlike the model answer which unhelpfully had 7.

1. Miss Tears could make sure netball is on the curriculum, so that students are playing it.

2. This will allow them to develop their basic skills, which will hopefully motivate them to participate in netball outside of school.

3. In addition to this, Miss Tears may arrange for some coaches from Westshore Netball Club to come into school.

4. She could run some taster sessions for students, to encourage them to attend the club on an evening.

5. To help with this, they will distribute flyers to promote the club.

6. This will enable the students to become familiar with the coaches at the club, which will help integrate them if they attend the club.

7. As this venue is familiar to students, Miss Tears could arrange for the club to move its training and matches to the school site.

8. This could encourage them to join the club, as they will not be going somewhere they are uncomfortable with.

Ok, but does it help them get full marks? Let's look at the criteria:

"Demonstrates detailed knowledge and thorough understanding of the ways that Miss Tears could help Westshore Netball Club attract junior membership through her role as a physical education teacher at the local secondary school.

Answers should include *three explanations*, **two of which must be detailed**.

Students spell, punctuate and use the rules of grammar accurately and use a wide range of specialist terms precisely."

Do eight complex sentences force the student to write with at least three explanations? I think so – they have to add explanations in order to reach eight sentences, and in order to make the sentences complex.

Does using complex sentences force the students to write some detailed explanations? Yes, look how discourse markers 'in addition to this', 'to help with this', 'as this' make the sentence complex, and simultaneously force the sentence to become complex.

Finally, will using a comma in each sentence gain the extra marks for punctuation? Undoubtedly, and much more clearly than the examiner's model, which is allergic to commas and wouldn't know a subordinate clause from Santa's elf (come on, I'm here all week).

The flipside of this is that, without complex sentences, it is entirely possible, indeed likely, for the student who knows the full answer to fail to write it in such a way as to gain full marks. That same student who is trained in writing complex sentences must get 100% – it would be impossible not to be detailed, not to give at least three explanations, not to be accurate with punctuation.

I've used a PE example to show you that this technique works with any subject which is assessed partly in writing. Your job is to work out what the rules are. One of the rules will *always* be about complex sentences.

The same principles are evident in AQA GCSE history. Let's look at a question and ask what the language features are that will force students to get closer to 100%:

(d) How useful is **Source E** for understanding why men made voyages of discovery in the sixteenth century? **8 Marks**

Explain your answer using **Source E** and **your knowledge**.

Target: An evaluation of utility (AO1: 2 marks, AO2: 2 marks and AO3: 4 marks)

I've decoded the mark scheme and examiner's partial exemplars to distil what is key to their writing skills. There is some key vocabulary that your history students must use:

- *Cause, consequence* or *consequently, characteristics*, all handily beginning with C.
- And because we must look at alternative interpretations: *alternatively, however*, and *interpretation*.
- We would also teach them to use conditional language: *could, might* and *would*.

- You could find ways to make this memorable: 3Cs Have A Lot In Common. (***Cause, consequently, characteristics*** are the 3Cs. Have = ***However***, A = ***Alternatively***, L = ***Language*** and C = ***Conditional***.) Students themselves might come up with different ideas to help them remember it.

I also try to find ways to make this memorable for them – often students will do this for you. You would need to write a model answer that included these skills. And before we leave this example, remember the model is not just so that students can see what they have to write. It is so that the mark scheme will make sense, in all its nuances, to you. Only then can you make it make sense to your students.

2. Write Together

Model how you are thinking, as you type, so that your writing is visible through your projector:

"I need a new idea that connects it to the last. Who has one? Good, before I hear it, what connective should I use that will show the idea is linked? Has anyone got a better word than "also"? We then write the new idea. "Who has some evidence that contradicts this? Good. What connective can I use to show this is a contradiction? Alternatively. Ok, which of these opposing views do I think is most valid? What point should I make next in order to force the reader to agree with me?" *Etc.*

3. Combining Writing with Multiple Choice

Here is an exam answer from the AQA Geography exam.

"Composite volcanoes occur at destructive plate margins. Here, plates move towards each other due to convection currents. Pressure builds up over a long period of time as the denser oceanic plate sinks beneath the continental plate. Melting of this occurs in the subduction zone due to friction and heat and the crust becomes magma. This process causes a build-up of pressure which is released in an explosive eruption – giving volcanoes that are formed of sticky slow flowing lava and ash often in alternate layers along a line of weakness/fault."

The question was, "Explain the formation of a composite volcano". There are a number of ways of using this answer in a multiple choice.

A. A Cloze Exercise
Take out 5 of the key words. Give students a list of 10 words as choices from which they have to select the right 5.

E.g. Destructive, convection, denser, subduction, friction, weaker, heat, attraction, conviction, unstable. (Note to self, mix these up). The student will need a high level of subject knowledge to get all five right.

Now, what would happen if you gave your students this answer BEFORE you studied composite volcanos? This would give you some feedback on the words they already did not understand (it won't be all of them, so again teaching time will be saved). But more importantly, they will have learned something they didn't know before simply by having to closely read the model answer. So, speed up learning by giving them the test BEFORE you teach the content. (Remember mastery learning?) But before giving them the test, give them an answer that gets 100%. As teachers, we feel this is wrong, as though it is like cheating. But, if students can reproduce this answer in two weeks or a month, they've learned. That's not cheating – it's teaching and learning.

You also have a wonderful baseline for each student now, when you give them the multiple choice test at the end of the unit, or a month after that, etc. You can then easily demonstrate progress to the students, creating a virtuous circle: students who can see they are learning are keener to learn!

B. Sequence
Another way is to mix the sentences up:

- This process causes a build-up of pressure which is released in an explosive eruption – giving volcanoes that are formed of sticky slow flowing lava and ash often in alternate layers along a line of weakness/fault.

- Melting of this occurs in the subduction zone due to friction and heat and the crust becomes magma.

- Here, plates move towards each other due to convection currents.

- Pressure builds up over a long period of time as the denser oceanic plate sinks beneath the continental plate.

- Composite volcanoes occur at destructive plate margins.

Now, ask students to number the correct order to write the paragraph. A further advantage of this is that they have to focus on a logical sequence for their answer.

C. True or False
Composite volcanoes form only at destructive plate margins.
True

Plates move towards each other due to convection currents.
True

Pressure builds up over a short period
False

The oceanic plate is lighter than the continental plate.
False

The continental plate begins to melt.
True

This melting occurs at the abduction zone.
False.

The crust becomes lava.
False

The build up of pressure causes an explosive eruption.
True

Volcanoes are formed entirely of lava.
False

The volcano is formed along a line of weakness or a fault.
True

D. Force the Passive Voice
Another alternative would be to get rid of the first word of each sentence. Students often fail to start sentences with a verb: "melting". This replaces clumsier phrasing: 'the continental plate now begins to melt' is replaced by "melting of this occurs"

This speeds up their writing, meaning the exam is done more quickly with more time to check answers. Another crucial benefit is that many exams, like geography, mark out the number of lines available for the answer. Long, waffly answers will run out of room, even where the student has the correct subject knowledge.

E. Focus on Common Misuderstandings: The Discriminator
Another way to use it would be to make one mistake in each sentence. These mistakes need to be plausible as likely student errors, and also test vital understanding. I've italicised some sample ones below;

Composite volcanoes occur at *tectonic* plate margins. Here, plates move towards each other due to *convection* heating. Pressure builds up over a long period of time as the *larger* oceanic plate sinks beneath the continental plate. Melting of this occurs in the *suction* zone due to friction and heat and the crust becomes *lava*. This process causes a build-up of pressure which is released in an explosive eruption – giving volcanoes that are formed of sticky slow flowing lava and gas often in alternate layers along a line of weakness/fault."

F. Reconstruct

Choose the three best key words per line. Delete the rest of the text. Students reconstruct it in their own words, but using the given words, in the same order. This will reveal how well they understand the process.

G. Rewrite Using Connectives

"Composite volcanoes occur at destructive plate margins. CONSEQUENTLY, plates move towards each other due to convection currents. THEREFORE, pressure builds up over a long period of time as the denser oceanic plate sinks beneath the continental plate. CONSEQUENTLY, melting of this occurs in the subduction zone due to friction and heat and the crust becomes magma. BECAUSE this process causes a build-up of pressure, IT is released in an explosive eruption. THEREFORE, volcanoes are often formed of sticky slow flowing lava and ash in alternate layers along a line of weakness/fault."

Another advantage of using connectives, is that it guides students to write about a process in each sentence. They won't simply describe (which would miss the marks) but explain the relationship between events.

H. Combine Techniques, One After an Another

And, because repetition leads to memory, you could offer all these tasks in the same lesson. Your explicit teaching will all be about how to write and structure a full mark answer.

Now consider how much geographical knowledge about volcanoes your students would learn without your even teaching it? When I tried this with teachers I gave them an online multiple choice to test what geography they had learned in 15 minutes. They averaged over 90%, and I had taught them none of it – instead I had taught them how to use model answers in their lessons.

Now, let's get really time efficient. What if you used the test with another class next year? What if you made it available to your department? What if each of you made a different one for different parts of the curriculum? Now you are looking at radically reduced burdens of time. No time spent marking homework, less time spent preparing homework. And these are merely the fringe benefits. The main benefit is that your students will learn more. That means more job satisfaction and less intervention. Intervene in lessons, so you can still get a life outside of them.

4. Give Frequent Quizzes

Your skill is in offering incorrect answers. These should be chosen to reflect the most common mistakes students make. If you design questions around typical misconceptions, all your interventions are immediately planned. Moreover, the students who get it right are ideally placed to teach those who did not. Again, no extra time for you, but faster learning for them.

5. Modelling Genres of Writing in Order to Get 100% or go Beyond GCSE

Write a newspaper article on deforestation in Brazil, we say. Write an interview with Pontius Pilate after he has crucified Jesus Write an unofficial school prospectus to give to the incoming year 7. Write a leaflet for a French exchange student on how to find their way around your town or school. Write a poem from a First World War soldier the day before he goes over the top. Write a training guide to prepare an athlete to play your sport to county level. And so on.

We routinely assume that students will know intuitively how to write a letter, a newspaper, a leaflet, a poem, etc. We assume that they are well read. We assume that there is a code, and that they have the key to it. We assume, in short, that they are middle class like us.

And so, what is to be done? Ban administration in department meetings, and meet weekly.

Whatever your subject, life will be improved if you teach some things in common. Decide on the pieces of writing you will all teach, and train each other on how to teach it. This forces you to compare notes, to depend on each other, to collaborate, to develop each other's skills. It also allows you to improve the lesson or series of lessons for next time. If you share ideas, you both improve the quality of your teaching and do so within a real time limit. In fact, because it takes place in department time, you will probably plan more quickly.

How you all changed and improved the lessons in practice gets shared and written up, thus further improving your lessons. Another bonus is that colleagues will have considered ideas that never occurred to you, and you will employ them elsewhere in your teaching. Finally, there are too many occasions in school where we feel we are working in isolation, which causes division at worst, discontent at best. Working together will increase your sense of professionalism and enjoyment of school.

So, start small. Most teachers can see the point of this collaborative approach to writing at key stage 4: this is where writing will be rewarded in exams.

6. Look at Language Features

Annotate examples of the writing for language features. You might need some support here, but it can be done very quickly in your planning if you grab the literacy co-ordinator. For example:

1. Is the writing in the third person?

2. Does it use the passive voice?

3. What subject specific vocabulary is included?

4. How are terms explained, in brackets, using dashes etc?

5. What vocabulary choices has the writer paid close attention to? These might be easily identifiable as the words students can't give an immediate definition to.

6. What verbs are used?

Students will need to see you annotate the text, but also apply this knowledge themselves, then report back what they have discovered.

Annotate the topic sentences of each paragraph. Firstly, decide what the topic of each one is, and write it in no more than two words in the margin. Students will now clearly see how ideas are presented in the first sentence of a paragraph. They can also examine the sequence of ideas.

It may be appropriate to present students with four to six paragraphs on separate pieces of paper, and get them to decide what order they must follow each other. They then have to annotate for the clues that told them what the order was to be.

A more advanced version of this is to give students the same number of paragraphs without their topic sentences. They must now write a topic sentence for each that will make sense, and link to the previous paragraph.

Present paragraphs without connectives, get students to choose which connectives would best fit. This is especially useful because many students use 'therefore' and 'however' to mean 'in addition'.

There may be particular sections of the writing that students will need to have modeled, especially introductions, conclusions and topic sentences.

Provide students with a planning sheet in columns:

Topic	Connective	Technical vocabulary	Evidence	Other vocabulary	Presentational features

These are example headings, but you can modify your own. It will perhaps work best on A3. You might decide that students need a full topic sentence, for example, or the word that will link back to the previous paragraph.

Give students an essay to annotate, then use the note taking table above. Then take away the annotated essay, and ask students to reconstruct it. I have even done this as an experiment with a whole essay, and found that though the original was the same for each student, their own versions were very different from each other. This is less contentious if it is done at KS3 and is great way to teach both planning and note taking.

7. The Big Picture: Why should you show them the model first?

Many teachers feel that showing the model first is akin to cheating. We instinctively recoil from this choice. However, consider other types of learning.

How did you learn to drive? Probably, you had a half hour session in a car park getting used to the controls, but as soon as was practically possible, your instructor took you out on the road. Forgive me for also pointing out that your instructor is probably a less able teacher than you are.

Nevertheless, this is a tried and trusted technique of driving instructors everywhere. Why? Because they are able to show you the big picture straight away. The singular advantage of showing the big picture straight away is that your instructor immediately responds to what she can immediately see you don't know. And it's what you don't know that lets her earn her money.

It's exactly the same in the classroom. Going straight in with the model allows you, and the students, to see what they don't know. But, there is an even bigger advantage than this: the model *always* allows your class to learn more than you teach.

For example, in a history lesson, you might be teaching the 'underground railway' for escaped slaves in America:

"The Underground Railroad, a vast network of people who helped fugitive slaves escape to the North and to Canada, was not run by any single organization or person. Rather, it consisted of many individuals – many whites but predominantly black – who knew only of the local efforts to aid fugitives and not of the overall operation. Still, it effectively moved hundreds of slaves northward each year – according to one estimate, the South lost 100,000 slaves between 1810 and 1850." From pbs.org

Your objective might be to learn that **each paragraph should contain at least three pieces of evidence to exemplify your topic**. But there are myriad things your students might also learn from this paragraph, depending on what they already know. In good history writing:

- Sentences might begin with qualifiers like 'rather' and 'still', instead of 'however' or 'on the other hand'.

- It contrasts ideas about the evidence, hence the qualifiers above.
- It involves adding in extra information.
- Dashes can be used to add in extra information.
- It attempts to be balanced – so it points out that there were both white and black rescuers of slaves.
- It qualifies that balance – "predominantly black".
- It signals that a source may not be enough to be definitive, but might still allow a certain bias by quoting it anyway – "according to one estimate".
- It uses words that convey judgement – "it effectively moved".
- It includes numerical facts, like the 100,000 moved slaves.
- It includes date ranges, not just a single moment in history.

Your model therefore works much harder than you can, and indeed much more efficiently than you can. That learning came from just one paragraph. How much of that learning would help them in an exam? All of it. How much of it would make them a better historian? All of it.

Rather than giving them this big picture, we make life difficult for ourselves, and by extension, our students. Instead, what we tend to do in teaching is anticipate all the problems that students will have, and therefore construct lots of little building blocks in stages. We throw words like differentiation and scaffolding at our lesson plans. But these actually get in the way of learning, much like scaffolding gets in the way of our view of the building, seeing the big picture. By trying to anticipate all the little stages, we effectively slow learning down, putting the brakes on, parking the car and fiddling with all the pedals and the gears. This, I would suggest, is one of the slowest ways to learn.

8. What Swimming Tells us About the Dangers of Scaffolding

Another analogy. I also trained as a swimming teacher. Although swimming skills can be scaffolded into component parts, it would be crazy for the swimming teacher to teach this way. I might model how in front crawl your hand is linked to the movement of your head. I would use the analogy of having some chewing gum from your mouth stretched to the thumb of your dominant hand. As your hand passes by your mouth, it pulls your head to that side, causing your head to turn, and allowing you to breathe. I would model this at the side of the pool for perhaps 10 seconds.

However, if I were to use the approach seen in many classrooms, I would model this with both hands, breathing both sides, an unnecessary piece of scaffolding.

Then I would straighten both arms, put them out in front of me and move them swiftly up and down to mimic kicking. Again, this is not helpful scaffolding – when do you kick? How does this relate to the arms? All the scaffolding causes my children to grow cold or restless.

Instead, I model the big picture. So, what I would actually do at the pool side is get them swimming front crawl as quickly as possible. They would only be focusing on one thing, the "chewing gum" movement of their hand and head, in order to breathe correctly.

Why wouldn't I get them to stand, just using their arms in the pool, to focus entirely on breathing? Because that is slow learning. If I make them do the big picture at the same time (swim front crawl kids), their bodies will be figuring out how their legs work, and at what speed, and where to put their hands into the water, and how hard to pull, and whether to move the hand below them or to pull wider to their side; whether to keep the body straight in the water or whether to roll it etc. In other words, most of their learning will be outside of my teaching, outside of my learning objective of trying to teach them how to breathe while doing front crawl. The more opportunities we give students to engage in this kind of learning, beyond and outside our learning objective, the better they will be in our subject. This means getting them to practise the 100%, not scaffolding a C, then a B, then an A, then an A*. Instead, for a middle set, you might go straight in at B, or perhaps A. For a top set, A*. And your endgame will also be to take your middle set to A* sometimes too.

We convince ourselves that the big picture is hard. It isn't. We just make it hard, because we make sure our students are unfamiliar with it, through constant scaffolding.

Don't believe me? The most stupid student you've ever taught can probably drive. The most stupid student you've ever taught can get by in a language. The most stupid student you've ever taught can probably swim. But I can guarantee the one thing they can't do is your subject. That's how you know they're stupid.

But I'd like to make the case that it is our scaffolded curriculum that is stupid.

9. How to Edit Writing

Students who don't write concisely, don't think precisely. They use far too many words to express themselves because they don't fully understand a concept. You can teach them to be concise, and help them to have a precise understanding – the act of writing better about the concept will teach them the concept.

To do this, challenge students to get rid of as many words as possible, while still making sense. Techniques for doing this are:

Get rid of any repetition that is not for effect.

Substitute words that mean the same as a phrase and can replace it.

Insert the best vocabulary.

Choose the most powerful verbs

Put verbs at the beginning of the sentence, modelling the passive voice.

Model this with the students. This can be done many times, because you have at least one student write their version on the computer each time you engage in writing, don't you?

Chapter 28

'When people come to me with a movie concept or a script, I always ask "What is the poster? What is the image? What are we trying to sell here?"'

Arnold Schwarzenegger

Concept Mapping   d = 0.6

What Does a Mind Map Do?

Tony Buzan has made mind mapping famous. Perhaps he has also made it infamous in teachers' minds. A gimmick. A money making exercise. This was my prejudice. But I was wrong.

This is how Buzan defines mind mapping on his website:

"7 Steps to Making a MindMap

1. Start in the CENTRE of a blank page turned sideways. Why? **Because starting in the centre gives your brain freedom to spread out in all directions and to express itself more freely and naturally.**

2. Use an IMAGE or PICTURE for your central idea. Why? **Because an image *is* worth a thousand words and helps you use your imagination. A central image is more interesting, keeps you focussed, helps you concentrate, and gives your brain more of a buzz!**

3. Use COLOURS throughout. Why? **Because colours are as exciting to your brain as are images. Colour adds extra vibrancy and life to your Mind Map, adds tremendous energy to your Creative Thinking, and is fun!**

4. CONNECT your MAIN BRANCHES to the central image and connect your second- and third-level branches to the first and second levels, etc. Why? **Because your brain works by** *association.* **It likes to link two (or three, or four) things together. If you connect the branches, you will understand and remember a lot more easily.**

5. Make your branches CURVED rather than straight-lined. Why? **Because having nothing but straight lines is** *boring* **to your Brain.**

6. Use ONE KEY WORD PER LINE. Why **Because single key words give your Mind Map more power and flexibility.**

7. Use IMAGES throughout. Why **Because each image, like the central image, is also worth a thousand words.** So if you have only 10 images in your Mind Map, it's already the equal of 10,000 words of notes!"

Yes, I hate the relentless use of cliché, the exclamation marks, the TM use of capitals, the overbearing cheerfulness of the whole thing, which is designed to make you buy, buy, buy the books that show you how. But hang on Dominic, let's go back to its usefulness for learning.

1. The research is quite clear that mind maps have a powerful influence on learning and memory.

2. When a student constructs a mind map, they have to see how each piece of their knowledge links to the whole.

3. The whole structure will be much easier to revise, as opposed to revision notes which will focus only on one component at a time.

4. It forces my student to think through what knowledge is essential, which is actually a very deep level of understanding.

5. It will allow my student to revise a whole topic in a single sitting. Then they can test themselves with an exam paper to find out where the gaps are. These can then be filled in on the mind map.

6. Any new knowledge already has a place to go – it is much more memorable if my student can see how it links to existing knowledge.

7. It looks simple and attractive. Your students are much more likely to put them on bedroom walls and look at them several times a week, than they are to look through their exercise books. Indeed, will your students ever revise from their exercise books? How long do we spend making students fill a book which they may never look at again? Don't they buy a revision guide? Or go to YouTube, or to SparkNotes, or to Bitesize or any other avenue, except your books?

But what if all they had to know was succinctly, memorably, beautifully and individually tailored for them in mind maps?

You know it makes sense.

If you still have doubts, read this anecdote (but feel free to skip it if you are already convinced).

Becoming a Mind Map Convert Happens When You Look at Learning and Impact

This year we've organised some revision sessions for the whole of year 11, using some videos I had put on YouTube.

We started with a mind map of the reading paper: "put everything you know about each of the three questions on your mind map." Bearing in mind that each student had sat the paper as a year 10 and year 11 mock, their knowledge scratched the surface. Very little was in long term memory. The mind maps were sketchy.

But, because they had a structure in mind, the mind maps flourished as I taught from the videos. These were forensic in their attention to detail. Students clearly enjoyed the use of colour, felt tips, highlighters, the art work of what they were producing. Great, but did it help learning?

So I picked a male (because boys can be good at English) and started to ask questions. You've highlighted a word in blue in the third question. What is it? You've used three exclamation marks in the bottom left corner. What do they emphasise? You've drawn a rabbit. What does it help you remember? This was fascinating, as the boy answered a long stream of questions correctly.

This corresponded exactly with how Buzan claims a mind map aids memory. It also role modeled to the students how to revise from the mind map.

The point of this anecdote is that several hours in year 10, more hours in year 11 had been devoted to preparing for the mock exams. Then more hours in the mocks. Then teachers had obviously spent other lessons practising questions separately. But what most students had retained was minimal. And these are good teachers, with results this year in the top 6% of English departments. So, it is very likely that your students remember very little of what you teach also.

Mind maps load the dice in your favour. Visit *www.tonybuzan.com* and find:

1. An online course to teach you how to Mind Map for free.

2. A free 85 page guide to mind mapping.

Respect, Mr Buzan.

Chapter 29

*"To test yourself and grow, you have to operate without a safety net.
Forget Plan B. If there is no Plan B, then Plan A has to work."*

Arnold Schwarzenegger

Teaching Strategies   d = 0.62

This is a summary of all the methods of teaching. We might think this is a vote of confidence in teaching, rather than learning, because having a strategy for teaching is incredibly powerful.

However, the top strategies are **acceleration, reciprocal teaching, and problem solving teaching** (0.61). These are successful, claims Hattie, because they rely on peers, feedback and transparent success criteria. In other words, they rely on all the techniques outlined in my section on modelling and worked examples. Imagine an observer coming to your lesson to decide if your students were benefiting from these techniques. Would they need to focus mainly on you or your students, your students or you? (If I ask a binary question in class, I often frame it like this, because lesson observation has taught me that most teachers signal the answer they want through intonation, or simply putting the correct answer last or, more typically, both).

Anyway, what's your answer? The observer would have to focus on the students. In other words, the main focus is always on learning, not teaching.

These teaching strategies also demand that teachers teach content and understanding, *before* moving deeper to analysis and evaluation. If we think of Blooms' Taxonomy, we are all tempted to rush to the top of the pyramid. If we think of Solo Taxonomy, we are encouraged to move from structural to abstract too quickly. The research reminds us of the importance of teaching content and understanding in order for the higher order thinking skills to have value. After all, how can your students answer the problem of how we could live on a planet with 50% oxygen, without knowing lots of other properties of oxygen – that it is combustible for starters? What would the effect on plants be that breathe carbon dioxide? Would it depend on the level of other gasses in the air, and if so which? Even for students to ask themselves the right questions, they will need a lot of scientific content before their problem solving becomes meaningful.

So embed content first. Then keep changing teaching methods in response to students' learning – i.e. monitor the impact, and where it is low, change the method. You'll be familiar by now with my claim that the best way to change this direction is to get students teaching, because they will have ways of explaining that you have not considered, because it is so difficult to think your way into your students' level of ignorance.

Chapter 30

"In this country, it doesn't make any difference where you were born. It doesn't make any difference who your parents were. It doesn't make any difference if, like me, you couldn't even speak English until you were in your twenties."

Arnold Schwarzenegger

Study Skills   d = 0.63

These have to be taught in context. They are very hard for students to apply across different subjects. Students need to know how, where, and when to apply them – show them this while they learn.

Study skills include note-taking, transforming information into some other form, summarising, self-management, planning, and being motivated. This is a huge area, involving students learning how to improve memory, set their own rewards, visualise goals, and seek help from other learners or experts. It seems to be as much about the student's motivation as it is about their skills.

Hattie highlights that "note-taking effects were higher when students were given instructor's notes to work from", d = 0.82. In other words, just as with modelling, rewards are greater when students are given the answer in advance. There is no value in letting students grope their way toward an answer when you teach them.

The easiest skill to improve is memory, for example using mnemonics, which had an effect of d =1.09.

Clearly, not everything can be learned in this way. My favourite example is AHFASTERCROCH which we met earlier. How many of these persuasive writing techniques can you still name?

Some Advice from Elevate (Other Study Skills Companies are Available)

Hattie's summary of the research on study skills is that concentrating on how your students should revise your own subject will pay dividends. We use a company called Elevate to deliver talks on revision to our students and their parents. Elevate break revision down into 8 practical and helpful steps:

1: Use Your Syllabus

"Top performing students use their syllabus to structure their revision across the year, and then as a checklist before exams...encourage...students to use a 'traffic light system'..."

There are real issues with this approach, due to the language of the syllabus – it is written for teachers. Consequently flashcards may be appropriate. You should already be familiar with Brainscape now. Students could each be given 1-3 pages of the syllabus to translate and type as flashcards in Brainscape, so that the whole syllabus can then be uploaded as a series of decks.

Alternatively, you could simply put their translations together, so they all have a syllabus they understand. You would need to mediate this first, to check for misunderstandings.

A more forensic way of doing this is to write a Personal Learning Checklist for each part of the syllabus, and get students to use this as the basis of their revision. The huge advantage of this is that students won't just identify gaps in their knowledge, they will also identify gaps in their skills. Moreover, the PLC will usually identify what the student must do in order to attain that skill.

2: Take Notes During Term

"Top performing students finish their exam summary notes as they go during term which frees up time before an exam to spend on 'high end gains' like practice papers."

This has profound implications for the way you teach, and the sorts of homeworks you set. A solution to make this manageable for you is to get rid of exercise books for your exam classes.

3: Use a Folder for Every Subject

"Use folders rather than exercise books to file their notes. Students memorise information most effectively using a system called 'chunking' where similar information is grouped together."

4: Take Effective Notes

Avoid writing in sentences, and in one colour. "The top students reduce the amount of words in their notes by 80% to just focus on the key words or 'memory pegs' or 'trigger words': that is the key information and ideas that trigger more information about that topic."

Use a colour-coding system for note taking, so that similar content is in the same colour in each subject. The categories they suggest are five: formulas and definitions, dates, quotations, names, word endings in languages.

A further suggestion is that colours should contrast: "The right combination of colours is important because it can produce higher level of contrast, and this can influence memory retention." *The Influence of Colour on Memory Performance*: A Review by Mariam Adawiah Dzulkifli and Muhammad Faiz Mustafar.

Clearly this suggests having the same colours across all subject areas, categorised in this way, will be beneficial when revision notes are made. You might even colour code your PowerPoints this way.

Take in Your Students' Revision Notes
This will show you how they have been revising, whether they have been revising, and how effective it has been.

You will also be able to see what the most effective forms were for your subject, especially if students hand them in as they enter the mock exams.

The final, considerable advantage, is that you can photograph the successful notes to use with the rest of your class, or with different students next year. Even better, you could film your successful students' explanations of why and how these revision notes worked.

5: Use a system of review

Spaced Learning, and the forgetting curve, the work of Robert Bjork suggests that content should be revised first within 10 minutes of being learned. Similarly, students should review in ever increasing gaps. Of course, this is even more important to your teaching than it is to their revision.

6: Use Mind Mapping

7: Do practice papers & practice questions

"We found the biggest difference between top performing students and lower performing students to be the number of practice questions and past papers they did."

We have seen that testing should happen at all times – with flashcards, with the mind maps, and here with past papers. Research is counterintuitive here: it is much more beneficial to test than reteach. So, teach, test, test, test, test is a much more effective method of increasing memory than teach, test, teach, test, teach. It's important to remember this during the moments of self doubt when you feel you are becoming an exam factory. You are not – all tests of memory demand that brains make new connections, and learning becomes deeper. Robert Bjork describes it like this:

"Testing effect
Taking a test often does more than assess knowledge; tests can also provide opportunities for learning. When information is successfully retrieved from memory, its representation in memory is changed such that it becomes more recallable in the future (e.g. R. A. Bjork, 1975); and this improvement is often greater than the benefit resulting from additional study (Roediger & Karpicke, 2006). *Interestingly, taking a test can modify memory for information that was not explicitly tested initially (provided that the untested information is related to the tested information in certain ways;"*

Anderson, R. A. Bjork, & E. L. Bjork, 1994; Chan, McDermott, & Roediger, 2006; Hamaker, 1986)." From the UCLA website at: *http://bjorklab.psych.ucla. edu/research.html*

My italics also emphasise another advantage – testing even improves your students' memories of ideas, concepts, facts *not included in the test*. This is because many of these will be related to what you have tested, and the student will revisit these briefly during the recollection for the test. This is easiest to imagine if you try to recall something on a mind map – you will automatically see much more than the information you are looking for, as you zoom in on it.

8: Independent Learning

"Our aim at Elevate isn't to turn students into exam machines...Invariably the students who do the best at school are the ones who have gone beyond the syllabus". This is the kind of approach I've recommended in the sections on modelling – teach students to go beyond 100%.

The Implications for Mock Exams

We need to remember this because testing itself has a lower effect. For example, simply taking a mock is likely to have a d 0.34 effect. This is how Hattie's research ranks it.

Effects of Testing   d = 0.34

Perhaps this is a surprising statistic. However, the effects of frequent testing, or testing without feedback on how to improve seem to be the key reasons for this low effect of d = 34. Hattie points out when testing is accompanied by feedback, d = 0.62.

Another problem is the effect of large tests: students do better with a large number of short tests than with a small number of long ones. This suggests that the traditional sitting of mock papers we see in schools is not the best form of exam preparations.

Coaching toward the test also improves performance, but not by much, at d = 0.22. This figure increases if more time is spent coaching, up to a figure of d = 0.70. The implication, though, is that mocks should not be the full test, it is much better to model the type of questions from an exam, and do more examples of the same type. Mocks should therefore be much shorter, and much more frequent.

Chapter 31

Homework d = 0.29   But in Secondary Schools   d = 0.64

Homework gets a very bad press. Hattie does not help, in that he deliberately puts forward this lower figure, even though it is dramatically affected by the low and negative effects of homework for primary school children.

However, there are some lessons about homework at secondary school age that are also rather surprising:

- The effects are highest when the material is not complex
- When the material is novel
- When it takes only a short time to do
- When it does not involve higher level concept thinking
- When it is not project based
- Effects are highest when homework involves rote-learning or practice

Learning of new material is appropriate to more-able students; obviously the older the student, the more likely they are to benefit.

The most beneficial homework doesn't look as we would expect. Blooms' has seduced us into thinking about analysis, evaluation and synthesis or creativity. The research suggests these are not the best approaches to homework. Instead, students should be tested.

And that should mean multiple choice questions. Why? Because you can include answers which target the typical mistakes that students make. Because you can reuse them again and again. Because students will remember the content you actually want them to know. Because you can get results in percentages, so students can see how they improve. Because you don't have to mark them. Because you can share them with your whole department, and other teachers will start preparing your homework for you.

The Case for Multiple Choice Testing as a Means of Learning Through Homework

You will probably resist this initially as not real learning:

Typical Objections to Multiple Choice

1. You have been trained to believe that marking is the mark of proper teaching. Only if it tells you what to teach next, and to whom. A multiple choice will tell you that.

2. If there are four possible answers to each question, students will get 25% correct at random. True, so set a high pass mark, 80, or 85%. Or write 5, 6, or 7 alternatives.

3. They take time to create. True, but 30 minutes spent designing a test that marks itself is better than a homework you have to spend 45 minutes marking, or indeed 30 minutes.

4. They are called quizzes, which makes them sound slight and inconsequential. Ok, but you determine the content, which you can make very taxing if you choose. You can also set time limits per question if rigour is an issue.

5. "It sounds too easy. Everything in my job is getting harder. So you must have an ulterior motive for pushing this." No, I just want students to work hard on the right things. Research says this is the right thing, and if you work less hard, that has to be good.

6. "What will Ofsted say, if they don't see lots of marking?"

   "Show me the impact." Your scores will give you a precise impact.

7. "It feels superficial; how will students be fully prepared for GCSE?" 80% (my contention) of most exam marks are awarded for memory. Memory benefits from frequent rehearsal, which multiple choice will do. The other 20% are skills, which you focus on in class.

8. The forgetting curve works best when gaps between learning is increased – and you can do this simply by resetting old multiple choices at intervals – again minimizing your planning.

And, if your students are getting progressively lower scores, fair enough. But they won't, and you will simply show Ofsted your impact. Ditto SLT, or head of department when you sell it to them.

Do it. Do it now. Get into the chopper.

Chapter 32

"I knew I was a winner back in the late sixties. I knew I was destined for great things. People will say that kind of thinking is totally immodest. I agree. Modesty is not a word that applies to me in any way – I hope it never will."

Arnold Schwarzenegger

Prior achievement   d 0.65

This is not really an intervention, but a prediction of how students will do based on their prior attainment. We might see this as not very useful to us, other than to use it to set students high targets. Progress 8 will already do that for us.

But there are other ways of looking at prior attainment which are more useful.

How Much New Information Should We Give to Students?

"We need to already know about 90% of what we are aiming to master in order to enjoy and make the most of the challenge (Burns, 2002). In developing reading skills, this target is somewhat higher: we need to know more like 95 – 99% of the words on a page before we enjoy the challenge of reading a particular text (Gickling, 1984)."

Let's imagine your lesson. Would this mean that a lot of the lesson should involve retesting of prior knowledge? We already know that it is less efficient to simply test most recent knowledge, but also retest what was learned last week, one month ago, two months, etc. To do this as a starter may well be too disruptive to learning. Instead, you might want three 4 minute sessions interspersed in the lesson. This is actually incredibly easy to do, because you can simply do it verbally, through questioning. Remember to ask the question first, so everyone has to answer in their heads. Then use the lollipop sticks to choose a responder. Because this is revision, quick fire questions will be appropriate, with simple recall of knowledge. Again, you can see how allowing volunteers to reply will damage the learning of your class here.

It is just as easy to get your students to ask these questions for you. Indeed you might set it up like this: first 10 students on the register, write 10 recall questions from the work we did last week. The next 10, write 10 from two weeks ago. The next 10, write 10 from a month ago. This could be their homework.

In any one lesson, you will call on only a few of these questions, so the bank remains extremely useful for the whole week. But if we look again at the idea of spaced learning and the forgetting curve, I hope you have got ahead of me here and realised it is even more beneficial. You will be able to ask students to repeat questions from last week's homework, or the week's before, etc, so that you will always have questions available for ever increasing gaps between the date of your lesson and the date the knowledge was first learned.

Finding Out What Students Know

David Ausubel states: "If I had to reduce all of educational psychology to just one principle, I would say this: 'The most important single factor influencing learning is what the learner already knows. Ascertain this and teach him accordingly.' " Ausubel, 1968

But you will also find that different students in your class have very different starting points. One solution to this is the 100% model. By typing mine live, as the students do an exam practice, they are able to have their memories jogged – "ah, yes, I need to consider the religious perspective". "Oh, I haven't used the words from the question in my first sentences." "I remember, quotations can be one word long." Etc etc. You get the idea.

This is also great discipline for me, as I realise what the students can realistically achieve in the time. Where I write more than this, I add it in a different colour, so I can teach them to go beyond the A* grade.

Writing your notes, in this case an essay, live with the students is also an excellent way to model what effort looks like. I've mentioned before how quickly students give up in an exam, and you are no longer allowed into the exam room to see. Your classroom is the best place for you to model proper exam behaviour – it's not over till the fat lady tells you to put down your pens.

Another is your knowledge of the students, based on frequent quizzing.

It is very rare for teachers to plan for this. Here's an example of what you may see in PE lessons. Even though many students will be club players of a sport at a high level, their starting points are ignored. They are not used in lessons to coach, or not asked to play with a handicap. For example, a football striker for a club team will learn a lot if you ask them to marshal a defensive line, or refuse to allow them to dribble, so that they have to lay off the ball in a maximum of two touches. It is quite easy for you, as a specialist, to think of the right conditions that will force your student to develop their prior knowledge in this way, even in the context of a mixed ability lesson, where their peers will know less. But I rarely see it done.

Prior Achievement

We've met the PLC (Personal Learning Checklist) before.

What would happen if we simply gave students the exam question before studying the content? "How does Armitage make the characters in *Gooseberry Season* memorable and interesting?" They will use this to look back over their essay. However, what if I gave it to them before writing the essay as well?

Personal Learning Checklist	
Organising your answer	**Yes, no or comment**
I wrote in paragraphs	
I underlined the title of the poem in my essay	
I managed to finish in the time limit	
I wrote a conclusion	
I used the key words from the question – **memorable** and **interesting,** not just at the beginning	
I used **connectives** to link my paragraphs	
Using quotations	
Each time I made a point, I used a quotation to back it up	
Each time I quoted, I made sure I used quotation marks	
I did not start my sentence or paragraph with a quotation, I started with the point I wanted to make	
I used some short quotations, 1 – 4 words long	
Using the right vocabulary	
I did not use the word quote, quotes or quotation, because I know that the "……" already tell the reader it is a quotation	
I called the speaker in the poem the **speaker, protagonist, persona** or father	
I mistakenly called the speaker in the poem Armitage	
I called the paragraphs of the poem **stanzas**	

I mentioned irony	
I used words instead of "**shows**" such as **reveals, suggests, indicates, implies, signifies**	
Punctuating my writing	
I ended each sentence with a full stop	
I always had a full stop before "**This**"	
I avoided "**quotation.**" **This** and instead wrote "**quotation,**" **which** in order to continue my sentence	
Meeting the B and above criteria	
I made sure I wrote about the structure of the poem, and why the stanzas were shaped as hands	
I wrote about the break in the structure with "razor's edge"	
I tried to give more than one interpretation for some of the quotations	
I wrote about why Armitage created this strange family, or the homeless man	

You can see, even if you have never written an essay about a poem, that all but the last section is concerned with skills that are generic to any poetry essay. I hope you can also see how explicit they are in allowing me, and the student, to diagnose their own starting points.

Similarly, the PLC will now have direct relevance, as your students will know exactly which parts apply to them.

What would happen in year 9 if you gave your class a GCSE paper? If nothing else, you would learn what the easiest marks to get are. You'd also discover what needed teaching first, the stuff they knew least about. Then, through interleaving and spaced learning, you could retest these topics more frequently, and have time to do so.

Imagine how motivating it would be to discover that they can already score 40%, with over two years to study. Some students might score far higher. Would you start them on an AS course early, but sit the GCSE at the right time, while they are studying the AS? If you taught students AS biology in year 11, would they still learn what they needed for the GCSE A or A* grade? Could you skip the GCSE? It would certainly work in Languages, in English literature, in maths.

The very least that will happen if you test students first is that you will know exactly what to teach next to each student. For that reason alone, the technique is worth making a favourite of your teaching.

Chapter 33

"Start wide, expand further, and never look back."

"The worst thing I can be is the same as everybody else. I hate that."

Arnold Schwarzenegger

Acceleration   d = 0.68

What might this look like in the real world of your school? To answer this, perhaps we should first consider what would happen in your ideal school. If we start here, we'll have a measure of what we want. Then we can see how far we are from that ideal.

I find this useful because any change from the status quo is easily dismissed as blue sky thinking. However, when faced with a real picture of how schools ought to be, a change that gets us only part of the way there seems like a sensible compromise, and not blue sky thinking at all.

What Sugata Mitra Teaches us About Accelerating GCSEs

This week (as I write that is, in 2016) the TES reports on two studies by Sugata Mitra. In one, he takes a primary school class of 8 year olds. They study GCSE science questions in groups of 4, around one computer linked to the Internet. At the end, the group takes a test, and on average each group scores 75%. Now, three months later, the students are tested individually. Now they each score an average of 80%. The experiment is repeated with different groups, different countries, and also with A level questions. Each group has only 45 minutes to answer and research their question. This is not robust research, as Mitra admits. However, if it happened in your class, with your students, you'd definitely be curious.

There are many possible interpretations of this, but the one that concerns acceleration most is the nature of our exams. Mitra also points out that nearly all the content for our GCSEs are for memory. This is not to start a debate about the relative merits of what should be examined. It is much more obvious and basic than that.

If working memory is all that a student needs to pass an exam, then age is not the determining factor as to when students should take the exam. Clearly, we should enter students when they are ready, when their memories are ready. Or, like Michaela, train their memories beyond the exam, and enter them when you, the school, are ready.

As a child I attended a school in Ibiza where students took exams when they were ready. I vividly remember my 12 year old friend taking O level maths. That this is not commonplace in the UK is a puzzle to me. I taught with a colleague whose husband was Greek, and she an MFL teacher. Her three daughters all spoke English, Greek, French and German. This was simply a matter of memory and practice.

In inner cities, teachers will regularly meet students who are fluent in three languages, because memory is easily trained through practice. But when we look at our own schools, we are tempted to see only barriers.

It is a tragedy that our education system is based so overwhelmingly on memory, but the skills of remembering are so rarely taught. Moreover, we persist in believing that GCSEs demand much more than memory – analysis and evaluation. This simply doesn't stand up to scrutiny of what students actually have to do in an exam. We've already seen this with a history question.

Now let me show you with a GCSE science question. Even the ones that claim to be about "application of knowledge": e.g. "Suggest why a sea slug or aphid will grow more in conditions that are well lit." This really just asks students to recognise that photosynthesis is the name of this process, growing in conditions with more light. The student would therefore suggest photosynthesis, even though it is traditionally associated with plants. This isn't really an application of knowledge as it does not extend the student's thinking. It is simply memory.

Students do not need to master the scientific way of reasoning and questioning proof, the scientific method. We should teach the scientific method, because it is a much better curriculum model for 90% of students, who aren't going to go to university to study a science. This way of thinking will reward them whatever they do in life – the scientific method will always be a useful approach to thinking generally.

What Being Head of Department Taught me About Acceleration

As head of English, you may remember, I put my money where my mouth is. I allowed 100 students a year, of mixed abilities, to take GCSE media studies in year 9. Their results would match or exceed FFTD targets for year 11. Were my department geniuses? No, we were teachers much like you. Many of the more able scientists would choose to take AS English literature in year 11, and still get B to A*. This also meant their taking GCSE literature in year 10, and GCSE language in year 10. Did it work? Yes, of course it did. We just told the parents and students that it was possible, and so it was.

By and large the barriers in school are our own limited expectations.

What Should we do in Year 7?

If students are now arriving at level 6, there is even more case for accelerating them. This should be about broadening the curriculum. My son took AS maths a year early, an opportunity offered to 25 or so in each cohort. But this was a gamble, as he knew that he wanted to pursue maths at A level and perhaps university. My AS literature course, in contrast, was not a gamble. It was aimed at students who loved reading, but suspected that they would take sciences and maths at A level. This year we are offering AS creative writing to students, simply for the joy of it, for students who love writing.

Likewise, media studies was simply available to the curious, it was education for education's sake. What if we also offered GCSEs in other subjects in year 9? Photography, astronomy, a second or third language, a design subject?

If we were to start our own school, we'd be much more likely to opt for a broader curriculum, one that developed the whole child. A curriculum that charged at learning every week. We'd be delighted for students to gain qualifications earlier, without worrying if it was too soon.

Moreover, we would consider this our moral duty. If GCSEs are so much about memory, it would be a sign of our personal failure that all students could not pass them until year 11.

Another powerful reason for acceleration is the slow progress in languages. If I ask MFL teachers to think how they would teach their own child or a friend to be able to speak the language abroad, they immediately recognise that their curriculum is inadequate. They would teach it much differently. That they don't is the fear of the masses who find languages difficult. What would happen if the new curriculum did not work?

I understand this fear, but still see it as groundless. To see how unlike blue sky thinking this is, consider an evening class. This is taught in two hours a week over about 30 weeks. That's it. And everyone sits a GCSE at the end of it. The typical riposte I get is that these learners are motivated. But what motivates is not so much that you have paid for the course, it is the promised rate of learning. Would I sign up to an evening class that told me I would take the GCSE after three or four years? No, that is demotivating. Even if it only cost £1 a lesson, you'd be reluctant to do it (and it would still be faster than a language GCSE in school). And that's why students are demotivated by the MFL curriculum. It is designed to take so long.

I use this as an example we can all relate to. But the same will be true in your subject.

Chapter 34

*"Positive thinking can be contagious. Being surrounded
by winners helps you develop into a winner."*

Arnold Schwarzenegger

Ability Grouping Acceleration   d = 0.88

Hattie asks "If acceleration is so successful then why is it one of the least used methods for gifted students?"

We know that setting damages the middle and low ability and adds only a small benefit to the more-able. Consequently, if schools are going to set, the only justification for doing so is to accelerate. Here the evidence presents us with two moral imperatives.

1.   The more-able have to be taught beyond A* or the new levels 8 and 9.

2.   We teach everyone else in mixed sets, in order to avoid giving them low expectations, and keep them with high target grades.

At the same time, the Toolkit suggests, we put our strongest teachers with the lower attainers, or disadvantaged:

"Some studies have shown that reducing the size of the lowest attaining groups and assigning high-performing teachers to these groups can be effective, as can providing additional targeted catch up support."

That's it.

Chapter 35

"There are no shortcuts — everything is reps, reps, reps."
Arnold Schwarzenegger

Meta Cognitive Strategies   d = 0.69

Self Verbalization and Self Questioning   d = 0.64

Meta cognitive strategies, or thinking about thinking. Does the very language annoy you as it does me? It is the very definition of wishy-washy.

It is more helpful to me to see it as self regulation. Getting students to make the right decisions about learning – checking the success criteria, working hard, showing resilience when things are difficult, seeking help from others and the teacher, setting challenging goals. Looked at this way, I can simplify it to getting students to seek feedback. To do this, I simply have to organise my lesson so that feedback is constant, not just from me, but from peers.

The EEF Toolkit summarises the research for us like this:

"What should I consider?
- Have you taught students explicit strategies on how to plan, monitor and evaluate specific aspects of their learning? Have you given them opportunities to use them with support and then independently?
- Teaching how to plan: Have you asked students to identify the different ways that they could plan (general strategies) and then how best to approach a particular task (specific technique)?

- Teaching how to monitor: Have you asked students to consider where the task might go wrong? Have you asked the students to identify the key steps for keeping the task on track?

- Teaching how to evaluate: Have you asked students to consider how they would improve their approach to the task if they completed it again?"

The most obvious demand on your behaviour is the requirement to try the task again, or a different task that involves many of the same skills. To do this, you will no doubt be using many of the techniques in previous chapters: modelling, mind mapping, mastery learning, using personal learning checklists, applying the teaching sequence of See, Try, Apply, Secure, etc. These all become "meta cognitive" when you ask a simple question – "how much or how well have you learned?"

Meta cognition is simply getting students to seek feedback on their learning, and how they are learning. This must work, *whatever* technique you or they are using.

A word of caution about your students' emotions. What your students feel about how well they have learned, is no more than interesting. What they can remember and apply is the only true test, and that involves testing or quizzing.

Very often, trying some new approach with students will activate their limbic system and they will immediately claim it did not work. Don't accept this on face value – assess the learning, and find out for sure. Of course the opposite is also true – "that was great Miss, let's do that again." "I'm glad you liked it. Let's take a look at the results" is the appropriate response.

Chapter 36

"If it's hard to remember, it'll be difficult to forget."
Arnold Schwarzenegger

Spaced Practice v Massed Practice   d = 0.71

Mock exams. Important, aren't they? Common sense tells us that students need to practise the real thing, the full two hours in the exam hall, so they get an exact flavour of what the real exam is like. Similarly, they need to get used to doing at least two exams a day, as this will also happen in the real thing.

Ok. But if these are our reasons for having full mock exams, then common sense will also tell us that they are best placed quite soon before the real exams – say in April. Yes, this would mean that teachers would not have much time to mark the answers, but why shouldn't students self mark at this stage? After all, they will need to know how to do it for themselves in six weeks' time. They would then get feedback on what they need to know about exam conditions just when they need it: oh, I do need to learn to write at speed; my hand will hurt if I don't spend Easter practising some prolonged writing; I do need to manage my time better, I missed the last two questions; oh, not checking my answer meant I lost a whole grade – I won't just sit back once I've finished the paper, I'll check it. Etc.

Instead we have our mocks in December, or January. Then we have too much to feed back on, and students have too much information to retain. It has an impact, of course, but not enough.

Now contrast this to doing an exam question, or section, every three weeks of the GCSE course. Here you would have ample time to feed back, and for students to act on feedback. They would do each section of the exam (obviously from different papers) several times over the two years. The content you studied earliest, they would have most attempts at this way, another advantage, as older knowledge is harder to recall.

The research is very clear – you must do this. It takes no more effort from you, just a change in thinking.

Spaced Learning and Interleaving

Research into how memory works, and in particular, how it grows, has been fascinating because much of it is counterintuitive. Professor Robert Bjork is possibly the leading light in this research. You'll find more in depth discussion of this at his website: UCLA Bjork Learning and Forgetting Lab.

The Testing Effect

Not only does the reseach show that testing leads to greater learning than simply re-teaching a topic, particular kinds of test are also very beneficial. "We believe that multiple-choice pretesting is more beneficial than is cued-recall pretesting because the multiple-choice pretest directs attention more broadly during subsequent study – not just to information pertaining to the question, but also to information pertaining to the alternatives."

So we should deliberately test using multiple choice questions, as these will make students link to other knowledge they might have. But more strangely, we should do this first before teaching the content, as it will strengthen what the student already knows. This is true even though their overall marks are likely to be low.

Desirable Difficulties:

"Imagine a scenario in which a teacher has students practice different examples of a single type of math problem for an hour in class...On a test two weeks later..." the learning has not stuck. "In contrast...imagine that the teacher had interleaved many different types of problems during in-class training drills. Recent research reveals that difficult training of this type produces higher scores on the test than the easier version described above."

Other desirable difficulties "include spacing rather than massing repetitions of to-be-learned information...testing rather than re-studying information... and varying the conditions of practice instead of keeping them constant".

Spacing

"The study-phase retrieval theory (Thios & D'Agostino, 1975; R. A. Bjork, 1975) of spacing proposed that the benefits of spacing arise from the retrieval of the first presentation upon repeated presentations...longer intervals create more potent learning events than shorter intervals."

Generation

This suggests that key words in a text, or in revision, should be made more difficult either by revealing only their beginnings and/or endings, or as anagrams. This is fascinating and easy to achieve.

For example: B...k's research reveals that s.....g and i..........g are both great ways of giving the brain the d.......e d..........s they need.

Or kjbors research reveals that isacpng and eritnevalgni are both great ways of giving the brain the edeiasrlb fifitedsiucl they need.

To be fair, you might want to have fewer such words per line, but you get the idea.

Interleaving

The act of interleaving different areas of learning in the sequence is the creation of a "desirable difficulty". The example he gives is of different subjects, "Study a little bit of history, then a little bit of psychology followed by a chapter of statistics and go back again to history. Repeat (best if in a blocked-randomized order)." However, these stand for the different types of knowledge that you will find within your own subject.

Perceptual desirable difficulties

I used to advise teachers to simplify their slides, often with font that was too small, or packed with too much information. And then I read this: "when you encounter fonts that are difficult to read or words in very small print, you may experience a sense of disfluency— the unusual or small typefaces are more difficult to process than more common typefaces." This disfluency causes the brain to think harder – it knows that the information is likely to be difficult – and so memory is enhanced.

What is clear from this, however, is that we need to dramatically alter the curriculum we teach in our subject. Having taught fractions, we might teach area, and then percentages, and then fractions in more depth, and then volume, and then area in more depth, and then randomly retest 3 questions on fractions, two on percentages, one on area, one on percentages, and then teach simultaneous equations, then one question on fractions, two on volume, etc. It might be that you would spend only two or three lessons on the same topic, before you switched. This feels impossibly hard. Psychologically, it is just as hard for the teacher. So, a rational response to this research would be to plan the curriculum from the beginning of the year, so that the teacher could stick to it.

This would also demand a full explanation to the class, with a clear sense of what desirable difficulties are for. To do this takes courage. To quote Arnie again, "There are no easy answers, but there are simple answers. We must have the courage to do what we know is morally right."

Chapter 37

"Your levity is good, it relieves tension and the fear of death."
Terminator, 'Terminator 3: Rise of the Machines'

Teacher Student Relationships   d = 0.72

Show the student you believe in them. Try to understand how the individual student learns, and in particular, to spot the barriers to their learning which are nearly always emotional. An emotion led student will opt for a subject they have little passion for, but where they like the teacher. They won't opt for the subject they are passionate about, if the teacher is one they don't like. Isn't that a typical student?

Student Centred Teaching   d = 0.54

Many teachers feel they display warmth, trust, and empathy. However, the key is whether your students feel that way. As I have mentioned, there is a case for faking it. I find it very difficult to empathise with some students who are completely dictated to by their emotions. However, I will still take the time to ask them how they are feeling at moments of stress. I tell them that I know I am asking them to do something difficult (when actually I can conceive of no such thing) and I will go out of my way to talk to these kinds of students when I meet them in the corridor, or on lunch or break duty. While I often find it difficult to empathise, I compensate with positivity which, in the lesson itself, is sometimes not possible.

The point of confessing my failings here is to suggest that we can all compensate for the parts of our personality that students might not warm to.

Imagine the effect of having a teacher who does not know your name. My daughter used to predict what grades her teachers would give her for attitude to learning based on whether they knew anything about her, including her name. Before we opened the envelope, she'd predict what she got on the 5 point scale from each teacher. Each 3 would be from a teacher who did not know her name.

Trust means that you believe in the student, no matter their starting point. This is the one that teachers find most difficult to exhibit. Do you have colleagues who label a whole class as impossible, because of the behaviour of four or five students in it? Colleagues who say a whole year group is the worst in the school, and tell the students? Colleagues who tell their classes they are the worst in the year group?

I know I do.

Meaningful Student Voice

Sail the 7Cs

In *Visible Learning For Teachers*, Professor John Hattie identifies the 7Cs of expert teachers. He also provides two questions for each C, 14 in total. These are adapted from the work of the MET project, which looks at 7 characteristics of teacher relationships with students: (www.metproject.org/downloads/Asking_ Students_Practitioner_Brief.pdf)

Secondary Version

Care
- My teacher in this class makes me feel s/he really cares about me.
- My teacher seems to know if something is bothering me.
- My teacher really tries to understand how students feel about things.

Control
- Student behaviour in this class is under control.
- I hate the way that students behave in this class.*
- Student behaviour in this class makes the teacher angry.*
- Student behaviour in this class is a problem.*
- My classmates behave the way my teacher wants them to.
- Students in this class treat the teacher with respect.
- Our class stays busy and doesn't waste time.

Clarify

- If you don't understand something, my teacher explains it another way.
- My teacher knows when the class understands, and when we do not.
- When s/he is teaching us, my teacher thinks we understand when we don't.*
- My teacher has several good ways to explain each topic that we cover in class.
- My teacher explains difficult things clearly.

Challenge

- My teacher asks questions to be sure we are following along when s/he is teaching.
- My teacher asks students to explain more about the answers they give.
- In this class, my teacher accepts nothing less than our full effort.
- My teacher doesn't let people give up when the work gets hard.
- My teacher wants me to explain my answers — why I think what I think.
- In this class, we learn a lot almost every day.
- In this class, we learn to correct our mistakes.

Captivate

- This class does not keep my attention — I get bored.*
- My teacher makes learning enjoyable.
- My teacher makes lessons interesting.
- I like the way we learn in this class.

Confer

- My teacher wants us to share our thoughts.
- Students get to decide how activities are done in this class.
- My teacher gives us time to explain our ideas.
- Students speak up and share their ideas about class work.
- My teacher respects my ideas and suggestions.

Consolidate

- My teacher takes the time to summarise what we learn each day.
- My teacher checks to make sure we understand what s/he is teaching us.

- We get helpful comments to let us know what we did wrong on assignments.
- The comments that I get on my work in this class help me understand how to improve.

The * denotes a reversal – negative comments are what is desirable in reply.

Many of these questions, we might feel, are loaded, making assumptions about good teaching with which we disagree. However, the MET project takes these questions for each of these 7 Cs, and correlates them to teachers in the top 25th percentile for progress, and for the bottom 25th percentile. This makes it very useful as a way of cutting across our assumptions – you can simply compare your results to those two percentages.

Hattie modifies this in *Visible Learning for Teachers* so that the students are asked a very manageable two questions for each C:

Taken together, these identify the characteristics of an expert teacher, defined by student progress, being at or above the 75th percentile.

Could we use these simple measures to decide whether we are expert teachers, and more importantly, what areas of our practice to improve?

7 Cs	Questions	At the 25th Percentile	At the 75th Percentile
Care	My teacher in this class makes me feel that s/he really cares about me	40%	73%
	My teacher really tries to understand how students feel about things	35%	68%
Control	Students in this class treat the teacher with respect	33%	79%
	Our class stays busy and does not waste time	36%	69%
Clarify	My teacher has several good ways of explaining each topic that we cover in this class	53%	82%
	My teacher explains difficult things clearly	50%	79%
Challenge	In this class, we learn a lot almost every day	52%	81%
	In this class, we learn to correct our mistakes	56%	83%
Captivate	My teacher makes lessons interesting	33%	70%
	I like the ways in which we learn in this class	47%	81%
Confer	Students speak up and share their ideas about the class work	40%	68%
	My teacher respects my ideas and suggestions	46%	75%
Consolidate	My teacher checks to make sure that we understand the lesson when s/he is teaching us	58%	86%
	The comments that I get on my work in this class help me to understand how to improve	46%	74%

Thin Slicing

Malcolm Gladwell, in *Blink*, introduces us to research on how easily students can judge the effectiveness of their teachers from non-verbal cues. Students watched video of a teacher teaching, with no students in shot, and no sound. How long did they have to watch before they could predict if the teacher was effective? 24 hours? 24 minutes? 24 seconds?

"Ambady ... compared those snap judgments of teacher effectiveness with evaluations made, after a full semester of classes, by students of the same teachers. The correlation between the two, she found, was astoundingly high. A person watching a two-second silent video clip of a teacher he has never met will reach conclusions about how good that teacher is that are very similar to those of a student who sits in the teacher's class for an entire semester."

David Munger looks at this study on his blog, *The six-second teacher evaluation*.

"These teachers were rated by their own students at the end of the term on a general effectiveness scale. I've created a table below to show the correlation of the ratings of the 30 seconds' worth of clips with the end-of-semester rating:

Active	.77
Competent	.56
Confident	.82
Dominant	.79
Enthusiastic	.76
Likable	.73
Optimistic	.84
Supportive	.55
Warm	.67

Concerned that their measure may only reflect a cursory evaluation of the physical attractiveness of the teachers, Ambady and Rosenthal had separate judges rate the teachers for attractiveness based on still photos. *Even after controlling for physical attractiveness, the correlation between student ratings and the video clip ratings was still significant. Apparently after seeing just 30 seconds of nonverbal behavior, we can reliably predict teaching ability.*"

These are my italics. We can clearly see the overlap between these correlations, and the 7Cs. It also reminds us about the impression we create on our students when they first meet us.

These are the same impressions, it seems, that we create in our line managers

– the first correlation was to principals' ratings of the teachers, then with the students' perceptions at the end of the term.

The section on body language should help you here – after all, none of these impressions were conveyed by voice, or words – it is entirely body language and facial expression. And, the only way to assess your body language is through video. Roll out the iPad.

This should be a staple of the way you review your effectiveness, even if it is not one used by your SLT. After all, you are the one who wants to improve your teaching, and the learning of your students. You are in charge.

I tried a similar experiment in a whole staff training session. A Teachers TV video is at www.stem.org.uk/elibrary/collection/3597/secondary-design-and-technology-teachers-tv?page=2 entitled Design and Technology. The opening 16 seconds features 8 teachers, at 2 seconds each. I played these and asked teachers to identify who they had a gut instinct would be best.

Astonishingly, there was overwhelming support for two of these. We have no way of knowing their value added. But the research suggests it is likely to be good. The real lesson, however, is that your body language and face conveys a huge amount to your students, and makes them more likely to believe in you as their teacher.

Watch these clips, and note down what makes you prefer one teacher to another. Then ask if these are traits you have.

Chapter 38

"Come on Cohagen. You got what you want. Give these people air!!"
Douglas Quaid, 'Total Recall'

Non-directivity   d = 0.75

Hattie is vague in his description of what this involves. The term itself comes from therapy and psychoanalysis. Non-directivity is also called the "person-centred approach". Perhaps this quotation will help:

"The basic hypothesis of the person-centred approach is that potentially the person who can best understand and change the client is the client himself. The task of the therapist is to create the conditions where the client feels free enough, strong enough to do that.

The obvious advantages of this emphasis on the centrality of you, the client, are that:

1. Your "solutions" are more likely to be the ones which fit you.

2. You are more likely to be able to act upon your own decision than any of mine.

3. A longer term, "social educational", effect is that having seen yourself come to your own solution and act upon it you may be more-able to do the same for yourself on future problems."

(The Person-Centred Approach to Therapy, by Dave Mearns: Paper presented at the Scottish Association for Counselling, 31st May, 1980)

If we replace the word 'client' with 'student', this seems like an exact explanation of coaching. If I could condense that further, I'd describe it as the habit of listening to the student, and asking questions that lead them to realise their own solutions. Often, because we are dealing with teenagers, the problems will not be the demands of the work itself, but rather the student's emotional approach.

The student who:

- craves attention because parental attention is denied in early childhood.
- craves approval from other students they perceive as more dominant.
- demands attention as a way of maintaining their place in the social hierarchy.
- fears losing face, so tries desperately not to engage.
- fears responsibility, so seeks to distract.
- demands negative attention because this habit formed early and replaced positive attention, or lack of attention.
- Is a perfectionist who cannot risk mistakes in case it damages their sense of intelligence and self.
- Is anxious, needs control and cannot cope well with change.

The problem is very rarely the difficulty of the task you set. The behaviours that follow the types of examples I've listed can be defined most broadly as a fear of challenge, and taking the risk of being wrong. They are also likely to manifest in attention seeking, disruptive behaviour.

The solution to this is a coaching conversation, helping the student to think of themselves from someone else's perspective. Sometimes this can be extraordinarily difficult for them. The students know they should not do whatever they were doing, but they're still doing it. So telling them again misses the point. Questioning can force the student to consider another point of view. E.g.

- How many students will stop listening to my lesson when you turn around and start talking?
- Who else is likely to start talking when they see you do it?
- How many students are now not learning in my lesson?
- What did you want me to feel when you said...?
- When I had already asked you to stop calling out, and you did it again, how do you think I felt?
- What stopped me shouting at you when you ignored what I asked?

- How would Sophie describe her lessons with you to her parents tonight?
- What was different about last week, when you were focused in class?
- How can I help you to avoid this behaviour next lesson?
- How can you spot the signs that you are going to lose self-discipline before you enter my room?
- What can you do before you come in to my room to prepare you for learning when you get here?
- Once you were given a warning, what stopped you from behaving well?

Note, none of the questions begin with a 'Why', which invites a defensive response, because it begins an accusation.

The other feature is that these are questions, for the most part, to which you don't know the answer. It is therefore a genuine conversation, where you want to hear what the student has to say. Often they will be scared of this process, especially as they begin to perceive their own honest answer is one that will cast them in a bad light.

It is only when students see their behaviour as others see it that they begin to change. My favourite example of this happened with a very able student, who constantly sought reassurance. Having taught her in year 9, she had different class mates in year 10. Another girl exhibited exactly the same behaviour. My ex-year 9 stayed behind after one lesson, "Mr Salles, I've just realised, that's what I must sound like." Her change was immediate and permanent.

This is an even more powerful technique to use as tutor, head of department, or pastoral lead. I have often seen these conversations manipulated, "do you think that...did you know that...can you see that" which are simply pretend ways of getting the student to see their behaviour clearly – they are actually a way of getting the student to see things *your* way. This will work, the student is likely to give you the 'right' answer, because you have isolated the student, and they can see that they are in some degree of trouble. But it will not work to change future behaviour, and so it is a lost opportunity.

Many students, of course, are not ready to be coached. However, the second, third and fourth times you have that conversation, you will perceive an improvement each time. As a member of SLT called to remove students from class, I often build better relationships with these students than those in my own class, because I have had these coaching conversations – a lesson to me I periodically have to relearn.

It goes nearly without saying that these same conversations work brilliantly with other adults in the school!

Teacher – student relationships d = 0.72 Rank 11th

Relationships are defined in order of importance of effect as

Non directivity d = 0.75

Empathy d = 0.68

Warmth d = 0.68

It is very interesting that personality has a much higher effect than subject knowledge or even a focus on learning.

Empathy

For any teacher, it is much easier to ignore how a student is thinking or feeling, and apply your rules consistently. You can compensate for this by instead empathising with those you keep behind, like this real conversation with Harry, who had not copied down notes of a class discussion:

"You're finding this difficult Harry, what's making it hard?"

"I'm just a slow writer sir."

I watched him copy.

"I notice you only write two words at a time, and then look up to find where you were on the board. What if you tried to remember five words?"

"I can't sir, I'm dyslexic."

I asked him to read the first sentence to me, which he did without trouble.

I then stood in front of him, so that he could not see the screen, and asked him to repeat the sentence to me from memory, which again he could do easily.

"Harry, that was eleven words you just remembered. Do you think you could remember five?"

"Yes sir."

"Do you find it difficult to copy in all of your subjects?"

"Yes sir, but I'll try to do five at a time."

This is not an especially dramatic example of empathy, but it serves to show a specific focus. Empathy asks: "What do I have to understand about you in order to make it easier for you to learn and succeed?"

Warmth

Warmth is another related trait. I know a brilliant teacher, who has excellent control of her class, can instantly transition from silent writing to discussion, to speed dating, to whole class movement. Her students do whatever she wants, when she wants. But hers is an option subject, and many students are reluctant to choose it if they have her. This is almost wilful stupidity. Her students know they learn a lot in her lessons. They always feel safe, and secure. But they don't feel liked. They react entirely with their limbic system, and emotion trounces reason every time. This is because we are dealing with teenage minds.

So, you might also fake warmth. Be ambitious in your fakery. Pick as many students as you can to like. Then find the ones who are more difficult. Find something to praise in their work, or in their inexplicable decision not to mess you about today. "Lori, you've come in without your ring on today, thank you." "Douglas, this is the best piece of work you've done for me this half term, well done." "Benny, you're calling out". Benny puts his hand up. You smile at him and indicate with your hand that he is next, after Melina. Then it is Benny's turn. "Thank you Benny, that was worth waiting to hear."

You will always be asked about the reputation of a naughty class. "Are we the worst class you teach sir?" "Vilos, this is my favourite class, I always look forward to teaching you." They might suspect this is a lie, but it is one they will deeply appreciate. Because only a teacher who liked their students would take the trouble to lie to them about enjoying teaching a difficult class.

And this is why your warmth matters so much. They will work for you, not because they like you, but because they believe you like them.

Chapter 39

Feedback   d = 0.75

What would happen if you never marked a student's work, but instead asked students to do it? What progress would they make?

Below is a mark scheme from an AQA DT design question. The task is "Sketch a design for packaging the insulated mug." 12 -15 marks

I've separated the skills into ten component parts.

1. Very creative design highly suited to packaging of given mug.

2. Excellent use of colours, tones and given images.

3. Ideas drawn in proportion using two or more recognised drawing techniques.

4. Very accurate and detailed 2D net development and/or 3D of package showing clearly how solution goes together.

5. Glue, fold & lock tabs accurate and proportioned.

6. Evidence of dimensioning included.

7. Detail or card/polystyrene insets.

8. Locking tabs and security seals/stickers.

9. Possible mention or corrugated card for lightweight protection etc.

10. Evidence as notes or sketches of how mug will be secured. Not just placed in a box.

Now, imagine that for each of those ten you introduced a four-point scale: very good, good, OK, not OK; or bodacious, better, borderline, basic – a four-point scale is simply a judgment call (which is essentially what we all do when faced with such criteria).

Right, now imagine that each of these is given a number 1 – 4. It would be easy for students to grade each component of the design, to arrange them in ascending pairs, according to their total mark. *Even easier, and much more quickly, they could judge the 10 holistically, and just assess with a gut reaction, e.g. mainly bodacious, mainly better, mainly borderline, mainly basic.*

Next, you could standardize the marking.

Students briefly look at the pair and decide which is better, moving the better one up.

It might look like this.

A	B better
C better	D
E	F better
G better	H

The new pairings would look like this:

	B
A	C better
F	D better
E	G better
	H

The new pairings would look like this. Then simply number the winners out of each pair.

C 1	B 2
A 3	D 4
F 6	G 5
E 7	H 8

Only 5 minutes are spent using the 4 point scale with the 10 criteria and a gut reaction, because you ask students to make their judgement quickly. Once work is paired, deciding on the relative merit of each one – is this one better than that? – might take only one minute.

Let's say there are 3 such reviews of pairs – a total of 5 minutes marking, 6 minutes sorting the pairs, leaving you 3 minutes for the physical movement around the room, displaying the work so your students can assess it.

That's 15 minutes. Now ask students to award whatever mark is available from the mark scheme, using the 10 points more critically.

The students will have a clear idea of what made one piece of work more successful than the one they downgraded. These then become the areas of improvement. In the process, they have developed a much greater understanding of the criteria – not just what the words mean, but what the skill actually looks like.

Now what? Ask students to write down 5 things they need to do better? Get them to photograph 5 pieces of work, each one demonstrating one of the skills they wish to improve in? Get them to do something that tries to meet those 5 things right now? Or just one right now?

As you can see, once you start to think in this way, you move further and further away from having to give the feedback yourself.

Let's imagine a worst case scenario, where 50% of the students' overall grading is wrong. Will 50% of their chosen targets for improvement also be wrong? Unlikely – a student who says that they have not done something well is usually right. They are often harsh on themselves, and award a low mark, but they won't pick a skill that they do well and criticize it. A student might also self assess themselves too highly, but that will not happen here – everyone is potentially assessing everyone else's work, so they have to choose targets that come from the range of options suggested by your assessors.

So hardly any of that potential inaccuracy is dangerous, because the improvements suggested will still be entirely valid.

Now imagine you are teaching a binary subject – science, maths, languages – binary, because most answers are simply right/wrong. As a maths teacher, you can simply get the students to mark their work every time. But what if you gave them no individual feedback at all, to explore why they were making mistakes?

Ok, what if we gave out the books in pairs after the students had marked them? Your skills as a maths teacher will allow you to predict what the three or four most common problems are for your students. You would write a sentence to describe each one, or show an example of each mistake. Mine are generic, to fit what I think would happen to nearly every maths problem faced by a maths student:

1. You did not recognise which method to apply
2. You had problem x in the method
3. You had problem y in the method
4. You had problem z in the method

The peer then has to write 1, 2, 3 or 4 next to the mistake, so the student knows what their problem is, other than not getting the correct answer.

Those who have made no mistakes, or few, become teachers. Send these students to teach those who need the help.

Then, give everyone 1 – 3 questions to see what they have learned, and try the process again. Your skill is devising the right questions, that will keep nudging the students' knowledge a little further, applying it in slightly different contexts, or with more operations.

Would your students still learn? Yes. Would the pace of their learning be high? Yes, higher than a lot of instances where you are assessing them, because the feedback comes right now – not delayed by when you can take in the books, and then when you can actually mark them, and then when you actually see the students again.

In this thought experiment, NOT marking the books or work has dramatically improved your feedback.

You can, within these rules, still grade students' work, but not correct it. You know where the students are in relation to where you want them to be, or to their starting points.

When you do look at the students' work though, your attitude can shift significantly, as can your work load. How many books would you have to read in order to decide on what you had to do next with the whole class in order to make them better? I'm going to suggest just 10, if you don't know the class. But if you know two from the top, two from the middle and two from the bottom of abilities, 6 will do. You will know the main 4 things to focus on.

Again, the feedback comes just in time – we can all read 6 books before the next lesson, especially if we don't have to correct anything. So, in geography, the four might be:

1. to give details of a case study,
2. to explain cause and effect,

3. to link to a long term consequence,

4. to use three geography specific words.

If you teach these briefly next lesson, would you be confident that students would correctly identify which ones were relevant to them? I think, by and large, they will be safe to do so.

Would those who had 100% learn nothing? No, they would still identify a weakness, and go beyond what the task required. Once more, feedback is improved because you have NOT marked the books.

How has the book dealt with feedback already?

Well, we have met the techniques already, in the sections on modelling:

1. Feed forward

- Show worked examples exhibiting all the skills you want your students to master.

- Keep parts of the model, and use these as clues for students to attempt to reconstruct it.

- Use the Personal Learning Checklist and the knowledge organiser to distil precisely what they should master.

- Give these out before studying the topic.

- Show examples of student work at the middle attainment for your class, and get students to bridge the gap by reworking it.

- Make instructional videos that students can always refer to, so your best teaching lasts for ever.

2. Feedback Live

- If it is work students are doing in a book, one person always types or writes on the board. This is always assessed in class.

- If it is something students make, photograph it to assess.

- If it is an activity, like our swimming example, get students assessing each other live.

- Film students performing a skill, and play it back for the class to assess.

- Have a demonstration group, as we did when teaching group work, or you might have in a PE activity.

- Use the pink highlighter pen to highlight mistakes that students must instantly correct.

- Give a highlighter to your TA.
- Use frequent testing, such as multiple choice.
- Use the teaching sequence – See, Try, Apply, Secure, so your students have a feedback loop that keeps leading to improvement.

3. Feedback from the group

- Use random questioning (I've explained why lollipop sticks are the most efficient method) to find out what students do and don't know. Again, adapt teaching accordingly.
- Keep digging deeper, till you find what students can't do. That might be through questioning, increasing the number of connectives students must use in their answer, taking a concept and making it ever more complex by varying the conditions.
- Retest, using spaced learning, to keep gathering information on what students still need to practise.
- Quick fire questions where students can answer on whiteboards, or an app that allows you to instantly see who knows what. If you are lucky enough to work in an iPad school, this should be a regular activity every lesson.

Our thought experiment might guarantee us excellent feedback to all students. But will it pass an Ofsted inspection? Here's one Ofsted friendly solution, if your students are not taking account of feedback and marking.

You take a set of books home. You forget about them till Sunday, then spend two hours marking them, underlining things students need to pay attention to, commenting. Then you apply your school marking policy – perhaps a spelling correction, a What Went Well, and an Even Better If.

You reward, recording these online or in your mark book. Next lesson, you give the books back and sprint the class towards new knowledge.

Well, no one can say you're not doing your job properly. Not your head of department, not the SLT, and not the parents. So you're covered.

But what difference did your two hours make?

Now imagine that this is not a thought experiment, but actually a description of typical marking in typical schools. Marking that follows a school code, but has little impact on the students' learning, because the student rarely does anything as a result. Or you have to pay real attention in your next set of marking to see if indeed the student has tried to take your advice on board.

One solution is Think Pink Go Green.

Here, any advice you want the student to think about you mark with a pink highlighter – a line, or a box, to make it very visible to the student and to you.

With a green highlighter, you delineate the space where you want the student to complete something to show they have attempted to take on board your advice. You don't have to double mark this – knowing that the student has had another go simply increases their chances of success.

The green highlighter helps you remember to give them time in the lesson to respond to the advice. If the feedback is important, then you will give time to them trying to improve the work. Knowing that you will give this lesson time really helps you focus on what to mark and what feedback to give.

Let's not shy away from the other advantages here. Your SLT will be able to see that students are responding to feedback, and that feedback is taking place regularly. Yes, Ofsted will also be able to see this.

Goal Setting

Hattie tells us there are only three questions that feedback asks:

1. Where am I going?   (What are my goals?)

2. How am I going?   (What progress is being made toward the goals?)

3. Where to next?   (What activiites need to be undertaken to make better progress?)

This is a fascinating area not much practiced in schools, which in the UK have been driven much more towards performance. We therefore tend to substitute targets for goals – "I want to get an A" rather than, "I want to become an expert in History as I am thinking of taking it for A level, and I know I'll be interested in history when I leave school".

Goals concern the whole child. I don't want an A* grade because that is my target, or because that will keep me in a top set, or because that will keep my teachers and parents happy. Now I want the best grade possible at GCSE, because I know I might want to take that subject at A level, and I might want to study it at university.

Or, my goal is to overcome dyslexia – I'll read out loud to someone for 10 minutes every day; I'll develop mind maps to summarise what I am learning in each subject, adding to them each week; I'll make flashcards on Brainscape for subject specific vocabulary and test myself on it every tutor time, with the help of a partner.

Similarly, my goal is to teach all my students how to get an A or A* (even in bottom sets I'll often teach to A and usually B).

The obvious weakness of this approach is that these are my goals, not necessarily shared by each student. Some keep getting stuck at D grade. I always believe they have the capability to get beyond this, if only I gave them more time, if only I were tougher, if only I were more encouraging, if only I involved parents more. But, I am only slightly awesome in my goal setting, because there has to be a limit on time.

Do Plenaries Work as Feedback?

Excellent lessons are often sacrificed at the altar of the plenary. The teacher comes up with various ways of students articulating what they have learned, which actually do nothing to embed that learning.

Students Self Report – thumbs up, thumbs down; red, amber, green

How students feel about their learning is much less accurate than what they can show they have learned. Test them to find out what they know.

The plenary is at best an ephemeral way to summarise learning. Students are much better writing it or annotating their work. This too is largely useless, unless it is reviewed, next lesson, next week, next month, so that students have a chance of remembering it.

The idea of sharing learning at the end of the lesson is counterproductive. If new learning will come from this sharing, then that too needs to be recorded, probably with a student typing notes at the board, or all students adding to a mind map, so that again, learning is not ephemeral.

However the best use of your 8 to 10 minutes at the end of the lesson is to revise what you have just learned. This is the hardest habit to break – we all want to teach up to the bell, because the pressure of the curriculum is so great. But, in terms of getting students to learn that curriculum, testing students for the last 8 minutes is far more beneficial. I have to relearn this every day.

Chapter 40

"Come with me if you want to live."

Terminator, 'Terminator 2: Judgement Day'

Reciprocal Teaching   d = 0.74

75% of what students learn in a lesson, they learn from their peers. We also know that 50% of it will be correct. There are a lot of advantages, therefore, in making sure that teaching from other students is good.

Where Are Your Teaching Skills?

Pair your students. Hattie points out that the greatest predictor of whether a student will succeed on transition to a new school is "whether the student makes a friend in the first month". You can allow students to select a partner, being alert to pairings which you know might not work due to poor self regulation. Or you can maximize the teaching opportunities by placing a more-able with a less able partner, which means that the quality of information received by the less able will always be high – ahead of the average 50% accuracy.

This reduces the number of times you intervene, and each time you answer a question it has an audience of two instead of one. A lot quicker, but not quick.

Quick happens when you are slow to help. "Eugenie and Olga need help on question 7, has anyone answered it correctly yet?" Devonte and Amal indicate that they have, so Devonte is sent to teach. This can happen every lesson in some subjects, like maths and MFL.

Listen to the quality of teaching. Often students will perceive a fellow student's lack of understanding or misconception which, as the expert remember, you will find hard, being too far removed from ignorance.

Berkley University, California, provides a useful summary of research on memory which gives us some clues as to why reciprocal teaching is so successful, especially for the student teacher:

"**Students take control:** Strong memories depend on 'top-down processing,' in which learners select and elaborate on what they perceive, actively shaping their learning as it takes place...(learning is more effective when the student engages brain regions responsible for volition and executive function as well as for memory.)"

"**Make information meaningful:** People remember information better when something is meaningful to them ... known ... as 'elaborative encoding,' by connecting course content to students' lives in any of a variety of ways." The student teacher can make it relevant to their partner's lives, in ways that you can't (because you don't watch Vines, get make up tips from Zoella, or watch KSI play Fifa whatever – these will date so quickly, as you and I have. However, your student teachers will always be current, riding the flotsam and jetsam of popular culture while we sit comfortably on the shoal and bank of time.)

"**Repetition and mnemonic study:** ... take advantage of the way the mind and brain privilege memories that have been repeatedly encoded." The student teachers, both in preparation and delivery, will have repeatedly encoded what they teach.

"**Testing as learning tool:** "moderately stressful exercises in memory retrieval, such as quizzes and tests, enhance learning for the future. Testing may therefore be seen as another study tool rather than simply an end goal." Clearly each moment of teaching acts as such a test on the memory of the teacher.

What Will Stop You Developing Reciprocal Teaching?

Fear. You don't want to lose control, you don't like the consequences of it all going wrong, with student teachers getting the wrong end of the stick, and student learners not engaging with what they are taught.

So start small – a four-minute section of your lesson where the successful travel to teach others in the class. You stay in control by nominating who they are, and perhaps who they can teach. We can all afford to sacrifice four minutes, even if no one learns anything (which actually won't happen).

Build up confidence by getting students in groups of three or four to research some information – you can specify the sources they use. They then present a five-minute lesson to the class at the beginning of each Tuesday period 2 when you know they are at their most biddable.

Once you have had small successes, you will be more inclined to take bigger risks. Good luck.

Chapter 41

"I am the most helpful and open up doors for everyone and I like to share."
Arnold Schwarzenegger

Classroom Discussion   d = 0.82

This happens when "teachers begin to probe children's thinking and understanding, in which students ask question (more than teachers ask them) and in which students comment on ideas" according to Hattie. Learning is often done together, mistakes are welcome, and talk is about learning and how to learn.

You will remember the Pose, Pause, Pounce, Bounce idea of discussion. Also that discussion is wasted if the ideas are not remembered – and to aid this, note taking needs to be taught. Consequently I'd suggest much classroom discussion is wasted: between 5 and 8 of the most able offer excellent ideas, while another 10 listen and contribute haphazardly, and another 10 chill out. These are very good reasons for limiting class discussion. However, if you ask the question, "how are we going to learn from this?" note taking will be a default solution, and the discussion will have increasing impact.

Moreover, discussion allows students to develop two of the most important learning skills also: how to reflect, and how to speculate. These are higher order skills, enabling them to gain grade A's or above.

We need to know how to express our opinions, back them up with evidence, ask for help, share a problem, offer solutions, negotiate a tricky conversation with a parent, colleague or student: we do it every day. These skills are central to many jobs. Discussion is perhaps the very heart of how we socialise our students. Can we afford not to teach discussion skills?

Look at the DfE performance tables. Schools in middle class areas do better than schools in working class areas. In every town, in every city in the country, that is the pattern. If we are not prepared to admit it is a social problem, we are suggesting it is a simple matter of the working classes being unintelligent. And, when you look at students' CAT scores, or Midyis scores, this is demonstrably untrue. So we must accept an offensive premise: working class children provide us with far greater problems than the middle class. We deny that it is a social problem, and so perpetuate it. Yet, when you reflect on your own experience, the disruptive students, the students who don't do homework, those getting detentions, the students taken off timetable, the students excluded temporarily or permanently, they are overwhelmingly male, and overwhelmingly working class.

Discussion is where we start to make a positive difference.

Many of us spend a lot of time expecting students to work well in pairs and groups. However, we spend very little time showing them how to do it well.

How to Teach the Skills of Group Work Discussion

If you insist on group work, pick student observers. Because you ask observers to comment on the performance of the group, the students automatically wish to acquire the skills. Similarly, because performing well in discussion will be rewarded, they also seek praise by doing well.

Your discussion checklist or criteria might look like this:

Skills	Name	Name	Name	Name
Wild card choice (optional, in which the group decide what they think they will be best at; it scores double points)				
Content, relevant contributions				
Body language open and supportive				
Including other people in discussion				
Asking speculative questions				
Developing the point of view of others in the group				
Staying on task				
Points Total				

Award one point if the person has mastered the skill, zero points if they have not demonstrated the skill. Total points at the end. It is easy to see who has performed well in the group, and of course, each student has ready made targets to improve for next time.

As I said when dealing with collaborative learning, group work is often a very slow way of learning. There are many lifelong advantages to training students in how to work effectively as a group. If you are in any doubt, take the sheet to your next team meeting, and secretly score everyone. They all have degrees. But could any of them be better at exhibiting the behaviours above?

Discussion also allows students, especially boys, an outlet for their humour. Again, this is often misplaced in class, and you stamp on it. Yet, in a small group, unsupervised by the teacher, it can lead to a lightening of the atmosphere, and actually help the group to gel. If the humour is disruptive to the group, the presence of the observer is an added peer pressure to abandon it.

Finally, discussion is very often a total change from the normal teaching diet they experience. It is also, whisper it softly, fun.

Socratic Dialogue

The pot at the end of the teaching rainbow is probably the students who can teach each other and themselves. In your classroom, this means students who can question each other and their own assumptions. An excellent way to prepare for this is through Socratic dialogue.

I mix this up with some ideas stolen from circle time and *Lord of the Flies*.

Sit all your students in a circle if possible. Number them one and two, around the circle. These form the pairs for discussion. Decide on an overarching topic e.g. did Napoleon's invasion of Italy create the conditions for unification? Will genome manipulation save or damage mankind? Is artificial intelligence dangerous? Would an atheist society be more equal than a religious one? Should we invest in flood defences, or build on higher ground? You might come up with a list of questions though it is often beneficial for students to ask questions of their own. Hold yours in reserve, either as models of good questions, or in case students miss a point you want them to explore.

Students answer questions in pairs.

Ask students numbered one to stand, and rotate clockwise more than one space for each new question. This forces your students out of their comfort zone, and builds cohesion.

They quickly become skilled at questioning each other about the topic, and short 1 – 2 minute time limits prevent socializing. Because they can all see each other in the circle they are much more likely to stay constantly on task.

Now share their answers in the circle. Choose a symbolic object or conch. The rule is only the person holding the conch may speak. It is important that you enforce this absolutely, even to the extent that you yourself cannot speak, unless you leave your chair and take the conch.

Everyone answers questions, and the ideas of the more-able consequently get shared. In this activity students offer answers or a question they would like solved. Each student passes the conch around the circle. If they do not wish to contribute they can pass. Initially you will probably find that most students are embarrassed and choose to pass the conch. Do not be discouraged by this. It is a clear litmus test of how reluctant your students are as learners. If it is not working, initially, they are self diagnosing themselves as poor learners. This is the very reason you must persevere.

One volunteer will instantly spark another and another, and you can quickly change the social mindset of your students. Because questions are genuine, and from the students, each student can clearly see their relevance, and consequently the worth of their answer to another student. This is a powerful way to create a learning environment.

The Socratic Element

The next stage is to prep six students in class to have the class debate for you, around the overarching question you planned earlier.

Thus, six students are picked at random and sat in an inner circle, facing outwards towards the rest of the class in the larger circle. Students on the outer circle train the student sitting closest to them on the inner circle as to what they might argue in their answer to the overarching question that you have given.

Sometimes it helps to put the inner six on two opposing teams, to argue opposite viewpoints. This does lead to very good debate. However, it is also worthwhile giving students time to argue their own point of view at some point during this activity.

Allow four minutes for the inner circle to be prepped by the outer circle. This ensures a high degree of challenge, and also minimizes opportunities for off task behaviour.

The Class Debate

Those in the inner circle then turn their chairs inwards, and debate amongst themselves, potentially using every idea in the class. It is an excellent way of modelling what an argument or debate looks like, both in public, and within an essay answer. It is, in many ways, an essay written out loud. Thesis, antithesis, synthesis, as each point is framed, challenged, re–examined from a new perspective.

The students on the outer circle now make notes. It is essential for you to narrate this as they do it, pointing out how good an individual's note taking is.

Students engage much more with this, and write much more than they would have simply listening to a class debate. Because the students themselves have proposed the questions in the debate, and invested in their champion to put forward their point of view, they are very invested in the discussion. The debate therefore has a live purpose for all of them, over and above the fact that they are learning something in your subject.

Chapter 42

"I am paid to lead, not to read"

President Arnold Alois Schwarzenegger, The Simpsons Movie

Strategies for Summarising Reading Material   d = 0.82

Which really means: How to Differentiate Texts

Here is a simple rule of thumb: if you are working hard, your students aren't.

But what if you had a reading and note taking technique that you frequently used, so that they could read independently? Indeed, what if your department taught the same technique, so that all students arrived with these skills? And what if it were followed by every department in the school? How much more quickly might stduents learn?

Meet **SQ3R**.

SQ3R   (Skim, Write 6 Questions, Read, wRite, Review)

Reading for Information

How do we get students to sift through a text for information? To differentiate the text for themselves? To face a lot of reading in an exam, when we cannot support them? How do we help them cope with swathes of Google in research and revision?

I've taught many a cover lesson where, using this technique, students have got through the questions on a textbook in half the lesson.

S Stands for Skimming.

Students skim a text.

Show the text for 30 seconds, deliberately too short to read it. Ask them to think through what they will do: look at pictures, read anything in bold, headings, titles, any dates or numbers. Look at the first and last paragraph. Let their eyes wander over the page in an S shape.

You can model how this is done, reading words that the finger approaches, and what this reveals about the text.

Q stands for Questioning

- Hide the text. Turn the books over, so that students no longer look at it.
- Pairs now have to jointly come up with 6 questions. The answers to these questions should contain all the most important information in the text (up to A3 size – a double spread of a textbook).
- When you take feedback on the first question, you model what makes a good question. Usually they will include **How** or **Why**, as answers to these questions will usually be more detailed than those beginning with **Who** or **What**.
- Students have 3 minutes to find 5 more questions.
- Ask pairs to rank their top 3 questions in 30 seconds.
- Take feedback from pairs on their best question, trying not to repeat a question from another group.
- Get your scribe to type these up on screen. You'll end up with about 10.
- Ask the class to rank the usefulness of each question.
- Select the top 6.

Now students are introduced to the 3Rs

Read

W **Rite**

Review

- Swap pairs: this will improve differentiation and help ensure that weaker students do not rely on a better reader to do the work for them.
- Pairs read the text and find the answers to their questions in 6 minutes. They write these down.

Review

- Students now review the text to see if it contains any important information that their questions did not predict.

What Would Happen if This Were a Whole School Approach?

- Students like routine.
- This routine encourages self reliance: students develop their own strategies for understanding a text.
- Rehearsal means students improve rapidly.
- Less able readers in particular are liberated, as they realise that they do not need to understand all the words in the text to understand the text itself.
- Students do not become reliant on the teacher, but take responsibility.
- These are the very reading skills students will need in their exams.
- Students support each other: this is far quicker than the teacher going round to a series of hands up.
- Teachers do not read the text to the students initially – normally this just allows passive learners to switch off until they are actually told what task they must do.
- They build a big picture, an overview of the text very quickly, which builds both a context, and confidence.
- The teacher models good questioning and prediction. These are the real skills of reading.
- SQ3R works with every text, and is therefore entirely a cross curricular set of skills.
- Students are forced to talk about the text, and how it is organised, rather than merely about its content. They therefore become expert at 'decoding' texts generally.

Chapter 43

"Just like in bodybuilding, failure is also a necessary experience for growth in our own lives, for if we're never tested to our limits, how will we know how strong we really are? How will we ever grow?"

Arnold Schwarzenegger

Micro Teaching   d = 0.88

This is expensive. You film a lesson, have an observer, and give the teacher a group, smaller than a class.

How to get the impact of Micro Teaching without the hassle

The advantages of arranging a small group, who are likely to respond to what you are doing, are somewhat offset by the fact that it is not quite real teaching. It is no good learning brilliant questioning techniques if you are missing the skills of managing classroom behaviour which would enable you to question the whole class.

So be filmed with the whole class. Feedback will then be about the skills you most urgently need.

Invite an observer with an iPad. I hold my iPad to my chest, as though I were carrying a clipboard. The wide angle films most of the classroom. Any observer has some impact on the class visited, but this is much less intrusive than you might imagine. Because I'm not looking at the screen of my iPad, it is often the case that students don't notice they are being filmed.

Another precaution is to film from different parts of the room, misdirecting students. For example, looking at the books of a pair on the right hand side of the room, but standing so that the iPad has a view of the middle and left hand side of the classroom.

All my conversations with students are also recorded. For example, you may want to find out what they thought of particular pieces of work, or particular pieces of marking, and you can film their book/folder/work while their comments appear as voiceover. This is much more useful to the teacher, because nothing is theoretical or abstract, or the observer's opinion, it is all concrete.

Questions about the activity they have done, or about their behaviour, or about some help they received or gave to a partner will all reveal much more than the teacher could notice during the lesson.

A final advantage is that I am able to leave the room after 10 to 15 minutes, to record my observations or thoughts on the lesson so far. This means that parts of the video to rewatch are far easier to find. Much of my feedback will also be speculative, in the form of questions, which is far more useful than simple judgements. It becomes entirely a developmental process. Indeed, all the observer's feedback could be in the form of questioning in a coaching role, rather than mentoring.

The act of dipping in and out of the lesson allows you both to gauge how your presence affects the lesson. I often pause before re-entering, unseen by the door, so that we can hear the noise of the classroom. We are all able to distinguishing between the hum of purposeful talk and the subtle sound of them moving off task.

There is never any disagreement about what actually happened in the lesson. We can also make much better interpretations of the effects of what happened. The teacher always spots things for themselves, and is therefore motivated to improve, unlike a traditional observation which is imposed.

When we identify what to improve, I often return to the same class. Interviewing the same students is a powerful way for the teacher to see the impact of their changes.

The video becomes the property of the teacher. I do show extracts to other teachers, but only of good practice, and only with the permission of the teacher.

There are expensive systems like Star Lesson and Iris Connect that allow teachers to film their own lessons, as discussed. There are huge benefits in allowing teachers to film their own lessons, and then choose which ones to offer for review. Harvard's 2015 study, *The Best Foot Forward Project: Substituting*

Teacher-Collected Video for In-Person Classroom Observations shows how teachers benefit both from the sense of control, and how their choice of video reveals relevant areas to improve. However, there is as yet no measurement of impact on students.

Both the cheap and expensive versions of filming do allow your school to build up a bank of very short clips of good practice on every conceivable skill in teaching.

What makes this even more useful than a brilliant book like *Teach Like a Champion 2.0* is that there is no disconnect – none of it will feel foreign to you, because you will recognise the students, and everything you see is therefore relevant to your own experience.

Chapter 44

"I'm sure a lot of people out there make mistakes.
I made my fair share of mistakes."

Arnold Schwarzenegger

Providing Formative Evaluation   d = 0.90

This means finding out what the students don't know. So not assessment *for* learning, but feedback *of* learning. It simply assesses the impact of teaching and shows what to do next to the teacher. This also involves students doing it for themselves, working out what they don't know based on the feedback you or their peers give them. Consequently, it demands that students are pushed to make errors – which is your role. To do this, you need to test what has been learned in a series of lessons, not a whole unit or end of term, which will be too late. You need to seek feedback quickly, so that you can adapt your teaching.

If you are a BYOD school, or an iPad school, there are many online ways of doing this. Quizlet, Show my Homework, Socrative, Edmodo, Google Docs, Kahoot, Padlet and no doubt dozens more.

If you teach in a school which has only a projector and a computer, the chapter on modelling lists all the ways you might seek feedback about what the students do and don't know. The most powerful effect of feedback is telling you what to do better.

In the low tech world this is achieved most easily through the mini whiteboard. Here, because everyone displays an answer, you can instantly judge what students are getting wrong. It is probably only a slight exaggeration to state that every classroom in the country has a set of mini whiteboards. How often do you see them used?

A Thought Experiment

Imagine you had to teach your subject without exercise books, without your students being allowed to keep notes or records of their learning. And imagine that your crazy SLT demanded that students still made progress. What would you do?

You would ask questions for students to answer on mini whiteboards. You would gauge when to move on, or when to stop and get those with right answers to teach those with wrong answers.

How would you know if knowledge had entered long term memory? Retest in later lessons, using multiple choice.

With no books, students would revise from Brainscape decks, GCSEpod, Memrise, your own videos or the textbook or study guide, or a knowledge organiser. You would set them exam questions, and see how they do, one question at a time. You would use spaced practice and interleaving.

But, how would students remember what they are learning, without writing in a book?

What makes you think that writing things down aids memory? If it did, why teach anything – wouldn't you just ask them to copy from the board or book? Asking students to write is just something we do because it has always been done like this. It is something you do so SLT can see stuff in books. But what you want, what you really, really want, is this stuff in students' heads. Low stakes quizzing will both put it there, inside their heads, and measure what has been retained.

Your exercise books are simply a record of what your students have studied, not what they have learned. Indeed, up to GCSE, how many of your students will actually revise from their books? I would be astonished if it is as much as 15%. They are allergic to their books.

But I hope you have seen that your mini whiteboard and quizzing has become indispensable to you as a way of measuring the learning of your class, in a much more immediate way than their exercise books ever are, or ever could be.

Make Students Type

Many classes are dominated by students who resist learning because it is difficult. Their interior monologue says, "This is difficult, therefore I am not learning". We need to invert this: "This is difficult, therefore this is exactly when I am going to learn".

I teach a dyslexic boy like this, so he often types at the board. We check his paragraphs in public. I ask him to punctuate. He gives me a comma. No – this is a comma splice, used instead of a full stop. I make him rehearse how we work this out – whether what comes before and after it makes sense on its own or not. The next one he gives me is a comma. Another comma splice. He has to rehearse again. The next 7 he correctly identifies, each time giving me the explanation as to why a comma is or isn't appropriate.

This was a real lesson where I was teaching creative writing, not punctuation. My feedback to the class was – 'here is our most reluctant learner, and you have just watched him learn.' I was also giving them feedback on how to avoid the comma splice, but this was of secondary importance. It is their mindset that needed changing before they could learn. Then, when they got their peer marked books back, they had to read out to me their scores out of 25 – one mark deducted for each mistake. They got some feedback about their position in the class ranking, but that was not what was important. I got feedback on what they all scored, with an average of 7 mistakes per 150 words. That too was not the most important. They got feedback that this was an urgent need for learning in the whole class. Even my top two students made 3 mistakes each.

Now I was able to show them that the quality of what we had written as a class was A grade (this is in a class where only 4 students are predicted B grades, the rest at C and D). We were able to see explicitly why it had achieved this grade.

However, their technical accuracy would count for around a third of their mark. Again, the feedback they received was that we would need to keep practising this skill, so that they might get A grades. The activity made them more, though not wholly, receptive to the feedback. And it also reminded me of exactly where I needed to go next in my teaching, in order to have the maximum impact on their grades.

If you teach a subject that involves writing, writing together in this way is a very powerful way to gain feedback from the class about what they need. Most subjects require this. Languages teachers have pointed out to me that writing counts for only 25% of their marks – why devote more than 25% of their time to it? This is a fair and logical question. However, if your students can succeed in writing, will those same skills translate into their other areas of assessment? In the case of languages, this would be reading, listening and speaking and listening. The answer, of course, is yes, yes and yes. It will be the same in any subject which has written answers in an exam. What the students type on the board is king.

Chapter 45

"My own dreams fortunately came true in this great state. I became Mr. Universe; I became a successful businessman. And even though some people say I still speak with a slight accent, I have reached the top of the acting profession"

Arnold Schwarzenegger

Teacher Credibility   d = 0.90

In *Visible Learning*, teacher credibility is defined as the difference between experienced teachers and expert teachers. Hattie suggests that expert teachers are characterised as follows. They:

1. respond to problems as they develop in the lesson
2. look for misconception and error
3. think through the teaching sequence
4. believe passionately that teaching can make the difference
5. develop mastery learning
6. provide the right feedback at the right time
7. Accept that "a typical lesson never goes as planned"

Only the first of these touches on behaviour. It is worth repeating this, because one of the messages of this book is that you do not have to be awesome at getting students to behave perfectly.

Let's look again at the learning described in points 2 – 7. How many of them will be covered in detail in the chapter on modelling and worked examples?

All of them.

If there is one chapter that you should take to heart then, I urge you to consider that one.

What is most interesting is that feedback is only slightly better from expert teachers compared to experienced teachers. In other words, what distinguishes the expert teacher is the feedback they seek *from* the class, which is point 2, looking for misconception and error.

The biggest difference is in the level of challenge, the feedback from students as a result of monitoring and testing, and the encouragement of deep learning. This again is addressed by the chapter on modelling – pitching your model above what the more-able students in your class can already do.

The most reassuring part of this message is that none of this impact depends on your personality. There is no requirement for you to entertain, to make learning fun, to relate to the students' own lives, to teach with engaging starters, skilful plenaries, group work, or limiting teacher talk. There is just an emphasis on learning, watching your own lesson, and reacting to the learning that is happening now.

The Slightly Awesome Leader

Chapter 46

"My relationship to power and authority is that I'm all for it. People need somebody to watch over them. Ninety-five percent of the people in the world need to be told what to do and how to behave."

"In the beginning I was selfish. It was all about, "How do I build Arnold? How can I win the most Mr. Universe and Mr. Olympic contests? How can I get into the movies and get into business?" I was thinking about myself . . . As I've grown up, got older, maybe wiser, I think your life is judged not by how much you have taken but by how much you give back."

Arnold Schwarzenegger

Instructional Leadership   d = 0.91

It has a much higher effect than transformative leadership – the vision thing.

Here are the effects of **Instructional Leadership:**

- Believing in evaluating one's impact as a leader: d = 0.91
- Getting colleagues focused on evaluating their impact: d = 0.91
- Participating in teacher learning and development d = 0.91.
- Focusing on high-impact teaching and learning: d = 0.84
- Being explicit with teachers and students about what success looks like: d = 0.77

- Direct involvement in classroom observation and feedback d = 0.74.

Transformational Leadership
- Strategic resourcing d = 0.60,
- Setting appropriate levels of challenge and never retreating to "just do your best" d = 0. 57.
- Establishing goals and expectations d = 0.54.
- Establishing an orderly environment for teaching, d = 0.49.

Hattie suggests that 80% of leaders see themselves as transformational. This is very much akin to many professionals' view on teaching – it is all about that professional, inspirational teacher persona. But I hope this book has shown this to be a false picture.

Just as you should monitor learning in your lessons, and how you model it, so it is with leadership. Leadership of schools is leadership of learning. The irony is that the visionary head ignores that – they lead people and teams and budgets. Necessary. But if every decision they make is not met with this question: "How will this impact on learning?", then the decision is poorly made.

If you are not a department head, or head of year, or senior leader, you may wonder what this has to do with you. Leaders are likely to evaluate themselves according to how they are perceived by teachers.

Most teachers judge their leadership teams on a transformational model. Do they ensure excellent behaviour? Is uniform up to scratch? Are they always visible around the school? (The answer to these is always "no" of course – behaviour often goes wrong, sometimes leadership can't solve it, sometimes it is the teacher's fault – though you never tell the student that – sometimes we don't care about a scarf worn in the corridor, a sandwich munched in an alcove, an untucked shirt or a micro skirt).

The other problem for the classroom teacher is the focus on teaching and learning, and impact. No, we don't want you coming into our classrooms. Yes, it is stressful if we don't know you are coming. No, you can't understand my lesson if you teach a different subject to my own. No, my value added data doesn't define me, it's just numbers in a spreadsheet.

So, very often, the classroom teacher is naturally opposed to the kind of leadership which will benefit them most, and by extension, reward the students most.

If you've got this far in the book, there is a good chance you'll welcome the evidence, and find ways to make your SLT better at an instructional role, rather than an inspirational one.

Chapter 47

"Unless you live outside the U.S.A. you know that Arnold Schwarzenegger is a Republican. When he came to America in 1968, the Richard M. Nixon – Hubert H. Humphrey presidential race was all over television. Nixon was talking about reducing government intervention in free enterprise, and that sounded just right to Schwarzenegger. From that time on, he has been a Republican."

Response to Intervention   d = 1.07

Hattie observes that "task predicts performance...the real accountability system is the tasks that students are asked to do."

In most schools, intervention is the job of individual teachers and of their departments – redo that piece of coursework, retake that exam, reteach that part of the curriculum. I've stated elsewhere that this is counterproductive, and much less effective than the intervention we call teaching – get it right first time in the classroom.

However, this level of intervention dealt with in the research is much more about school culture. The idea is that teachers are not individually responsible – the school as a whole has to make the the community a place in which conversations about impact, learning, and progress are routine.

For example, some of the new strategies we have tried are dramatically increasing the number of homeworks set, using Show my Homework. Increasing the quality of homework, so that it tests memory, for example with quizzing. Making homework less open ended, so that it is shorter – typically 20 minutes long – and rehearsing prior learning rather than introducing new learning.

Year 11s have been invited to revision club – selecting the right students, selling it to them as an opportunity rather than a punishment, staffing it for two hours a night with refreshments and online revision.

Underachieving, but reachable year 11 boys (and the odd girl) are put in teams to compete on behaviour for learning. Each student is rated once a week by each teacher: 1 if they have improved, 0 if they have remained the same, -1 if they have deteriorated. The groups meet with their competitive male teacher team leader, scores are added, and a senior leader awards the week's prize of bragging rights and chocolate.

Elevate, whom we met earlier, are brought in to do a session on how to revise. They modify and repeat the session for all parents of year 11.

GCSEpod is bought for all students, and years 10 and 11 are all registered in tutor time, and shown how to use and access the podcasts.

All pupil premium students are offered a tablet preloaded with all of GCSEpod for every subject (Cost well under £50 per student – what do you have to lose?)

Parents' evenings are put on for students in year 10 and 11, where students look at their chances graphs of results suggested by FFTD. They then choose their own target grades for GCSE.

Mock results are collated as they will be in August. Year 11 is taken off timetable to have a motivational assembly focusing on aspiration and revision, before opening their results.

Instead of one comprehensive mock in December, two slightly shorter mocks are done, in November and February.

Students who put in lacklustre effort in their mocks, are made to sit the mock again, and taken out of lessons to do so.

SLT mentor key students who are at risk of not meeting crucial targets.

This is not a comprehensive summary of what we do. Similarly, organisations such as Pixl suggest a whole raft of similar and more extreme interventions. I include these to illustrate how they become part of the culture of the school. The SLT have to support this, not simply ask teachers to do more.

For interventions to be sustainable, to have moral purpose, we can't simply ask teachers and heads of department to keep doing more. Instead, leaders need to show leadership by running these interventions. Then they need to measure impact. Then decide whether to modify, keep or abandon it.

Hattie's impacts however, appear to be based on *early intervention*. His website observes:

"Response to intervention seeks to prevent academic failure through early intervention and frequent progress measurement". From *visible-learning.org/ glossary.*

This is a truth frequently ignored in schools. In a secondary school, intervention should happen in the first term of year 7. You will notice that all the interventions I listed above, apart from homework and GCSEpod, are directed at year 11. They are essential, but they are a last resort.

The best intervention in year 7 is to make sure that each student can read, write, and understand maths. Remember how many teacher hours could be paid for by the cost of a TA? Remember the impact the teacher's intervention with 4 students will have compared to the TA's impact on one or two?

Spend intervention money on teachers of year 7 so that intervention will have impact as soon as the student enters the doors to your school. Don't wait till year 11.

Chapter 48

"Failure is not an option. Everyone has to succeed."

Arnold Schwarzenegger

Piagetian Programmes   d = 1.28

Piaget observed that children develop thought through a series of stages:

Concrete Operational Stage – Hattie characterises it as "logical thinking emerges, reversibility begins to occur, and children begin to explore concepts" at around 7-12 years.

Formal Operational Stage – "children can think in abstract or hypothetical terms, are able to form hypotheses and can reason through analogy and metaphors" at around 12 years to adulthood."

How might teachers move students from the concrete to the formal stage?

Shayler 2003, sees the goal of the teacher as developing a "cognitive conflict" in the student's understanding of the subject. This becomes a way of getting "cognitive acceleration". This involves teachers giving students "challenge or disequilibrium". Cognitive conflict occurs when the learner meets something new which appears to contradict what has already been learned, or what is believed.

Shayler found that the memory based nature of exams meant that teachers do not create lessons that force students to get into the formal operational stage. He claims that fewer than 50% of year 11 and 12 students are formal operational thinkers!

It is worth noting that this cause is purely conjecture – the research is only clear about the result. However, we should ask ourselves in school, is teaching to the GCSE limiting our students? Should we teach our students to go beyond it? Should we aim for more than 100% (because 100% of a GCSE is not enough)?

The premise of this book is that we should. Some solutions to this are suggested in the chapter on problem solving.

Chapter 49

"Well, you know, I'm the forever optimist."
Arnold Schwarzenegger

Self Reported Grades   d = 1.44

Ranking 1st   Number of studies 209

Possibly the most helpful steer he provides us is on the Visible Learning website:

"In a video Hattie explains that if he could write his book Visible Learning for Teachers again, he would re-name this learning strategy "Student Expectations" to express more clearly that this strategy involves the teacher finding out what are the student's expectations and pushing the learner to exceed these expectations. Once a student has performed at a level that is beyond their own expectations, he or she gains confidence in his or her learning ability".

Of course the high expectation alone is useless – the students have to see exactly where their performance lies in relation to that expectation.

I confess, I find this very hard. Do I have time for these 30 conversations? I am the obvious single point of failure here – I need to be consistent with 30 students in my class. But during each of those conversations, I might also fail because the student does not want to face how far off their expectations they are.

A simpler solution, because I will always manage to adopt it, no matter how rubbish I am on the day, is simply to teach all my class beyond their predicted grades. Once again, the chapter on modelling and worked examples will come to my rescue, and yours.

Hattie is certainly convinced of the validity of this extraordinary effect size.

"But here's the killer. What students so often do, is they set safe targets...Our job, I believe, is to mess that up. Our job is to never to meet the needs of kids. It's never to help kids reach their potential. Our job is to help kids exceed what they think they can do... and my major and loud message is...we need to raise those expectations and give the students the confidence and their skills and the understanding that they can exceed. Doing their best is never good enough."

Professor John Hattie at https://vimeo.com/41465488

Many teachers and academics question the validity of this effect size, and of the of the studies that Hattie has referred to. I find it impossible to judge the merits of either side's methodology. And I have to admit the effect size looks frankly ridiculous. It is the equivalent of three years' progress.

It is the equivalent of students taking a GCSE at the end of year 9. I mean, that just doesn't happen in the real world, because, well, that would be impossible. Right?

Chapter 50

Putting it all Together

Dear Reader,

Thanks for sticking with me so far. How do we put all this together?

These are the habits I have had to break:

Asking questions of volunteers rather than finding what my students don't know, and adapting the lesson accordingly.

Wanting the freedom to plan every lesson my way, no matter how little time I had, instead of relying on adapting excellent planning done by my team. I used to:

- give students activities to elicit knowledge from them, rather than teaching it to them first.
- plan creative homeworks rather than activities that rehearse, test and reinforce what they have already learned.
- keep my door shut, rather than invite people in to see my teaching.
- refuse to film my lessons because I'm fat and I talk to much. Instead of improving the quality of my explanations and teaching, I avoided seeing myself on screen.
- use dice for random selection of students, rather than the far quicker use of named lollipop sticks.
- do lots of engaging activities rather than focusing precisely on getting students to learn as much as I can possibly teach them in the lesson.
- train students in group work for class discussion, rather than using pairs and a scribe at the computer.

- write on my board, rather than typing everything so that I can save it to teach from in later lessons.
- mark my students' work in private, rather than displaying it instantly though the computer and projector.

Why does this matter?

When I was lucky enough to visit Michaela school, their head teacher Katharine Birbalsingh described teacher training to me as brainwashing. I wondered if this was extreme. Let's consider some of the ways she might be right. These are false messages given to new teachers:

1. Group work is king.
2. You can rely on volunteers to answer questions.
3. What you do as a teacher is far more important than what the students do as learners.
4. Entertaining starters are essential to gaining students' engagement.
5. Asking everyone to write down or say something they have learned is a valid plenary.
6. Asking students to self-rate as thumbs up, thumbs down, red, amber green etc has impact on learning.
7. Teaching the skills of the exam is not real teaching.
8. Giving students the answers before you test them is cheating.
9. The best marking happens in books, instead of right now, in the lesson.
10. Having lots of activities in the lesson leads to better learning.
11. Engagement means progress.
12. Teacher talk is not learning.
13. Elicit instead of being explicit. Be 'the guide on the side'.
14. Differentiation will lead to greater progress.
15. Testing isn't teaching, so only do it every six weeks.

Everyone who comes in to teaching has a degree. They are academically able, often high achievers, and determined learners. Yet I regularly watch NQTs and trainee teachers at interview. Most teach for a whole hour in which students learn almost nothing. I know they are brainwashed because they have no idea: they think the lessons are great. They have not looked at student learning, just at their damaging checklist of 'showcase' teaching skills.

This ought to be a national scandal. We take highly educated, highly motivated people, and fill their brains with rubbish. Don't let this happen to you. Don't let dogma, government, Ofsted and SLT fill your head with rubbish.

Choose to be slightly awesome.

Your Slightly Awesome Teacher Personal Learning Checklist:

The Slightly Awesome Teacher		Yes/No
Behaviour		
1	Only what is needed for learning appears on desks	
2	No coats, hats, earphones are worn	
3	No one speaks over anyone else	
4	The seating plan is the seating plan	
5	Narrate what you want	
6	Use descriptive language and positive framing	
7	Patrol the room	
Questioning		
1	Use lollipop sticks	
2	For deeper thinking, use paired discussion first	
3	Everybody answers	
Reading		
1	Everybody reads	
2	SQ3R	
Writing		
1	Students write in silence	
2	A student always types to display on the board	
3	Every time you assess, students get models *before* writing	
4	During writing, students ask questions by writing them	
5	After writing, students compare theirs to the model	
6	Students use the passive voice and complex sentences to write texts like those in textbooks	
Understanding the Exam		
1	Models always show how to get the top grade	
2	Every assessment has a PLC	
3	The exam criteria is written in language students understand	
4	Tests are short and frequent, rather than relying on big mocks	
5	You call back exam answers from past students to teach from	

Curriculum		
1	See, Try, Apply, Secure	
2	You teach beyond A*, so students can become experts	
3	You interweave topics	
4	You increase gaps in testing, using spaced practice	
5	High expectations begin in year 7	
6	Homework = quizzing, testing, rehearsal, not new learning	
7	Videos explain exactly how to get to A* and beyond	
8	Schemes of work are planned lesson by lesson, in one software (e.g. PowerPoint)	
9	All your resources are available online to your students	
Feedback		
1	Everything is displayed	
2	Everything in class (not everyone) is assessed live	
3	Students sit in teaching pairs	
4	Students teach from the front	
5	You only write in books to get students to redraft or respond	
6	Pink Highlighter	
7	Photograph (or video) and display each practical piece of work before and after teaching	
8	Peer assessment uses models and PLCs, so it is explicit	
9	Content that is assessed through writing, is taught through modeled writing	
10	You examine your impact and value added	
11	You film your teaching and ask what works and what can be improved	
Memory		
1	Brainscape, Memrise or equivalent	
2	Low stakes testing, quizzing happen frequently	
3	You teach note taking skills	
4	Mindmaps	